The Right Kind of Suffering

The Right Kind of Suffering

GENDER, SEXUALITY, AND ARAB ASYLUM SEEKERS IN AMERICA

RHODA KANAANEH

University of Texas Press   AUSTIN

Copyright © 2023 by the University of Texas Press
All rights reserved
Printed in the United States of America
First edition, 2023

Requests for permission to reproduce material from this work should be sent to:
 Permissions
 University of Texas Press
 P.O. Box 7819
 Austin, TX 78713-7819
 utpress.utexas.edu/rp-form

♾ The paper used in this book meets the minimum requirements of ANSI/NISO Z39.48-1992 (R1997) (Permanence of Paper).

LIBRARY OF CONGRESS CATALOGING-IN-PUBLICATION DATA
Names: Kanaaneh, Rhoda Ann, author.
Title: The right kind of suffering : gender, sexuality, and Arab asylum seekers in America / Rhoda Kanaaneh.
Description: First edition. | Austin : University of Texas Press, 2023. | Includes bibliographical references and index.
Identifiers: LCCN 2021062297 (print) | LCCN 2021062298 (ebook)
 ISBN 978-1-4773-2638-1 (hardcover)
 ISBN 978-1-4773-2672-5 (paperback)
 ISBN 978-1-4773-2639-8 (PDF)
 ISBN 978-1-4773-2640-4 (epub)
Subjects: LCSH: Political refugees—Legal status, laws, etc.—United States—Case studies. | Political refugees—Arab countries—Case studies. | Gay political refugees—Legal status, laws, etc.—United States—Case studies. | Gay political refugees—Arab countries—Case studies. | Asylum, Right of—United States—Case studies.
Classification: LCC HV640.4.U54 K36 2023 (print) | LCC HV640.4.U54 (ebook) | DDC 362.870973—dc23/eng/20220518
LC record available at https://lccn.loc.gov/2021062297
LC ebook record available at https://lccn.loc.gov/2021062298
doi:10.7560/326381

For Laiali and Malaika

Contents

Acknowledgments *ix*

INTRODUCTION: Narrow Pathways *1*

1. "I've always been looking for my freedom" *11*
2. "My life is a Bollywood film" *47*
3. "I wish it was a happier ending" *79*
4. "Many reasons to leave" *119*

CONCLUSION: Of Stories, Traumas, and Happy Endings *145*

Notes *167*
Index *185*

Acknowledgments

THIS PROJECT STARTED OVER A DECADE AGO, and many people, institutions, and organizations have helped me along the way. I was fortunate to have my research buoyed, shaped, and pushed along by numerous people who shared information, voiced opinions, expressed emotions, offered advice, bestowed funding, and posed questions, and I am thankful to them all.

First and foremost, special thanks are due to the many successful asylees who agreed to talk with me. I am deeply grateful to them for allowing me to write about their experiences and trusting me with information that was often delicate—in particular, the four at the center of this book. After their harrowing asylum experiences, their willingness to revisit and discuss the past, to give me their precious time and to share their thoughts, is truly appreciated. I hope that what I wrote will encourage some reader out there to think differently about the processes they were forced to undergo. In addition to asylum seekers, there were others connected to them who helped me: their friends, social workers, and advocates, all of whom I also cannot name. You know who you are, and I am indebted to you for helping me.

I also owe gratitude to a large number of kind souls who agreed to read various portions and incarnations of my manuscript—many of them slogging through confusing rough drafts, giving me challenging feedback, and nudging me to explore new directions. Some are esteemed academics, others are personal friends (some are both), several had relevant expertise, and yet others were just in the wrong place at the wrong time. I thank them all for their energies, time, and wisdom: Lila Abu Lughod, Gabriella Amman, Sa'ed Atshan, Nadia Awad, Asli Bali, Moustafa Bayoumi, Becky Carpenter, Karo Durr, Sondra Hale, Roger Lancaster, Anne Langston, Margot Lourdel, Sarah Rozen, Aseel Sawalha, Sarah Schulman, and Sandra Stevenson. Jim Burr has been a thoughtful editor and guide for this book, and I thank the two anonymous peer reviewers he commissioned for their incisive detailed feedback.

I spoke with many people who generously offered advice and connections to organizations, lawyers, researchers, other academics, or asylees. I thank them for going out of their way to help and for trusting me with their contacts: Ahmad Amara, Abed Awad, Evan Chang, Diane Conway, Huma Hasan, Ibtisam Ibrahim, Sarah Ihmoud, Hebah Ismail, Hani Khoury, Nick Lomuscio, Christine Moore, Nadine Naber, Isis Nusair, Dan Smulian, Elissa Steglich, Bassam Kassab, Ori Kleiner, Mezna Qato, Parvez Sharma, and Emrah Yildiz. Thanks also to the unnamed asylum officer who agreed to discuss her work in general terms. I have also benefited from numerous exchanges with colleagues who constructively suggested readings and ideas. Some who stand out in my memory (though there are many others I am forgetting) are Ayse Caglar, Tarek Ismail, Ruba Salih, and Lana Tatour.

The Department of Anthropology at Columbia University, the Center for Palestine Studies, and the Middle East Studies Institute enriched my research with three visiting researcher appointments. A number of conferences and workshops helped ripen my ideas and provided valuable feedback. Thank you to the Hagop Kevorkian Center for Near Eastern Studies at New York University for inviting me to give a seminar and to Miriam Ticktin for providing ground-laying suggestions there. I am indebted to O. Hugo Benavidez for inviting me to speak at the National University of San Martín in Buenos Aires and encouraging me to expand my North American lens. Suad Joseph and Kamala Visweswaran kindly served as discussants for papers I presented at meetings of the Middle East Studies Association and the American Anthropological Association and provided important input. The Jean Monnet Alumni conference at the European University Institute helped me consider European parallels and differences, both in asylum and in academic trends. I thank the organizers of the International Relations Within workshop at the University of Tokyo for inviting me and to Taro Tsurumi for his probing queries.

Finally, I thank my family. My daughters, Malaika and Laiali, put up with my repetitive stories during a decade of asylum interpretation work and with my research-related absences. Along with my husband, Seth Tapper, and my parents, Hatim and Dolores Kanaaneh, they were essential in helping to center me after emotionally draining work sessions, wrapping me in the warm embrace of family life, something that many of the asylum seekers I worked with longed for as well. There is no doubt I could not have sustained this work without their support.

The Right Kind of Suffering

Introduction
NARROW PATHWAYS

SUAD WAS CALLED IN FOR ANOTHER FINGERPRINTING APPOINTMENT—scheduled, coincidentally, on the biggest Muslim holiday of the year.[1] US Citizenship and Immigration Services did not take note that it was *Eid* (Arabic for "holiday"). Nor did the team of lawyers who had been helping Suad prepare her asylum case pro bono. Suad knew the fingerprinting routine. The night before, she had set aside the suit jacket she bought at Strawberry and ironed her clothes carefully. In the morning, she spent extra time fixing her hair into a low, neat ponytail. This was her fourth fingerprinting—or was it her fifth? She had lost count. She told me she didn't mind that it was on Eid, really. It would break up the monotony of her daily routine, one that she had developed during the months, and then years, of waiting for asylum. Most days she put in long hours at the drugstore, where she was not formally a pharmacy technician though she did the job of one, but her boss gave her the day off for fingerprinting. A lawyer from the pro bono team traveled to accompany her and make sure the appointment went smoothly—and, given what they had been hearing recently, that she was not suddenly detained or thrown onto an airplane headed back to Sudan. Suad was happy to have her lawyer there, but he had no new information for her: her asylum hearing had been postponed yet again, and it was still not back on the court calendar. The lawyer knew Suad was considering giving up. She had been living in limbo for years, and her nerves were worn thin. He tried to sound encouraging and optimistic. His team would not schedule another harrowing session—where they would have Suad practice recounting her pain and suffering—until after her case was back on the judge's calendar.

    Fadi couldn't really afford a cell phone, but it felt like a lifeline so he decided he had to keep it. He tried to meditate for at least half an hour everyday. And he walked in the park regularly, even in bad weather. His pro bono therapist—and he was fortunate to have found her—told him he should get out of his small room every day to avoid sinking deeper into depression. He still couldn't really work: "Americans are afraid. Who is going to give me a job? I'm an Arab Muslim without a work permit!" One well-off friend of a friend hired him to clean his house. It was not enough, but anything was better than nothing. In the next few days, he had to make a difficult phone call to his brother back in Jordan. Not long before, an angry friend had called the brother to tell him that Fadi was gay. The brother was not exactly pleased, but he did not shut Fadi out either. Fadi had to ask him for a favor: to write an affidavit for his asylum application. He needed to get this affidavit to his American lawyer—the one who remarked upon meeting him, "You don't look gay. That's a problem." When he succumbed to feelings of loneliness and isolation, he felt unlucky, cursed, doomed.

This book follows the experiences of Fadi, Suad, and two other Arab asylum seekers, Fatima and Marwa, as they navigated the twists and turns of an often ridiculous process. But these four are some of the luckier asylum seekers out there, because they made their ways to the United States on tourist visas and figured out they were eligible for asylum (and happened to do so before the Trump administration created huge new obstacles). They each managed eventually to find strong attorneys, and mostly pro bono ones, to help them apply. The lawyers provided much-needed guidance to navigate a complicated, scary, and dysfunctional system. They helped the applicants frame their suffering in the most legally impactful way, though that process itself was traumatic, and advised them on the immigration system's counterintuitive measures of truthfulness and worthiness.

What is considered evidence that accounts of persecution such as Fadi's and Suad's are truthful is rather arbitrary, like hidden rules to a bureaucratic game—rules that require a law degree to unlock. Suad had to memorize the number and exact sequence of what initially were jumbled memories, because this imposed grid order made her more credible in the eyes of adjudicators. Similarly, some aspects of persecution are considered worthy of asylum, while other forms of suffering, particularly economic hardship, need to be set aside. Fadi had to emphasize the homophobic motivations for his arrest and torture in Jordan while eliding its class dimensions. Fadi and Suad were fortunate to have found lawyers who explained these rules to them, helping them to frame their narratives in the fashion the immigration system prefers.

With that technical expertise, Fadi, Suad, Fatima, and Marwa stood a chance to eventually—after much torturous delay and a dehumanizing process—legalize their lives in the United States. Together, the chapters about each of them paint a picture of a deeply flawed yet life-saving system and tell us not only about the individual asylum seekers but also about America and its gendered vision of the Arab world. Thanks to the diligent work of feminist and gay rights activists, the Unites Stated would slowly admit and (symbolically) embrace Suad, a circumcised well-educated woman from Sudan, and Fadi, a middle-class gay man from Jordan. However, it simultaneously barred from asylum many men and women with similar experiences from those countries. In this book, I explore what this narrow path to asylum for a select few says about our politics beyond the asylum office or courtroom.

WRITING WHILE CHILDREN ARE CAGED

As I write in 2021, telling stories about the dysfunction of asylum and its toll on relatively privileged applicants like Suad and Fadi seems like an odd choice, perhaps even misguided. Asylum seekers who enter the country through the US-Mexico border without visas are much more vulnerable. And the forty-fifth president of the United States had repeatedly threatened to eliminate asylum altogether and, during the months of writing this book, came awfully close to doing so. Trump introduced policies that significantly worsened the conditions of asylum, from child separation to "Remain in Mexico," placing it even farther out of human reach. Nevertheless, the liberal belief that the problems with the asylum system are caused only by Republican administrations is not supported by historical fact. A reversal of Trump's changes is certainly urgent but is hardly enough to repair a system that has been cruel and unjust for decades.

Why write about a few relatively lucky asylum seekers who submitted their applications before this downturn? And why point out the older shortcomings of a system that was recently transformed into something far worse? Because it is now more urgent than ever to humanize asylum seekers. And it is urgent to humanize applicants from the region known as the Middle East, who are often demonized in current political discourse. They are routinely suspected of being dangerous terrorists, particularly if they are men, for no other reason than their country of birth. Or they are viewed as the female or gay victims of said terrorist men. But Fadi and Suad's lives are much more complicated than that. Moreover, they have aspirations that may sound familiar to many readers—aspirations for things like a nice home, a good job, kind friends, and a stable life. Perhaps I am naïve, but I see the accounts of such struggles in this book as an antidote to the dangerous stereotypes that fuel immigration politics. And as the forty-sixth US president puts forth his immigration policies, viewing asylum seekers as people rather than hordes is vital.

Statistically, only a minority of asylum applicants in the United States in recent decades have arrived from Arabic-speaking and primarily Muslim countries (many more hail from China and Central America). But those who do arrive from that part of the world are targets of a particular form of hostility and vilification that rest on powerfully gendered images of the dangerous and oppressive Arab man. Other pathways to US citizenship from Arab and Muslim countries have dwindled since September 11, 2001. At the same time, the various prongs of the so-called war on terror, along with other conflicts and crackdowns, have displaced more and more people in the region. These trends make the admittedly narrow pathway of asylum increasingly significant.

In this book, you can read about a few Arab men and women from different backgrounds who struggle and strategize to carve out a space for themselves in the United States using this limited legal opening. I hope that my recounting of these complex experiences will elicit not pity but some degree of identification. Readers are invited for a moment to walk in someone else's shoes. Seeing the world from that angle—even if that view is brief and limited—makes it harder to ignore the injustice of the asylum structure and indeed our immigration system overall. I hope it drives home the ultimate arbitrariness of the laws and borders that divide us.

CHANCE INTRODUCTIONS

Back in 1996, as a graduate student in anthropology in New York, I procrastinated from doing my schoolwork by answering an email posted by a lawyer from Catholic Charities looking for a volunteer Arabic interpreter. She asked me to go with her to an immigration detention center in New Jersey, where she would be meeting a new Arabic-speaking client for the first time. Honestly, I didn't know much back then about the process of applying for asylum. Nor had I even heard about immigration detention. This was long before the current asylum-focused political moment in the United States. When I read that asylum was given on five central bases, where individuals were persecuted in their countries because of their race, religion, nationality, political opinion, or membership in a particular social group, it sounded vaguely familiar. I soon learned that feminists and gay rights advocates were pushing to expand asylum to include people persecuted because of their gender and sexuality, often using the membership-in-a-particular-social-group basis.

Aside from my initial cluelessness, my memory of that trip is hazy. I can't clearly recall the face of Hakim, the young Algerian man—boy, really—we traveled to see. But I have a distinct memory of sensing his palpable discomfort, his mumbling in a low voice I could barely hear, and his squirming over and over in his seat. He was visibly anxious while telling two strange women, the attorney and myself, about getting caught in Algiers with his boyfriend, being beaten by his father, and stowing away aboard a ship that took him to Europe and then to Elizabeth, New Jersey.

My job was "just" to interpret—as I would hear repeatedly later on. Aside from being bilingual, I had no formal qualifications or training as a language interpreter. I quickly realized that interpreting was neither simple nor neutral. That day, using my choice of words and my demeanor, I strained to reassure Hakim that, despite the bars surrounding him, he had done nothing wrong. The lawyer would be helping him apply for asylum and, in the meantime, try to get him released from immigration detention. But she had to set realistic expectations. It would take a while—months, or perhaps longer.

I continued to interpret on and off for asylum cases after that. When I responded to requests for volunteers, I knew little about whom or what the cases involved. Coincidentally, quite a few also centered on gender or sexuality. More than a dozen years later, I decided to make this volunteering a central focus of my anthropological attention. The idea of being somewhat useful as an interpreter during what could become research appealed to me. If I would eventually write about the asylum seekers I met (with their permission of course), I would not be writing from some kind of neutral outsider's standpoint, but as an advocate—though not a particularly powerful one—for their attempts to legalize their lives in the United States. That legal status was a privilege that I myself enjoyed because of an accident of birth: being born to an American mother. I possessed the documents the men and women in this book worked so hard to try to get, not because I did anything to deserve it, but by random circumstance.

Over the decade leading up to this book, I met more than forty asylum seekers through two main avenues. One group I met through connections made by my network of friends, colleagues, and nonprofit workers, who introduced me as a researcher to individuals who, like Fadi and Marwa, had already succeeded in gaining asylum. Another group I met while volunteering as an interpreter, something I had been doing anyway—and wanted to do, regardless of whether I wound up writing about the case or not. For these asylum seekers, I waited till after their applications were decided to ask them for permission to write about their experiences (like I did with Suad and Fatima). I felt that, if I had asked them earlier, the fact that they were still relying on me for interpretation help would make their agreement to participate in my study less meaningful, regardless of how much I emphasized that it was optional. Once granted asylum, they gained a bit more security as well in making a choice whether to consent or not.

When I began this research, asylum was not yet the hot topic that it is today. While it has existed in some legal form since World War II, the numbers at the time I began my study were much lower than today. In 2012, less than forty-five thousand asylum applications were submitted in the US. This number has since risen steadily, with over two hundred and twelve thousand applications submitted in 2019.[2] When I embarked on this project, asylum seekers from Central America were arriving at the US-Mexico border, but an official "crisis" had not yet been manufactured in the media. The Syrian civil war had recently begun, but Syrian refugees had not yet been given a central place in the European political imagination. Trump would not be elected for a few more years, and his Muslim ban and caravan fearmongering would come later. My choice of topics appears more obvious today, but the rationale has been there from the start: to think critically about who can become an American, how, and why.

OUR WOMEN/GAYS ARE BETTER THAN YOURS[3]

Asylum applications contain within them a distillation of the life stories of the applicants and, in the case of gender and sexuality asylum, stories about sex and bodies. While certain individuals' scenarios are chosen as the basis for granting them entry into the American polity, eventually making them eligible for US citizenship, other life stories are rejected. The personal accounts at the heart of asylum applications therefore give us a strong sense of the flavor of narratives Americans like to hear about immigrants and about themselves, especially around gender and sexuality. My book delves deeply into some of those stories and what they tell us about who Americans like to think they are and why that should change.

The four asylum seekers I chose to focus on come from Egypt, Lebanon, Sudan, and Jordan—four incredibly different countries. They were all roughly middle class, which is basically a prerequisite for their access to tourist and student visas to enter the United States (so from the get-go, many poorer individuals are locked out of this pathway). But they varied, not only in terms of their genders and sexualities, but also they ranged in age from early twenties to late fifties, as well as in educational background from fourth grade of primary school to three years of university. They also diverged in terms of their racial experiences in the US, with one occasionally passing as white, two often racialized as Arab, one racialized as Black, and all four racialized as Muslims in America to different degrees.[4] These differences and similarities shaped their varying experiences of asylum and beyond.

I passionately supported the asylum applicants' attempts to make their lives in the United States legal, as mine was. Yet I found parts of the process that they had to go through strange. I cringed at some of the ways in which the system pushed them to frame their experiences. There seemed to be an unspoken imperative that they vilify and flatten their cultures in the process of throwing themselves at the mercy of America, a country they had to hail as superior and perfect in all ways. Because of my privilege of being a winner of "the womb lottery" (a US citizen), I can reflect critically on this without fear of deportation.[5]

Using asylum to paint a heroic picture of America as savior is not surprising, given that the system grew up in the shadow of the Cold War and was used to reaffirm the oppressiveness of communism and the benevolence of the west.[6] In many asylum cases I interpreted for, women were encouraged to present themselves as victims of a kind of timeless Eastern oppression, and gays and lesbians as persecuted by nothing less than Islam itself, all of whom are to be rescued by the United States, where gender and sexual liberalism are assumed to reign. These simplistic narratives of American superiority ignore US involvement in the creation of conditions in the countries in question and disregard the forms of violence that persist here against women and lesbian, gay, bisexual, trans, queer, intersex, and other gender-nonconforming people (LGBTQI+). It also obscures the torture and retraumatization to which asylum seekers are subjected in the very process meant to rescue them from trauma. Moreover, by casting the small number of successful asylees as "worthy victims," many others get blanketed as unworthy.[7] Built as it is on "us" saving victims from "them," asylum can harden the very border momentarily cracked open for a few, building it higher and harder for the rest.

A BROKEN SYSTEM

The research that went into these pages took close to a decade, much longer than I initially anticipated. The time horizon for my fieldwork was subject to the same lengthy delays asylum applications were subject to, though clearly the stakes were much lower for me. Many cases dragged on for months, and then years, increasing the burden of the process. I witnessed many ups and downs along the way, sometimes stretching human endurance to its limits. Though the four asylum seekers I focus on all eventually succeeded, their positive outcomes by no means came easily, nor did it mean an end to their struggles as immigrants. And yet, even in these success stories, the injustice of the system is undeniable.

Unlike the majority of asylum seekers, the people I met had lawyers to guide them. Two, Suad and Fadi, were connected by nonprofits to pro bono attorneys at prestigious corporate law firms, who accepted the occasional asylum case to bolster their public image. In contrast, Fatima's lawyer, like the Catholic Charities attorney I first met, dedicated herself to working at a nonprofit organization and managed a heavy immigration caseload. Marwa was fortunate to find friends who loaned her money to hire an expensive private immigration attorney. These different lawyers, with their varying degrees of experience in asylum and understandings of immigrant lives, all guided their clients to the essentially magical words they would need to access the perilous system. Since noncitizens are not entitled to free legal representation (even three-year-olds[8]), and since the nonprofits that provide the assistance of attorneys are dwarfed by the volume of the need for legal help, the majority of asylum applicants are without lawyers as they face a system that requires extensive knowledge of the law.[9]

Of the four people featured in this book, three applied for asylum affirmatively, meaning they were fortunate enough to secure tourist or student visas to enter the country and then applied for asylum within a year after arriving. Applying affirmatively is an advantage, as it affords applicants additional opportunities for redress in the system. Only one of the four, Fatima, had overstayed her visa (by several years) and was placed in removal proceedings, as is the case for asylum seekers who have no legal avenue to enter the country in the first place. All four faced multiple challenges, but fewer than are faced by most migrants entering through the US-Mexico border. None of the chapters center on people incarcerated in "justice-free" immigration detention, as tens of thousands of asylum seekers are.[10] In this sense too, the perspective into asylum represented in this book—though it includes nights slept on the floor of bus stations and work at grueling and exploitative jobs—is nonetheless a vantage point of a relatively privileged group.

I have reiterated that the four asylum seekers in the book are relatively privileged in their access to asylum, difficult as it was, though they are hardly a wealthy or powerful group. Yet, in comparison to migrants who cross the border without visas or to fellow Arabs suffering similar or more severe persecution but without the resources or networks to leave their countries, these four had easier access to asylum. My window onto these asylum routes was also shaped by my relatively privileged background as an educated, middle-class, straight, cisgender Palestinian woman with American citizenship, who easily migrated to the US at age 18.[11]

To say that the asylum system is dysfunctional is not particularly controversial. At a minimum, it is widely recognized that it is hugely understaffed and that its backlog of cases is appalling. In early 2020, even before the coronavirus pandemic hit, there were over eight hundred and fifty thousand pending cases for about four hundred judges. And, as the head of the National Association of Immigration Judges put it, "justice delayed is justice denied."[12] Immigration court is not an independent judiciary and is therefore subject to the whims of each administration's policy preferences. One Kafkaesque caprice by the Trump Department of Justice in 2018 was to reverse the order of pending cases so that those who had been waiting the longest were placed at the end of the queue and thus would have the longest to wait going forward.[13]

Along with unpredictable and often logic-defying policy shifts, asylum seekers are subject to a kind of "refugee roulette,"[14] where applying is, as one asylum officer put it, "like buying a lottery ticket."[15] Grant rates change over time: when I started my research in 2012, one case succeeded out of every 4.27 submitted, three times higher than in 2018 when only one to 12.51 did.[16] And within any given year, there are huge disparities in the grant rates of particular judges and cities, independent of the merits of the cases.[17] These factors can determine the fate of asylum seekers in ways they have little control over. Sadly, due process and justice are, for many, often just an illusion.

Yet, despite its hypocrisy and contradictions, asylum can be important for individuals like the four in this book. It represents the overcoming of a major hurdle, even as Fatima, Marwa, Suad, and Fadi faced many others. They fought hard and long and on many fronts to gain admission to this country and, in the end, their lives were better for it. But in the shadow of these four difficult journeys, and in the contours of this warped system, one can make out the faint outline of many other people's blocked paths—those who couldn't overcome the many obstacles or who were not even able to start on the difficult journey.

The four people whose experiences I dwell on are not immigrant superheroes. Though they persevered in the face of extreme challenges, Suad, Fatima, Fadi, and Marwa, like most humans, are not perfect. They are ordinary, multifaceted beings who were positioned—by their birth in formerly colonized countries—in a way that forced them to navigate a difficult asylum system to improve their lives. They are neither docile victims who should be pitied nor apolitical leaves blown in the winds of fate. They had to be strategic and actively struggle to create better futures for themselves using the strange tool of asylum. And their struggles continued afterward, with more maneuvering required to try to stabilize the American lives they aspired to. They in fact pose a threat, but not to individual Americans or to western culture or to the white middle class's young daughters, as anti-immigration politicians would like you to believe. Rather, they push back at what is at some level a global apartheid system that separates people along national boundaries and by class and opportunity.[18] Their journeys highlight the ultimate arbitrariness and injustice of the rules governing who gets to live where and how.

"I've always been looking for my freedom"

ON A PARK BENCH IN MANHATTAN ON A SUNNY AFTERNOON, Suad declared to me: "When I came to America, I was just looking for my freedom. It was a long process, but now I am so happy. I have a good job. I have a nice life. As a woman I can do what I want to do. I am no longer afraid of being recircumcised." When I first met Suad years earlier at the offices of a large New York law firm, she seemed shy and hesitant. She spoke in a low voice, slowly and in short, unsure sentences, and she rarely ventured to use English. A team of lawyers from the firm would be helping her apply for asylum pro bono, and I was the volunteer interpreter. By the time I started to write this book several years later, Suad seemed transformed. As we sat eating sandwiches in busy Bryant Park during her day off from work, she was talkative, confident, expressive, and articulate in both Arabic and English. She had gained a stronger footing in her new home and, as she insisted many times, her life had improved in many ways: "I want you to know how important it is to me that I never want to live anywhere other than in America. Only here can I really be free and exercise my right to live my life as I decide I want it to be."

Suad's passage through asylum could be seen to represent a system functioning slowly—at a brutally crawling pace, with extremely lengthy delays, and in traumatic fits and jerks—but, ultimately, functioning nonetheless. It even had happily-ever-after potential. Suad saw herself as a success story and was happy to praise the country and system that, after an invasive process and considerable torment, minimally lived up to some of its promise as a place of justice and freedom. To her, asylum was ultimately a pathway to a better life. But framing her sense of freedom in terms that include "I am no longer afraid of being recircumcised" was something Suad learned from the asylum system. This is not to say that her statement is false, but rather that it uses a vocabulary she learned from the lengthy legal process. Though Suad knew nothing about asylum before she came to the United States, it embodied something close to what she in fact wanted without knowing its name or its rules: freedom from family restrictions and the ability to start a new life in America.

After a rough start, Suad was able to eventually position herself astutely in relation to asylum and to learn the nuances the legal process demanded of her. What is more, in the eyes of the system, as a younger, educated, middle-class woman, she fit the profile of the rapidly assimilating, American-dream-aspiring, citizen-to-be. She was a victim of her culture, a victim that America could easily save. Within a few years she was on her way to becoming a model immigrant. She held a steady job as a pharmacy technician, was studying for a clinical chemistry certification exam, and was dating doctors and lawyers.

A few months after she was granted asylum, I asked for her permission to write about her experiences. She enthusiastically agreed and often called or emailed to update me and tell me things she thought were important to include in my book. Though shaken by the threat of more numerous and more visible raids by Immigration and Customs Enforcement (ICE) after the election of Donald Trump, Suad was emphatic that day in the park that her new life in the United States was still her best option. Her beginning in America had been filled with loneliness, unemployment, isolation, and uncertainty. She had to wait a long time to get asylum, with an initial denial, a brutal preparation process, and then multiple stressful and demoralizing postponements of her hearing. But now she felt that all that was behind her and, after asylum, "even though I am not young, my life has started anew."

During our many conversations, she was taken aback whenever I asked her about any downsides to asylum. She had difficulty with the invitation to criticize the system, perhaps because of her ongoing insecurity in relation to it but also probably because asylum was a net positive. She had been traumatized, frightened, and diminished by the process, nerves worn so thin she had actually asked at one point to withdraw her application. Yet, in the end, she was here, dreaming of a house with a picket fence—an American cliché, but one that Suad embraced.

Suad's lawyers based her asylum case on FGM, short for female genital mutilation. She was able to gain asylum essentially because she had been circumcised in Sudan when she was six years old. The trauma of experiencing FGM was recognized in the asylum system at that point as constituting "ongoing harm" and the fear of one's daughters being circumcised as a legitimate fear of persecution. Suad happened to arrive more than fifteen years after the landmark "Matter of Kasinga," the first successful FGM asylum case in the United States, which was initially denied but then granted in 1996. After being locked up in immigration detention and subjected to a long ordeal, Kassindja (spelled "Kasinga" in court) won her case, and it became the first published asylum decision in the US that included gender as part of the applicant's "particular social group."

Writing about Suad's case has been challenging. The very term used in American law, "Female Genital Mutilation/Cutting"—as opposed to the term *khitan* ("circumcision" in Arabic) that Suad usually used—suggests the graphic sensationalism surrounding this harmful practice. In the US context, women are portrayed as the undifferentiated passive victims of a singular practice. But there are different types of circumcision, with different health impacts on women and different rates of prevalence. Women are variously its advocates, practitioners, reformers, and protestors. While the practice is harmful, its depiction is often inaccurate and racist. This is true of some academic studies and nonprofit organizing, including asylum advocacy in the United States.[1]

My challenge in writing about Suad's asylum case was to be respectful of her by recognizing her suffering and the complexity of her experience and avoiding simply reproducing the invasive sensationalism and drama the court system packaged it in—even though that sensationalism had likely helped her chances of asylum. I hope an appreciation of what Suad described as a "whole new world" in America does not have to come at the expense of flattening the world she left behind.

MEETING

The first time I met Suad was in a conference room at a large law firm, which I will call McCormick, in midtown New York. The windows looked out onto a beautiful vista of the city below. The giant table had stacks of crisp yellow notepads and pens neatly laid out for us by invisible hands. Over the course of dozens of meetings spanning over three years, I never met the staff who meticulously set up the rooms for us. On a side cabinet was a well-stocked spread of hot and cold beverages, assorted baked goods, and fresh cut fruit along with dishes and tidy rows of small silverware. Suad would later explain to me that she had been too nervous that day to touch any of it. A team of three attorneys, all relatively young (in their late twenties or early thirties) and white, were there to greet us: Steven, Julia, and Tom.

Suad had started her asylum case two years earlier at a more modest office. A friend had referred her to a private immigration attorney, who charged her several thousand dollars to submit a hastily assembled asylum application. That initial application was not granted—though FGM asylum case law was expanding, this did not mean that it was easy to win such cases. Suad's application was referred to the court, where she could try to make her case again. It was unclear to Suad if her initial application had failed because of sloppy work on the part of her lawyer. Regardless, she could not afford to pursue her case further. After months in a state of deep despair, out of the blue (or so it felt to Suad), she received a call from a human rights organization: "I don't actually know how they found me. I vaguely remember a form at the asylum office that asked if I could pay for a lawyer... It was lucky for me they found me because there was no one else who could help me at that time." The organization eventually connected Suad to the attorneys at McCormick, who took on a few pro bono cases each year as a service to the community and to boost the public profile of their firm.

By the time I met her, the money Suad had saved up and brought with her to the United States had long since run out. She had not yet received a work permit (her first lawyer had neglected to advise her to submit an application when she was eligible according to the regulations at that time: five months after her asylum application). She had lived with relatives when she first arrived, but moved out after they tried to limit her comings and goings. An ex-boyfriend from Sudan was sending her a couple of hundred dollars every so often, and she lived very frugally, renting a small room in Queens. She was too afraid of the authorities and too insecure about her English to work without a permit. Her economic situation was dire by then.

At this first meeting, one of the lawyers, Steven, told Suad that one of their first priorities was to submit a work authorization application on her behalf. They would need her to go to a nearby store at the end of the meeting to get passport-sized photos to submit with the forms. He added that the firm would be able to reimburse her for the cost of the photos. Suad seemed visibly relieved to hear this last detail. The cost of the photos in midtown Manhattan represented a significant portion of the small income she was surviving on in Queens.[2]

It was in this context, with four new strangers (the three lawyers and myself), that Suad had to now discuss her sex life, medical history, childhood trauma, and personal beliefs. This was not the first time she was forced to do so and certainly not the last. But all asylum seekers face similar challenges. Only a few lucky ones like Suad face it in such a posh setting. Suad eventually received her employment authorization after several months' delay. And while her case was still pending, she slowly worked her way up a small rung or two of the employment ladder. The McCormick office became more comfortable, more familiar, but it still remained otherworldly compared to the rest of Suad's life. The stark contrast between Suad's world working minimum wage jobs in Queens as opposed to the offices of one of the premiere law firms in Manhattan encapsulates the frequent role of "charity" and "pity" in the power structure of asylum. According to the standards and whims of the politicians of one of the wealthiest countries in the world, a few disempowered and vulnerable asylum seekers are chosen to be rescued, sometimes with the help of charitable organizations or publicity-seeking firms. Suad nonetheless benefited from this structure, though only after it exacted an emotional price from her.

ON HAVING TO INVITE THE STATE TO EXAMINE YOUR BODY

At our second meeting the following month, the McCormick team wanted me to translate the personal statement Suad's old lawyer had hastily assembled for her initial asylum application. Though that application had failed, they wanted to review it to see if there was anything in it that would be useful for her new submission. In order to refresh Suad's memory, I read aloud, sentence by sentence, first in English and then interpreted to Arabic, pausing for the lawyers to ask questions. The statement included descriptions of alterations made to Suad's genitals in childhood; a listing of sores, infections, and pain related to menstruation; and the difficult prospect of intercourse—all very personal, intimate information. I read these private details aloud in the conference room, wanting to cringe at how loud my voice sounded in the awkward silence. When I got to the part of the statement that talked about Female Genital Mutilation, Suad was confused. I had to editorialize, with the lawyers' permission, and explain to her that this is the term that would be used in court to refer to circumcision. The original statement briefly noted that, because of FGM, Suad had recurring medical complications linked to her monthly menstrual cycle. The lawyers, with Steven as lead, asked Suad if this was accurate and to please elaborate.

During this portion of the conversation, Suad spoke quietly, murmuring answers under her breath, and looked even more uncomfortable than during the earlier part of the meeting. She shifted in her seat, averting her eyes from Steven as he spoke. At one point, she fell silent and looked like she was about to cry. To say that this process was invasive is an understatement. I hazarded a guess that Suad might be more comfortable talking about her genitalia and sexual problems, if she absolutely had to, without the men in the room. After a particularly extended pause from her, I asked her in Arabic if she would be more comfortable if the male lawyers left the room. She nodded yes. I then suggested this in English to the lawyers. They all seemed a bit surprised. That this did not occur to them was perhaps a function of their inexperience in gender asylum, but it was also a reflection of the power dynamic at the core of asylum: asylum seekers are forced to invite authorities to probe their private lives. The McCormick team agreed to have the male lawyers step out, but before they did so, Tom asked me to explain to Suad that she would eventually have to get used to the idea of talking about these topics with men in the room—not only her lawyers, but also the male judge, probably a male interpreter, and maybe a male government lawyer. The message to Suad was: Tom and Steven would step out today, but don't get used to this momentary partial privacy.

In gender- and sexuality-based asylum cases, persecution is often linked to the asylee's body, whereby the immigration system must be essentially invited, as in Suad's case, to inspect the asylee's body, including in this instance her vagina, through medical reports and personal narratives. That women seeking asylum are often ashamed and reluctant to discuss gendered violence has long been established, but discuss they must.[3]

As Julia explained again that day when Steven and Tom left the room, Suad would have to get used to talking about this and do so in front of many people, including those whose job is to be skeptical, even hostile, to her retelling of her pain, her shame, whatever it might be. In fact, part of the purpose of the meetings with the attorneys, after piecing together a strong personal narrative, was to practice telling that narrative over and over until such difficult-to-talk-about topics become almost routine. Most of the asylum cases I have encountered, centered as they have to be on a well-founded fear of persecution, involve recounting difficult events and painful experiences. Asylum seekers need to delve into their past traumas as a prerequisite. But they also have to revisit them and revisit them and revisit them again—especially if they have competent attorneys assisting them to prepare.

The repetition is meant to dull some of the emotions so the asylum seeker can withstand an asylum interview or court hearing. They must be able to tell the story under the pressures, anxiety, and high stakes of a courtroom without being flustered by possible cross-examination. Though the goal is not malicious, the process is callous, and asylum preparation relies on what is usually a retraumatizing experience for the asylum seeker.[4] As Julia explained to Suad, talking about these issues "will never be *easy*, but it might get a bit easier or less embarrassing. After all, you did not do anything wrong."

This retraumatization is not unique to Suad's case. An immigration lawyer who read a draft of this chapter noted that attorneys get caught up in deadlines, documents, and legal arguments and do not focus on how their clients experience the asylum preparation, even if they were fortunate enough to have been taught about client-centered lawyering in law school (which not all universities teach). As a result, they often "feel that trauma is unfortunately an unavoidable part of the process, and that sometimes we might even further contribute to it despite all good intentions, as our role is so goal-oriented." As a volunteer interpreter, I was of course complicit in this.

However, traumatizing practice sessions during the preparation for an asylum case cannot erase an applicant's emotions entirely. In fact, lawyers hope that her feelings will reemerge in the courtroom to elicit sympathy and to bolster credibility before the judge. The Immigration and Nationality Act states that judges "may base a credibility determination on the demeanor, candor, or responsiveness of the applicant"[5]—all incredibly subjective categories. Suad would have to present the appropriate "demeanor," whatever that may be, in order to be believed. Her lawyers would have to somehow balance practice and repetition with rawness and fresh "appropriate" emotions.

In the months that followed, it turned out that Steven was the lawyer Suad connected with most comfortably. He was approachable, attentive, and kind. We all later teased him about what a terrible job he did in practice sessions pretending to be a mean government lawyer cross-examining Suad with aggressive questions. But at that early meeting, when Suad was relatively new to talking about these sensitive issues and still unfamiliar with the lawyers, Steven and Tom's maleness added to Suad's discomfort and embarrassment. When the men in their suits and ties left the room, Suad took a deep breath and slowly began to explain.

In the relatively short time remaining, Suad was able to give Julia substantially more detail about the daily intimate difficulties she experienced because she had been circumcised. The lawyers got the elaboration they were looking for: personal details that would enrich Suad's new statement, making it more credible and moving and therefore more effective within the asylum system. Suad explained that she suffered from repeated fevers, extreme cramps, swelling, and infections in her urinary tract and reproductive organs. During her menstrual flow, she was regularly debilitated for several days by severe abdominal pains. It was often hard and painful to pee. Sexual intercourse would have been difficult, because her vaginal opening was too small, as later detailed in an expert medical affidavit.

When Suad told Julia about her frequent infections and pain, Julia asked if Suad had any documentation that would support this. Suad did not understand, and Julia explained that documents showing proof of hospital visits or medical prescriptions would help strengthen her case. Suad took note, and several weeks later she brought records from an emergency room visit she had made when she was running a high fever and experiencing severe abdominal pain. She said that the physician who examined her was shocked—she had never seen a circumcised woman before, and Suad had an alarmingly large abscess. Based on the last meeting at McCormick, Suad thought the doctor's strong reaction and report might be helpful to her case. Julia was happy to receive the hospital records and said the team would add them to Suad's application.

All these painful personal details and the suffering caused by her "FGM" were included in Suad's statement and submitted to the court. They were backed up by expert testimony. Suad visited doctors and therapists with recognized degrees from elite American schools, who examined and interviewed her and whose expert reports confirmed her experiences—making them more real to the asylum system. She was fortunate to have her team of pro bono lawyers marshaling this type of evidence favored by the court. They were also connected with a network of nonprofits that trained doctors and therapists in writing effective testimony for asylum cases, thereby maximizing their impact. Asylum seekers without legal counsel, with language barriers, or too afraid to access the healthcare system would all be at a significant disadvantage in their applications. And asylum seekers not plugged into this network of asylum-trained specialists would not have the additional benefit of this expert support.

TROUBLES BECOME FEAR OF FGM

American views of FGM are deeply problematic and have had mixed impacts on women.[6] Yet advocacy based on these flawed understandings created an opening for Suad to apply for asylum. Unsurprisingly, to pass through that narrow legal opening, women like Suad have to present their experiences in terms that renounce their pasts. In this context, Suad's account of her childhood and of her suffering, fears, and hopes should be recognized as purposeful—it aimed to trigger a grant of asylum. It is only logical that, outside the context of asylum, her account of her childhood might emphasize other aspects of her life. It is therefore unreasonable to assume that Suad's asylum narrative is the same as a story of her life—or worse, that it represents the life of girls and women in Sudan in general. Nonetheless, feminist asylum advocates sometimes do exactly that.

The webpages of asylum organizations such as the Tahirih Justice Center describe former clients and their "success stories." The women's undoubtedly complex experiences are distilled into catchy one-liners. Readers are presented with a country (or sometimes world region) together with a stock color photo and a brief description of abuse. A headshot of "Kae," for example (and we are told this is not her real name), is accompanied by a caption that reads: "Kae was taken to an old house where two women forced her down on the carpet to perform a female genital mutilation."[7] In 2013, several of the photos on the website were of seemingly random women, perhaps from the same region as actual asylum seekers served by the organization, taken by an Italian travel photographer named Sergio Pessolano. This observation is not meant to discount the incredibly significant work of Tahirih, an organization founded by attorney Layli Miller-Muro the year after she helped win the first gender-based asylum case, that of Kassindja. Tahirih has been a pioneer group in the field since then, expanding its offices and pro bono networks from Washington DC to Houston, San Francisco, Atlanta, and Baltimore and helping many thousands of women. But these webpages easily lent themselves to the "saving brown women from brown men" scenario and were ripe for racist, even if feminist, harvest.

Though Suad didn't know about asylum per se before arriving in the US, she did know she wanted to leave the restrictions of her old life. Similarly, she didn't know that what her lawyers called FGM could help her accomplish this, though she knew she suffered in many ways from having been circumcised and hoped the next generation could be spared from having to suffer in that way. Circumcision was part of the world she was trying to move beyond, but she had to learn to articulate her desire in a particular form in order to use it as a legal basis for her asylum application. In more wide-ranging conversations with Suad over the years, I have learned that she had wanted to move beyond the whole package that was her life in Sudan—including the gendered expectations there regarding marriage, work, dress, and her body, as well as surveillance and restriction of movement, police harassment, and the various limitations on her ambitions. The asylum system pushed her to articulate this in a much narrower language: "I am seeking asylum in the United States to escape the danger of circumcision for my future daughters and of being recircumcised myself." Other issues may have been more present in her mind as factors in leaving Sudan, but, according to her lawyers, these reasons did not provide a legal foundation for her asylum case. She had to base her case on what essentially was an invitation to the authorities to probe her body. She learned how to describe circumcision to the asylum system using new technical terms. She could tell the judge that she had undergone "pharaonic circumcision," as a doctor had explained to her, "one of the most severe forms of the practice that involves the removal of most of the labia."

Suad's asylum claim was not fraudulent, but the system, when used with the proper legal assistance, narrows, sensationalizes, and warps the complex stories of applicants. Would Suad have become an outspoken activist against FGM had she not applied for asylum? She was not sure. She certainly saw herself as suffering extensively from the practice. If it gave her a pathway to US citizenship, then she would definitely take it. But she chose to come to America to escape a lot more than just FGM. She also wanted to get away from the restrictions on her movement as a woman, the family pressures to conform to social expectations, the ceiling on her career ambitions, and the lack of economic opportunities.

Friends and colleagues I shared my research with sometimes questioned the impact of my analysis. They worried that, by trying to be nuanced, I was simply confirming the suspicions of any readers already predisposed to disbelieving asylum seekers and thinking of them as cheats. But Suad did not cheat. It is the system that cheated her out of her right to a more complex story. Asylum seekers are forced by the legal process to tell simplistic stories in order to qualify for asylum. My goal is not to weaken Suad's asylum claim, but to humanize her and to counter the belittling effects of the narrow and sensationalized focus on FGM. Suad's circumcision is a drop in the cup of her lifelong struggle, as well as in an ocean of suffering experienced by men and women around the world who would be helped by immigration to the US or elsewhere. But, from the US perspective, Suad's is the right kind of suffering that we are willing to acknowledge under specific rare circumstances.

According to numerous international organizations, and as affirmed by the state department, FGM is considered widespread in Sudan. While this was documented in Suad's file, it was also most likely part of the judge's a priori assumption about the country. In the landmark "Matter of Kasinga" case, the applicant was from Togo, where FGM is actually not widely practiced. Experts reported "a low (5%) rate," a fact that, logically, could have complicated the argument about the threat of FGM to the applicant if she were forced to return to Togo.[8] Yet that detail was overshadowed by an American view of Togo as a place where women are oppressed.[9] Advocates for FGM asylum have been criticized for deploying such colonialist blanket descriptions of a dark savage continent—racist descriptions that have opened a narrow pathway for some women.

Asylum adjudicators in any case do not have deep knowledge of all the countries asylum applicants come from. They can't be, as one asylum officer put it, "an expert in the political, cultural, social and economic situations in innumerable countries around the world."[10] So they rely on the generalities they think they already know or can easily find. While Sudan had relatively high rates of "FGM" (as high as 88 percent[11]), a similar preexisting view of it as a place of female oppression likely helped Suad's asylum case, and the detailed supporting documents about the country may have been superfluous. That the judge in Suad's case seemed to have missed some major information in these documents, as I will detail later, reinforces this impression.

Suad's case was built on an argument that her experience and expectations around circumcision were commonplace in Sudan. Critics of using a widespread cultural practice as a basis for asylum worry that this makes almost all women of that culture eligible.[12] This objection to FGM asylum does not argue that the practice does not meet the standard of harm, but rather that it opens the floodgates to too many applicants. This ignores the fact that so few of these potentially asylum-seeking women can make their way to the door in the first place. In order to get a tourist visa just to step foot in America, Suad had to demonstrate that she was not poor by showing her bank statements and savings at the American embassy in Khartoum. This is only one of the many obstacles a woman in Sudan would have to overcome to enter the US and therefore be eligible to apply for asylum.

THE RIGHT WAY TO REMEMBER

Suad's application file included dozens of articles and reports assembled by her lawyers on FGM in Sudan and elsewhere. Her role was to personalize these reports and make them come to life. The McCormick team assured Suad that, although they were submitting a significant amount of information on FGM, it was helpful for the court to "hear your account firsthand, in your own voice." Suad therefore had to practice over and over again telling her memory of how her circumcision occurred when she was six years old.

She had to learn to narrate again and again her memories of being tricked as a child and being told by adults that there was a special Eid that day. She was given new clothes and candy. She remembered her mother, grandmother, and aunts taking her to a room with a cot that had a hole in the middle. An old lady she hadn't met before joined her female relatives. Suad remembered the woman's face, which still haunted her dreams. And being held down by the women and given a piece of cloth to bite down on. And the stinging pain of the razor blade cutting her. As a lab technician, she was horrified in retrospect by the unsterilized conditions, noting that the woman only used a bowl of salted water to clean the blade. Suad recalled her fever afterwards, her inability to urinate for what felt like days ("I must have had an infection"), and how a doctor was called in, who gave her antibiotics.

Suad had to repeat this story and its details endlessly, first to prepare her initial application with the private lawyer, then at her asylum interview, again when being screened by the nonprofit, then again for her new pro bono lawyers to include in her narrative, then repeatedly in practice sessions to prepare for her hearing, and yet again for refresher practices after each postponement, of which there were many. Each time I heard her give this account, she would get visibly tired and uncomfortable. Her lawyers recognized this but saw no choice but to push her to continue and to repeat. They urged her to "remember to go through it systematically, even though I know you didn't experience it like that. Remember to list all the impacts physical and mental." She had to remember to talk about the symptoms she had suffered since her circumcision, including repeated urinary tract infections. And the pain of her menstrual cycle, where she said her blood could not flow out freely. And her regular fevers, cramps, and cysts. During one practice session, the lawyer reminded her "you didn't say anything about your depression, flashbacks, fear of the dark, lack of sleep, and fear of intimacy. I know that's your everyday life, so it's obvious to you, but it isn't clear to someone who doesn't know you." And the lawyers persisted, with my assistance.

At one stage of preparation, Steven took on the role of government attorney and tried to ask Suad a series of hostile questions to help her prepare for such a situation in court. When he asked her: "How can you remember all these details of your circumcision from when you were six years old?" Suad answered that since it was a very significant event in her life, it was easy to recall, and, "in any case, I've heard my mother and aunts talk about it many times." When I interpreted this, Suad's legal team collectively winced. They warned her that this was a bad answer, explaining, "if the central story was claimed as a personal memory but turns out to be a parent's account, this will damage your credibility." To an anthropologist, this notion that a "personal memory" can somehow be neatly distinguished from a family account is truly laughable. Most current understandings of how memories are formed include, at a minimum, that they are shaped by social recounting of events.[13] Yet, in the world of immigration court, a clear and simple line needs to be drawn through these obviously interwoven areas to produce a supposedly pure memory.

Beyond remembering to give an exhaustive account of the physical and emotional suffering caused by her circumcision, accurately repeating her memory of being circumcised as a child, and absorbing clinical terms like "pharaonic circumcision," Suad also had to learn to frame this harm in terms of discrimination against women. Though the suffering she had to endure as a girl was unmistakable, she was encouraged to frame it in terms of "gender oppression"—language that she did not use at the beginning of the process, though certainly the sentiment was there. Early on, Julia asked Suad: "Would you agree that FGM discriminates against women?" Suad was a bit confused by this: "Discriminates? Yes, I think so." Julia rephrased: "Would you say that it is part of the oppression of women?" Suad replied: "Yes, of course."

Suad was told that her case would be stronger if, in addition to medical reports on her sexual organs, she got affidavits from her sisters and female relatives in Sudan that recounted her circumcision and her suffering thereafter. Given that these relatives did not know what asylum was (just as Suad did not know beforehand either) and that Suad was not on speaking terms with many of them, the process of collecting these affidavits was onerous. Compounding all this, the time period during which the lawyers asked for these affidavits coincided with a period of political unrest in Sudan when widespread popular demonstrations were occurring in Khartoum. News from the region reported curfews, electrical outages, and internet shutdowns in various parts of the country. Suad had to figure out which female relatives to contact, explain to each of them how to write the affidavit, have a draft emailed or faxed to the lawyers in New York (who would ask for clarifications or suggest changes), and then guide the women to write final versions that had to be notarized and then mailed via DHL to New York—all in the midst of electrical and web outages and movement restrictions in Sudan. The arduousness and cost of getting these affidavits was not apparent in the three short pages that were appended to Suad's thick file.

RECIRCUMCISION

A key part of the legal argument her team made was that Suad feared returning to Sudan because, were she to give birth there, she would be in danger of being recircumcised. Postpartum recircumcision was so naturalized in Sudan that, when Suad first discussed this with her lawyers, she thought that it was simply a matter of medical necessity. She knew that, when a severely circumcised woman gave birth at a hospital, her vaginal opening would need to be cut wider for delivery of the baby and had therefore mistakenly assumed that she would need to be sewed back up to the way she was before delivering (i.e., an artificially small vaginal opening) out of a medical necessity "to prevent her from bleeding to death." Suad was not aware that this procedure of reclosing was not necessary and that its likelihood in Sudan was something that could help her case. She eventually connected it to what she had heard from family members, noting the long postpartum recovery times of some of her sisters and girlfriends, many of whom were unable to care for their infants for weeks because of complications from these procedures. Suad's lawyers included scientific studies on the practice of reinfibulation that demonstrated its high prevalence rates.

Without the assistance of her lawyers, Suad would not have known to argue that she was afraid of being recircumcised. Much more germane in her mind was her desire to seek a restorative surgery to reconstruct her external sexual organs. Without this surgery, Suad said she would have trouble with sex, with conceiving, and certainly with delivering a child. Julia naïvely asked Suad why she hadn't had this surgery done in Sudan. Suad explained that the surgery was not available there and that she had only learned about it after arriving in the United States, from a doctor who tended to her during one of her emergency room visits. She said she could not even imagine discussing such a thing with a doctor in Sudan, as it would be considered shameful. Suad tried to enlist the help of the pro bono team to obtain this surgery. She sent an email explaining: "I need help. I don't know how and where can I do it. I share this with you guys because this is part of my asylum case." One of her lawyers wrote back to say that this was not their area of expertise but that they would make inquiries and connect her with a specialist, which they eventually did. However, Suad at that time could not afford the procedure, which was deemed elective. She wanted the surgery to be featured in her personal statement. Her lawyers placed a brief mention in the concluding paragraph on her hopes for the future. But fear had to be the basis for the legal case, not hope for a reconstructive surgery.

CREDIBILITY: NUMBER AND SEQUENCE

In addition to FGM, Suad's asylum application used a second legal argument as well, that she was persecuted because she refused to wear a hijab or headscarf. "The case law for FGM is much stronger than that for hijab," Steven explained to Suad, but, he added, in order to be consistent with her first submission, they would be using both.[14] When Suad lived in Sudan, she had been harassed on many occasions by the public morality police because of the way she dressed. On her way to work in the center of Khartoum, she would often pass by policemen who disapproved of the tightness of her trousers or the length of her skirt or her lack of a headscarf. Sometimes they pointed at her with their batons or yelled insults. On other occasions they stopped her and verbally chided her or even sent her back home to change her clothes and would not allow her to pass or to ride on the city bus. Once, a policeman hit Suad with a baton, though she remembers more the sting of the humiliation than the pain of the wood striking her body. According to the public morality law in Sudan, Suad could in fact be subject to flogging for such violations.

When Suad first told the McCormick lawyers (and me) about these incidents, she was visibly upset, and her sense of the injustice of what had happened was palpable. However, in order to include them in her asylum narrative, her lawyers had to impose two organizing frameworks on these accounts. First, they had to quantify the number of incidents of harassment and to establish the exact order in which they occurred. Second, they needed to frame Suad's resistance to the dress code as political.

To start with, Suad's lawyers wanted to know exactly how many times she had been stopped, as well as the dates and the details of what happened each time. Suad said that she was stopped many times over the course of several years, all more than two years earlier, so she could not remember the exact number, dates, or sequence. Her lawyers pressed her to do her best to estimate. As she struggled to organize her memories, four particular incidents stood out in her mind. She was not sure about their exact sequence but told them to the lawyers in a particular order that day. Once the incidents were quantified and written down by the lawyers, Suad then had to memorize that precise order with all of its details. She had to be able to answer questions such as "What happened on the third time you were stopped?" or "Describe the incident during which you were not allowed to board the bus." They explained that she might be asked questions like this in court and if she could not replicate the exact number, sequence, and details, her "credibility would come into question."

This task of memorizing the details of these incidents and their sequence took many hours of all of our time. The lawyers worried that the government attorney could try to slip Suad up by asking confusing questions about this. The ability to replicate the exact order of memories was clearly fetishized by the system as a test of truth-telling, even though the particular order being memorized was an artifact of the legal process. This forced Suad's cloud of memories into a clear, linear order that then became *the* story that she then had to replicate perfectly in order to prove that she was credible.

To drive the importance of this memorization of details home to Suad, the lawyers explained to her that her initial asylum application had been rejected in part because of an inconsistency in the date of her firing. Suad's written narrative said she was fired from her job in August, and she had said during the interview that she was fired in September—that small difference of one month had signaled to the asylum officer that Suad was not credible! Indeed, according to US law, the ability of the applicant to repeat information consistently is used to determine credibility, regardless of whether an inconsistency goes to the heart of the claim or is a tangential detail.[15] Such high stakes of course made Suad quite worried, and she mastered the sequence once she understood this expectation.

But this memorization was a tricky task and not something anyone would naturally do. Moreover, the lawyers warned Suad not to recite the sequence mechanically. She had to achieve a delicate balance between being well prepared and being over-rehearsed. The Immigration Equality manual for asylum lawyers insists, "You should never give the client the questions to 'study.' . . . if he [sic] memorizes the 'correct' answers, his testimony will sound rote and unconvincing."

The second thing the lawyers had to do was to establish that these incidents of harassment were motivated by Suad's political opinion. At the first few meetings, the lawyers asked Suad why she had refused to comply with the dress code required by the police. Her initial reaction was that the clothes made her feel uncomfortable. The lawyers followed up: "Uncomfortable physically or ideologically?" Suad looked a bit confused. She responded, "I'm not sure what you mean; I think it's both." The lawyers explained that the word "uncomfortable" was too mild: "The judge will not give you asylum if the Sharia dress code was just annoying to you." The following meeting, the lawyers asked her the same question, and Suad answered, "I was more comfortable walking and working at the lab in trousers." An asylum expert from an NGO who was in attendance that day flat-out told Suad that this was not a convincing argument.

The lawyers asked, "Were you trying to make a political statement that women have a right to wear what they want?" Suad said, "No, I was not trying to make a political statement. I was not affiliated with any political party." This threw the lawyers for a loop. They had difficulty connecting the personal to the political without Suad explicitly doing so herself. Indeed, they were wise to be concerned, as courts have tended to label punishments suffered by women, including those for "refusing to conform to societal norms," as "'private' matters outside the scope of asylum law."[16] They discussed among themselves in English how to proceed. Suad interrupted: "Guys, I want to put your minds at ease. I've always felt strongly about women's rights and, if someone told me wear this or don't wear that, I would react very strongly because my freedom was being limited."

Through this process, Suad learned to articulate her rebelliousness and the many instances of dress-code defiance as a feminism-inspired political conviction. This was not a lie or a fabrication—it was a particular framing of the issue that made it legally impactful. Within the asylum system, a woman who risks being flogged dozens of times for defying the dress code in Sudan, as Suad did, needs to say she defied it because of "political opinion" rather than because "I didn't like it."[17]

Suad had more frequent run-ins with the morality police after graduating from college and as she got older. When asked why, she explained that the Sharia police had been headquartered near her new place of work. The asylum expert told Suad that this was not a good argument because it would mean she didn't need asylum: she could just go work or live in a different neighborhood in Khartoum. Suad was also told to avoid bringing up differences between regions in Sudan. This is an example of geographic homogenization in the asylum context: applicants are incentivized to flatten their accounts of their countries by presenting them as oppressive everywhere, all the time. Over the course of the many meetings with her lawyers, Suad learned to emphasize the stronger arguments and to use a vocabulary recognized by the system as political opinion. Her first (failed) application read, "I wore skirts sometimes to avoid harassment and about twice a week I wore pants," while her new affidavit stated, "I continued to refuse to comply with the dress code despite harassment."

My point is not that there is fraud or lying. All of the elements of this drama were present from the get-go. But they had to be staged in a new way, thanks to the assistance of her lawyers—assistance that Suad was fortunate to have and that most asylum seekers don't have access to. The lawyers advised her on the most impactful way to answer a question: truthfully, but in the most legally relevant way and using language recognized by the system. As a reporter described it, there are "magic words" that applicants need to use.[18] Most asylum seekers who do not have the advice of a lawyer on this coded language are at a serious disadvantage.

GOVERNMENT LAWYERS

Suad did not realize until well into the preparation process that, unlike the initial asylum interview, her court hearing would involve a lawyer representing the government who was tasked with questioning her application. Soon enough, though, the figure of the hostile government lawyer loomed over the preparation, and different members of the team and advisers played that role so Suad could practice responding.

At one point, a government attorney I'll call Brodie, who had something of a notorious reputation, was assigned to Suad's case. Brodie was known in legal circles for being "a total jerk" and a racist. Suad's lawyers had heard rumors that Brodie's brother, a policeman, had allegedly assaulted an immigrant man. The victim filed charges against Brodie's brother but then suddenly disappeared—he was conveniently deported, presumably with Brodie's help—and the charges went nowhere. For a period, Brodie figured prominently in Suad's anxiety about her hearing, but as her case was repeatedly delayed, other government lawyers were assigned and reassigned.

Closer to one of the hearing dates, Suad, with her team of attorneys and myself, met for a practice session with Lisa, the asylum expert from the nonprofit. Though Lisa generally had a dry, no-nonsense demeanor, her tone when role-playing the government lawyer that day was even sharper—something sweet-natured Steven couldn't muster even when he tried. Lisa asked questions in rapid succession, impatiently and in an accusatory tone. Suad became confused, and tears rolled down her cheeks. Lisa explained that she was trying to corner Suad as the government lawyer would try to do in the hearing: "You should stay calm and not get flustered. Stick to what you have practiced. And do not give any new information you have not discussed with your lawyers beforehand."

Lisa also cornered the legal team and challenged them on some of the paperwork they had submitted to the court. The McCormick lawyers, normally confident in their home office, were deferential to Lisa and apologetic about not having all the correct answers. They had graduated from top law schools in the country and were hardworking. They would go on to other prestigious positions after leaving McCormick. And though Suad's asylum case was clearly more interesting than much of their other (dry and corporate) work, as they noted several times, they were nonetheless inexperienced in immigration court and had to lean heavily on Lisa's advice. Lisa explained that day that immigration hearings are different than regular court because judges have more control. Much depends on the personality of the judge, who can decide to skip the entire formal proceedings and ask all the questions themselves. Lisa reassured the lawyers that the judge appointed to Suad's case was reputed to be nice and had a high grant rate—an incredibly important element in the refugee roulette that Suad was betting on.

Lisa also gave me a hard time that day; she spoke quickly and did not pause. I struggled to keep up with interpreting, and she was visibly annoyed (though I would not be interpreting for court). Lisa's gruffness was construed as tough love—traumatizing Suad and her lawyers in order for them to be able to withstand the stress of the real hearing. One New York lawyer told me that this role playing is "probably the worst part of being an immigration attorney. . . . You know you have to get your client ready for the jerks but it still feels disgusting to do their dirty work during prep."

Such traumatization is, sadly, a regular feature of asylum preparation and proceedings where already-traumatized asylum seekers must pay an additional mental price to access the system. Suad was told, "your therapist is probably telling you to forget about the fear, but here we are asking you not to." On a number of occasions, Suad's lawyers told her that, if she felt like crying at her hearing, "that's fine, don't stop yourself" and that "the judge will be looking at your expressions to see if you are sincere." These were obviously nerve-wracking instructions for Suad. She was told that the judge assigned to her case was nice, but also at one point that the government lawyer assigned was mean, "so they will balance each other out, and it might even work to your advantage if the government lawyer is bullying you and the judge sees that." The fact that, although she could expect to be bullied, it might help her case was far from reassuring to Suad.

A CONTRIBUTING MEMBER OF SOCIETY

Suad's lawyers advised her to deflect any suspicion that her motives for coming to the United States were economic. Asylum is granted to individuals who are persecuted on five central bases: their race, religion, nationality, political opinion, or membership in a particular social group. Poverty or economic hardship is explicitly excluded as grounds for asylum. To paraphrase Miriam Ticktin, some victims, such as those considered to be gender and sexual victims, are sometimes allowed to travel across borders, but poverty victims cannot.[19] To gain asylum, gender and sexual victimization have to be presented "in isolation from other injustices or forms of exploitation."[20]

Suad's encounters with the morality police caused her to arrive for work at the medical laboratory late and distraught, and she was eventually fired for this. But loss of employment, even if directly related to the claim of gender or sexuality victimization, is not grounds for asylum and in fact could potentially weaken or taint an application. Suad's lawyers counseled her not to dwell in her narrative on the fact that she lost her job: "If you talk too much about that, it might sound like you are coming here to work, and economic reasons are not allowed in asylum." On Immigration Equality's list of attorney "Dos and Don'ts" in preparing an asylum application, the advice is: don't

> include economic motivations to come to the United States. When an asylum seeker leaves his country, there may be many reasons that he chooses to come to the United States. The hope of greater economic opportunity may be one reason among those, but this is not something to highlight in the applicant's declaration. Many asylum adjudicators fear that asylum applicants [are] really only seeking asylum for economic reasons, and there's no reason to draw attention to this fear.[21]

As a result, the array of restrictions in Suad's life in Sudan, as well as the package of hoped-for advantages in an American future, had to be represented more narrowly by banishing any element of choice and focusing on her coerced migration to escape circumcision.

Suad's initial failed asylum application stated that, if she were to go back to Sudan, she would be persecuted for the way she dressed and prevented from using public transportation and would therefore be unable to earn a livelihood. Her new lawyers did not like this emphasis. They explained that, if she said she started thinking about coming to the United States after she was fired, then it might seem like she was "coming here to find a job." Suad learned instead to emphasize her feminist refusal of the dress code. The conclusion to her personal statement emphasized her middle-class and upwardly mobile aspirations. As she practiced answering the question "If you were granted asylum, what would you do with that privilege?" Julia advised her to mention "wanting to be a lab technician. That is a respectable job and will be looked upon positively by the judge."

Some years after, in late 2019, the Trump administration announced changes that would in effect prevent immigrants from getting green cards if they had used (or were somehow considered likely to use) certain forms of public assistance.[22] This policy did not apply to asylum, but many asylum seekers heard about it and feared it would impact them.[23] Although this "public charge" rule was not the stated policy at the time Suad applied, a related sentiment underlay lawyers' advice to asylum seekers to signal their economic self-sufficiency and aspirations for future contributions to American society. Though it was not a legal requirement for asylum, self-sufficiency likely influenced most decision-makers' views. Suad's upwardly mobile trajectory fit into this framework of what one organization called "a wealth test" for immigrants.[24] Communication Arts professor Sara McKinnon has noted that the very ability of women seeking asylum to be perceived by adjudicators as "speaking well" is linked to class and social mobility.[25]

Though Suad came from a middle-class background in Sudan and would strive to work her way back into that class in the United States, she did become quite poor in the interim. She ran through the savings she had brought with her, since she wasn't able to work for almost two years due to a combination of the government-mandated wait period for work permits, poor advice from her first lawyer, and a delay with her permit "due to a bureaucratic glitch."

Delaying asylum seekers' work permits of course constitutes a huge economic burden—at that time, asylum seekers had to wait one hundred and fifty days to apply for a permit and would receive it thirty days after. This five-month waiting period for work permits was deliberately introduced in the 1990s as a deterring barrier to asylum seekers.[26] In August 2020, the Trump administration extended that wait to a full year and introduced delays to application processing, though NGOs filed lawsuits that resulted in an injunction barring this rule from applying to some categories of asylum seekers.[27] But even before these changes, and back when Suad submitted her application, inefficiency and delays in processing applications were not uncommon.[28]

Unsurprisingly, in addition to the economic burden caused by work permit wait periods, the delays are also linked to social and psychological strain. Once Suad started working, her morale improved. She had been isolated and bored, staying at home, worrying about her future, and waiting day after day for progress on her case, which seemed endlessly stalled. Having a bit more income and more human interaction seemed to effect a positive change in her. She said she was happy to have somewhere to go to outside the four walls of her small room. She soon switched from working in the back of the house at Burger King to a job interacting with customers at a Dunkin' Donuts. Even though it was not particularly exciting, paid poorly, and was a significant step down from her position as a chemist in Sudan, she was struck by how she felt some of her anxiety lift.

She enjoyed practicing her English with customers and became friendly with a number of regulars at the shop. She told me that just saying "good morning" to people and giving them their favorite pastry felt like an improvement in her daily life. One regular at the donut shop, an older Egyptian man, was a manager of a nearby pharmacy. As they chatted and he learned of her background in chemistry, he told her that, if she did a two-week night course, he could offer her a job at his store. Once she made this transition to a job she considered closer to her field, her mood again visibly improved. Though she initially was not given many hours, she was thankful the manager was willing to adjust her schedule for asylum-related appointments, of which there were many. Three years later during a conversation we had over lunch, I asked Suad what had changed for her since she was granted asylum, she answered: "To be honest with you, in terms of daily life, not very much has changed. The big change happened earlier, when I got the work permit. People work and study and buy homes and build families, and that is what I started to participate in. This improved my state of mind a great deal. When I received my work permit, I felt like I had graduated, like I had taken a giant step forward."

After some time working at the pharmacy, Suad was able to afford a gym membership, and she moved to a new apartment where she rented a room from a nice Nepalese family she liked. She slowly felt an improvement in the quality of her daily life, and her growing confidence and lifted spirits were visible in our still upsetting meetings with her lawyers.

SIMPLE NARRATIVES AND COMPLICATED LIVES

Asylum cases favor simple narratives: Suad was a citizen of Sudan and left to come to the United States to seek asylum. But life is not always that simple. Suad had actually been born in Saudi Arabia, where her father was a so-called guest worker for many years. None of her family members had any citizenship rights there, yet Suad had to prepare for questions along the lines of "If you can't go back to Sudan, why don't you just go back to Saudi Arabia instead?" Her father was only a migrant worker, and Saudi Arabia was notoriously callous to this class of noncitizens,[29] and the family also experienced considerable anti-black discrimination. And, in any case, Suad's father soon lost his guest-worker status as well. During practice sessions, Suad had to learn to argue: "I have no place to go to except Sudan, and I absolutely cannot go there."

Her lawyers explained that even the fact that Suad had moved back to Sudan at the age of sixteen could be seen as a weakness in her claim, since she had "agreed to travel to the country she claims is too dangerous to return to." This sounded ridiculous to me, and I could not manage to interpret this to Suad without saying so. As a sixteen-year-old, she had little choice about where to live. Suad also had to justify her decision to go to university in Sudan. She had to anticipate naïve questions such as "Why didn't you go to study in another country in Europe or elsewhere?" She had to explain that she didn't have financial independence at the time, and the only option her family gave her was to study in Sudan.

Through their initial screening interviews, organizations that take on asylum cases or place them with pro bono attorneys attempt to select from among the many potential applicants those they consider to have strong cases that are likely to succeed. More complicated ones, such as, for example, those involving bisexual applicants using sexuality as a basis,[30] or women who married their abusers, can be deemed harder to argue and can therefore be passed over. Both judges and attorneys have "refused to believe respondents are gay because they have children or have had heterosexual relationships in the past."[31] Suad's case was considered winnable because of the strong legal precedents for FGM asylum. The complication of having been born in a third country was deemed surmountable.

TORTURE BY DELAY

While, on the one hand, Suad's ability to work improved her morale, the many considerable delays in her case dispirited her. She had submitted her first asylum application back in 2010. Suad remembers the anxiety and fear she experienced leading up to her first appointment for her asylum interview with her private lawyer that year. She had been unable to sleep that week and had arrived hours ahead of time (before the office building opened that morning) because she was worried about missing her appointment. However, she soon discovered that the lawyer had filed her application at the wrong office and they were directed to submit to a different location. This frustrating beginning foreshadowed what turned out to be a long series of Kafkaesque experiences well beyond Suad's control that spanned more than five long years. Though this first disappointment seems to have been due to an error on the part of her attorney, the multiple cruel delays and cancelations that followed were beyond the lawyers' control. Since I first met Suad, she had often asked her lawyers how much longer they thought her asylum application process would take. Much of the time, they could not give her a definite answer. Even when she was given court dates, these were often changed at the very last minute, sometimes even after they were scheduled to begin.

The first delay I witnessed firsthand was in late 2013. Two weeks before a long-awaited hearing date, we met for what should have been a final set of practice sessions. Her lawyers told her at the start of the meeting that there had recently been a government shutdown and that this meant there was a chance that her hearing date would be postponed. Upon translating this to Suad, her sense of disappointment could be felt hanging heavily in the room. She sighed and said it was so hard to live with the uncertainty and waiting. The lawyers tried to proceed with the practice session that day, but Suad had trouble focusing. She asked me to repeat questions again and again. She apologized and said, "My brain is distracted now." We met again a few days later, and Suad had to soldier on with the practices and the recounting of her painful memories and experiences, knowing that there was some chance the hearing would not take place the following week.

When we met two days before that hearing date, the shutdown had already been over for many weeks and the lawyers had not yet been notified of any delay. So they expected the hearing to take place as scheduled. Lisa had given them a checklist of things to explain to Suad at this stage. Number one was that, unlike with the initial asylum interview where applicants returned two weeks later to receive a decision, the judge would be making a decision at the end of Suad's hearing, which was scheduled for that Wednesday. Upon hearing this, Suad became emotional and worried. As they tried to reassure her, all three lawyers seemed on the brink of tears as well, and I was similarly emotional. We all could sense what a momentous and fateful hearing this would be for Suad. Lisa's second item to explain to Suad that day was that, while her case was very strong, there was always a chance that the judge would rule against her. Should this happen, the lawyers explained, there was an appeal process that they could help her with. This made Suad even more distressed. Steven told her that she did not need to think about that at this stage and to simply think about Wednesday. I made a comment about how confident Suad sounded that day. I hoped to encourage her, but it was also true, given how many practices she had already gone through.

On the day before the hearing at a scheduled final practice, Steven told me as soon as I arrived that they had just received a call an hour before from Brodie, the scary government lawyer whose reputation for nastiness preceded him and who was at that point still assigned to the case. Brodie told Steven that the judge had asked him to reach out to the lawyers to let them know that the case had been postponed. Steven was skeptical: it would be highly irregular for the judge to communicate with McCormick via the government lawyer. Steven called the court, and the scheduler still had the hearing listed for the following day. We therefore had to assume the hearing was going forward and had to plan to appear in court the next morning. Though the court would provide an interpreter, and Suad's English had come a long way over the months of waiting, I was still asked to join the team at the hearing for any complex communication before or after the formal hearing.

Suad was extremely tense on arrival at the court building the following day, where we all passed through the airport-style security check to enter. We waited in the assigned courtroom. A few minutes before the scheduled hearing time, Brodie came in. He seemed surprised to see Suad's legal team and approached loudly: "What are you guys doing here? I had the courtesy of giving you a call yesterday and told you not to come!" His demeanor was angry and unprofessional. Steven, who is soft-spoken, tried to sound firm: "We would like to speak to the judge because the schedule says the hearing is still on." Brodie shook his head, huffed, and went to his table.

Eventually, a middle-aged man wearing a colorful sweater and an ID on a lanyard around his neck came in from the judge's door. Eschewing the formal black robes, the judge introduced himself with a thick Spanish accent. Though this is naïve, to me it was somehow a little reassuring that he was from an immigrant family. In any case, Lisa had told us that he had one of the best records of granting asylum in the district. Still, that moment of hearing the judge speaking in a Spanish accent was one of the rare times I had warm, fuzzy feelings about the immigration system and its potential for inclusivity and humanity.

The McCormick lawyers then told the judge that Mr. Brodie had called them alleging that the judge had postponed the case. The judge seemed confused by this. Brodie jumped in and said, "The file has not arrived, judge." And to Steven: "What did you think, I was lying to you?" Of course, he *had* lied, because he had said that the judge had requested a postponement, when the judge had done no such thing. But the judge did not penalize or even reprimand Brodie. Throughout this time in the court building, I could feel my heart racing. I am sure Suad's heart was beating even harder.

Brodie claimed that the government shutdown had delayed the file and therefore he was not ready to proceed. This was perhaps convenient for him; he would now have more time to prepare for this case, though he had already had many months to read the file. According to the rumor mill among lawyers and law students, the government attorneys in immigration court generally do not prepare much, and they routinely try to postpone hearings to spread out their heavy workloads. Though this postponement was perhaps of minor benefit for Brodie, it had much bigger potential ramifications for Suad—sometimes rescheduling a hearing meant a whole year's delay or more. Fortunately, the judge rescheduled the hearing to just a few weeks later, a minimal setback compared to what it could have been. Downstairs the lawyers explained to Suad what had occurred, and I interpreted. Suad sighed, noting that she had already appeared twice at immigration proceedings where the file was missing. Though she had already experienced multiple delays, Suad would still have her hearing postponed at least three more times after. "This is really torture," she lamented.

Sure enough, on the following hearing date a few weeks later, just two hours before the team was going to leave for court and after several agonizing refresher practice sessions in the two weeks prior, Steven and Julia received a call from the court notifying them that the hearing had been canceled. They wanted me to be on their call to inform Suad of this frustrating news so I could interpret. This was a particularly painful conversation. As soon as Suad answered the call, she said, "Hi Rhoda, I hope they haven't postponed the hearing?" I had to tell her, "Unfortunately, they have." Steven said that he was very sorry, but the court had canceled the hearing and there was nothing we could do but wait. Suad's heavy silence on the other end of the line conveyed what was surely deep frustration and anxiety. The reason for cancelation given by the scheduler was a building function. We later learned this was a holiday office party at the courthouse. The warm, fuzzy sentiments I had when I first saw this judge were by now replaced by a heavy feeling of senseless cruelty. Julia said to Suad that day that "this is disgusting, and cruel, but it is the nature of the beast that is the immigration system." "This is infuriating," the other two lawyers repeated. At least at the last postponement, there was an excuse: the documents were not received. On this day, the court offered no justification for the postponement. The delay was just another symptom of an underfunded, slowly crawling, dysfunctional system: "We are sorry your case has been such a mess in terms of scheduling."

Zooming out for a moment, it is important to remember that Suad was fortunate, in that she had a capable team of lawyers to guide her through the long and arduous process, something that many applicants do not have. They helped her prepare for a complicated legal process that she would not have been able to face on her own, though this meant that they effectively traumatized her and invaded her privacy (with my linguistic assistance). Suad may not have been in detention awaiting the hearing in a jail cell, as tens of thousands of less fortunate asylum applicants are on any given day,[32] but her trauma from before she arrived in the United States was certainly compounded by her experience with the asylum system. The week following the postponement caused by the holiday party, she fainted at home. The family she lived with called Steven on the cell number he had shared with Suad. When I saw Suad at the meeting Steven arranged shortly after, her body language suggested to me that she was, unsurprisingly, depressed. As we waited for the McCormick lawyers to arrive in the conference room, I tried to make small talk with her to fill the time, asking about her job and her niece in Sudan. She distractedly asked about my daughters, and we talked about the news of rains flooding Gaza and causing the sewage system there to overflow. While we continued to wait for the lawyers, Suad sighed, "I'm really tired of these meetings."

Steven, Julia, and Tom arrived soon after. They wanted Suad to sign an application for Temporary Protected Status (TPS), a program that allowed immigrants from certain countries affected by armed conflict or environmental disaster to reside and work legally in the US until conditions improve. This would be extra protection for Suad because, legally, she was already allowed to stay while her asylum case was pending. But the lawyers knew that Suad now had her doubts about continuing with her asylum claim. They proposed discussing more details of Suad's case that day, but Suad said she was not feeling well and wanted to leave. She told me she had a headache and indigestion. I offered her some of the tea and crackers that were, as usual, laid out beautifully in the conference room. She took a sip of chamomile tea and wanted to leave. I walked with her to the subway, as we often did after our meetings, but this time she leaned heavily on my arm and moved slowly. I accompanied her farther than usual, because I feared she might pass out in the subway station. I felt that I was in over my head. I hoped Suad would reach out to her therapist, as Steven had suggested that day, and that the therapist would be able to help her during this difficult period.

Her hearing did not get back on the court schedule for several months. Suad would regularly dial the information line and enter her case number to receive automated status updates. For months, the recording announced that no new information was available. Suad considered withdrawing her asylum application. She told me she called Steven to tell him this, and he asked: "And where would you go? You are only saying this because you are upset." Suad said Steven explained that, if she withdrew her application, she would be giving up what she had worked so hard for and closing the door. At the following meeting, Steven elaborated that, if she just ignored her case and didn't show at the next hearing, an order of removal (meaning deportation) would be issued against her and she would not be able to reenter the United States again for at least ten years. If she decided to leave the country voluntarily to see relatives in a third country, she would not be able to apply to reenter for at least three years, and that would weaken her asylum claim. In any case, Steven explained, it would take months for her Sudanese passport to be returned to her, as it was with the government in a storage facility in Missouri. But Suad was unsure she would be able to continue to wait in this limbo status for much longer. She worried she was bothering Steven with her questions, and I reminded her that this was his job. She had not previously realized that, although the firm was offering its legal services to her free of charge, the individual lawyers were in fact paid.

Finally, Suad's case reappeared on the schedule for mid-2014. She and her team prepared yet again for a hearing, with multiple practice sessions for which Suad was forced to miss work. They dressed and traveled to court and appeared before the judge. A new government lawyer had been assigned, who again asked to postpone the case because the government was not ready to move forward. I was unable to attend that day, but Steven and Julia told me that the judge was furious. The government lawyer claimed that "the security check was not complete," a check her lawyers had not heard about before. This new government lawyer was apparently even more rude and unpleasant than Brodie had been.

So, the hearing was again postponed, this time to late 2014. However, it was then taken off the calendar *again*. Suad said her heart told her something was wrong one week, so she called the automated information line, only to discover that there was no information, meaning her hearing had been taken off the calendar and postponed again with no known reschedule date. Steven and Julia tried to push for a new date and prepared a letter urging the court to speed up Suad's process, as it had been delayed so extensively already. This was not so reassuring to Suad. It was soon after that Steven left his position at McCormick to clerk for a judge. Suad had gotten very comfortable with him and was sad to see him go. Tom, who had attended our meetings less frequently, had already taken a new job and left a few months earlier. And Julia would leave a few months after Steven for a different position.

While it was still unclear when she would have her hearing, Suad now had a whole new team of lawyers (similarly young and white): Jason, Melissa, and Charlotte. When the new team took over in early 2015, they arranged a short meeting. The main purpose that day was to have Suad sign documents to approve them as her new lawyers. Jason dressed more formally than Steven, appearing in a stiff starched shirt and cuff links. Melissa seemed nice, but busy, and did not make much eye contact. After we left, Suad apologized to me for taking up my time: "In the past, Steven would have emailed me the documents, and I could have signed them and express-mailed or scanned and emailed them back." Each time one of these meetings took place, Suad had to get time off from her job and travel almost an hour and a half in each direction. It took a while for the new team to learn Suad's strengths, and they never reached the same level of comfort and rapport as the original team. The new lawyers had to rely primarily on the notes taken by the earlier attorneys and were often, to Suad's frustration, unfamiliar with issues we had spent many hours discussing in the past. Suad told me that my presence at most meetings from the time she started with McCormick and through this transition period comforted her, and I was thankful for being able to continue to be present for them.

Jason noted that there was still no court date and, according to their inquiries with other lawyers who had cases before this judge, there were no dates for his other cases either. Apparently, the judge had been sent to another state to help process the many cases of asylum seekers crossing the southern US border, and it was unclear when he would return to the cases in New York. When the hearing was finally rescheduled, the date given was not until many months later in 2015. Leading up to that, Suad would have to attend practice sessions with the new lawyers, who seemed less detail-oriented and at some points unfamiliar with major parts of her personal statement and story. They also wanted Suad to practice with another interpreter, because she needed to prepare to speak at the hearing with a court-appointed interpreter she would be unfamiliar with. This made sense, of course, but it nonetheless made Suad nervous. She asked if I could come to these meetings as well, but we agreed it would be best if I didn't.

ANTICLIMAX

In the end, Suad's hearing, when it finally took place in late 2015, was anticlimactic. Luck would have it that the date coincided with a Muslim holiday.[33] That morning, I traveled by car service with the McCormick lawyers and the asylum expert, Lisa. Suad made her own way to the court building. The lawyers received information that they should go up to the third floor to the judge's room, but in the confusion of the day they forgot to tell Suad. As soon as we realized this, I called her cell phone, but there was no answer. I went downstairs to the lobby and, after dialing her two more times with no success, I was unsure what to do next. Just then, she appeared at the end of the hall. We went up to the third floor and into the courtroom. Suad's lawyers were huddled together, discussing strategy. I fell into the role of taking Suad to sit down and trying to keep her preoccupied and calm, to the extent possible, while her lawyers talked among themselves. The judge arrived at his bench before our scheduled hearing time. There was another hearing on his calendar for that morning and it proceeded ahead of us because the court-appointed interpreter for that case had already checked in. We went to a waiting room for what felt like much longer than the actual thirty minutes.

Eventually, we returned to the courtroom, and the hearing that Suad had awaited for years finally began. The judge said that he had carefully read Suad's file. He asked her to state her name, date of birth, and current address. He asked her why she was seeking asylum. Suad said, as she had long prepared to do, that she was seeking asylum to escape circumcision and to avoid being recircumcised. The judge did not understand what she meant by "recircumcised." It appeared that the parts on recircumcision in her personal statement and the multiple affidavits, as well as the many pages of expert testimony and supporting articles on reinfibulation, had not caught his attention, after all. But he did not seem hung up on this, and the hearing proceeded rapidly. He turned to the new government attorney that had been appointed, and she said that she had no questions on the merits of the case! Just like that. She said she was only waiting for a name clearance that was taking longer than normal because of a UN meeting in town, but she hoped to have it by the end of that day. Why the name clearance was being done on the day of the hearing (rather than in the many months or years before), and in what way the bad traffic near the UN affected it, remained a mystery to Suad's team. But the gist was that the government was checking on the name "Suaduna," which was the first part of Suad's email address, and it had not cleared yet—whatever that meant.

Very quickly, the judge announced he had reached a positive decision. Once the name clearance was completed, he would mail his decision to grant Suad asylum to the McCormick offices. He said he was very happy to see the pro bono team ("we see very few pro bono lawyers at this court"), and he thanked them for their service. He told Suad her lawyers should take her out to a nice meal with the pro bono money, but Suad seemed confused.

Jason told Suad: that was it. She was crying and did not quite grasp what had happened. She asked me, "Why didn't my lawyers ask me questions, and why didn't the government lawyer ask me anything?" She had prepared and practiced for so long in anticipation of these exchanges, but on the actual day of her hearing all that preparation was unused. Beyond stating her name, date of birth, and address, she only had to answer the basic question: "Why are you applying for asylum?" We went into a conference room, and I translated while Lisa explained to Suad what had happened. Lisa asked, "Is there anything about that name [Suaduna] that we should know? Did you ever use that name in any other context?" A dazed Suad said no. Suaduna was a nickname her family used for her. Everyone congratulated her, but she could not properly celebrate yet because of the pending name clearance. There was even some chance she would have to return for a hearing to answer questions about that name, and Lisa guessed that, if that happened, it could be in another six weeks, "but who knows." We all tried to comfort Suad. We took photos outside the courthouse, and the lawyers asked her if she wanted to get something to eat, but she said no. They agreed to plan a celebration meal when the final decision was mailed to them.

Just before we left, Jason asked me what holiday it was that day. He wondered whether it was the same Eid that Suad had referred to in her narration of her circumcision as a child. He said it would be poetic justice if it happened to be the same Eid, and that "twenty-four years later to the day, Suad had finally gotten her justice." But of course it was not actually that Eid, or any Eid at all, when Suad's family had lied to her before she was circumcised (as her narrative makes clear). It would seem that her own attorney had not read her file that carefully either. Telling Suad that it was an Eid and giving her candy and clothing was part of how her family got her to cooperate on the day of her circumcision. Neither the judge nor her main attorney had fully digested all the details the process had painfully extracted from her, but that hardly mattered to her, given the apparently positive outcome she had long hoped for.

When we talked about that day several months later, Suad recounted that she did not expect the hearing to go the way it did:

> I was so surprised, I was not able to process the information. Lisa congratulated me and I could not absorb it. I did not even say thank you to her. I did not feel relief or happiness because I was so tense. I was thinking that there was still more left and that the process was not over. I did not think that that was the end. I was waiting for the government lawyer to speak and was expecting one or two hours as they had told me. But it had only been twenty minutes. And then I had to wait for the name clearance.

Suad's name did clear the following week, and the decision was mailed to her lawyers the week after. But that celebratory meal never happened. I noticed a similar pattern in a number of other cases I interpreted for:

despite the desire to celebrate the momentous occasion, I suspect the last thing most asylum seekers want to do right after the stress of a hearing or an asylum office visit is spend more time with their lawyers.

IT'S NOT A DONE DEAL

Suad's asylum was a huge relief after years of delay and what felt to her like endless waiting. She looked forward to finally having a sense of stability to build the life she aspired to here, in what she saw as the just and equitable United States. However, not long after her asylum grant, the 2016 presidential elections ushered in a shift in policy and sentiment on immigration that undermined her newfound sense of security. After the inauguration of President Trump, his efforts to impose a Muslim travel ban (the first and second versions of which included Sudan), to escalate and expand the activities of ICE, and to reduce the number of refugees allowed into the country, along with the general anti-immigrant sentiment of his administration, all had a negative impact on Suad. She was initially surprised at the turn in discourse: the ideals of justice she had held to be American came up against increasingly frightening news reports of violent attacks against Muslim Americans and individuals thought to be Muslim. It didn't make sense to her, because: "I consider America my country and my place first and last." Soon her sense of disappointment turned into fear.

I received a panicked message from Suad in February 2017: "Good afternoon, Rhoda, I need any contact with human rights or help. The New York immigration attorneys have an alert for people from seven countries. Thank you, Suad." I called her that day, and it turned out that Jason had reached out to tell her that there had been reports of ICE raids in the New York area, and he advised her not to answer the door and to contact him should anything occur. Unsurprisingly, she was scared and worried. I tried to calm her down and reaffirmed what Jason had told her: that she could not legally be deported. She was lucky to have Jason's cell number to call in case of any problem, but accounts were circulating of swift deportations during which no phone calls were possible.

The following week, she wrote me again, concerned about ICE coming to her job and treating her like a criminal: "I have heard this has happened to good people and I am worried this could happen to me." Her anxiety was heightened by news reports and conversations with friends and coworkers involving ICE raids on restaurants and stores, racist attacks on nearby streets, shouting matches on buses, and more. She forwarded me a message she had received from friends concerned for her safety, warning that the US government had "speeded up deportation of all citizens of other countries.... Naturalised citizens especially black or anyone with [an] accent [should] order a citizenship card that you can carry in your wallet. General advise [sic]: Don't stay out late, don't run a red light, don't get involved in anything that will involve police fingerprints."

Conceptions of race are complex in Sudan, with some northerners (such as Suad's family) often identifying as "Arab" in opposition to "African" southerners (a legacy of British colonialism[34]). In contrast to their self-identification as Arab, Suad's family intimately experienced anti-African anti-Black (and anti–migrant worker) discrimination in Saudi Arabia. And in the US, she brushed up against a system where Black immigrants face egregious conditions in immigration enforcement.[35] She also experienced a sense of Black solidarity in New York when African Americans regarded her as a "sister." Though Suad identified as both Arab and Black, on the streets of New York, due to her brown skin along with her foreign accent, she was frequently perceived as an African immigrant, and this made her extra vulnerable to both racism and xenophobia.

The safety warning email Suad received concerned her. Jason had sent her a letter on formal McCormick stationery stating that she had legal status in the United States and listing his personal cell number to call. She carried it everywhere, along with her valid work authorization card and her ID. Suad remained nervous for many months, and wrote me a number of times: "Do you think they will stop me if I am walking in New York? Even if I carry my documents?" She said that after receiving asylum "my life has started anew," but the uncertainty of the past haunted her in the form of immigrant harassment. Suad and I had planned to go together to an Arabic music concert in March 2017 (I had hoped the concert would be fun for both of us in the midst of considerable gloom). Unfortunately, the concert was canceled, because the singer was denied a visa to the United States.

Suad had broken off the relationship with the ex-boyfriend from Sudan and began looking for another suitable partner for her new life. As we met occasionally during this period to listen to live music together and visit exhibits, she mentioned several eligible men she had met—a Sudanese doctor from Pennsylvania, a Sudanese restaurateur from Canada who traveled to meet her to propose marriage, an "American" pharmacy manager who seemed to be interested in a serious relationship. Suad weighed her suitors' personalities, their financial situations, their former marriages, and their citizenship statuses. She considered her options but "didn't want to rush into anything."

Suad and I met occasionally at the New York Public Library, particularly the science branch in midtown Manhattan. She was eager to brush up on her laboratory science and to study for the certification exam necessary to have her university degree recognized in the United States. Suad said she could now finally again focus enough to study (when she was going through the asylum process she would constantly lose her concentration). The books necessary to prep for this test were costly, so we explored the library as an option, but because they were in high demand, most of the books she needed were checked out with multiple borrowing requests preceding ours. Eventually, Suad searched for an affordable university course that might help advance her career. She also tried to improve her work conditions in the meantime. She applied for jobs similar to her current one in other nearby areas. She had worked for four years in the pharmacy in Queens and had not been given much of a raise. Though she liked her boss and her coworkers well enough, she wanted to see if she could get a better salary. However, she was not sure if other pharmacies would accept her years of experience as a pharmacy technician in lieu of a certificate, as her current job did. This job hunt indeed proved harder than she had hoped. Suad's life post-asylum was not always easy, but as she reminded me, it was built on choices she herself made, regardless of whether they yielded the results she wanted.

AMERICA THE GREAT

Like many asylum narratives I have read, Suad's personal statement framed her travel to the United States as a journey to seek emancipation in a free and safe America: "All my life I've been looking for my freedom. And I realized America was where I would find it." Like in many narrative conclusions, Suad ends by supplicating to noble American ideals: "I knew I needed to go to the United States, not anywhere else, because there I would be safe and my human rights would be guaranteed." But this understanding of asylum as an inevitable call to freedom in the land of the free was complicated by the fact that some of the hardest times Suad ever faced as an adult were in the United States. During her first year here, she "experienced more stress than I had in Sudan. This is not the country that I expected." She was isolated, afraid, depressed, and, eventually, broke. Her path to asylum was long and bumpy, the postponements were excruciating, and the practices (even when they went well) had been traumatizing and retraumatizing. Her story had to be told narrowly and just so. But this was asylum at its best—Suad was one of the relatively lucky ones who eventually had skilled lawyers at her side to guide her.

Why did it take so many years for her to be granted asylum? The dysfunctional bureaucracy in this wealthy nation is not just a product of neglect and lack of political will to create a humane asylum system. The burdens and barriers are intentionally there to dissuade potential applicants from seeking asylum. The government has built a bureaucracy that makes it increasingly difficult for people to seek refuge here, thereby relying on administrative hurdles rather than outright bans to do so. And over the last decade, the trend toward increased hurdles is growing: wait times for asylum interviews have gotten longer and longer, and the guidance on adjudicating cases often more contradictory and arbitrary. This is not simply about a switch in the political parties—it is a general wariness among both Democrats and Republicans of people like Suad. We want the status of saving the victims of other cultures—but only a small, essentially symbolic number of them.

One evening in 2017, I received an email from Suad: "Rhoda ☺☺. Am sooooooo happy I got my permanent resident card yesterday. Sent from my iPhone." Suad's was a story with serious happily-ever-after potential, though it was almost derailed along the way by the despair the torturous process had caused her. Thinking back to the first time I met quiet, hesitant Suad at the McCormick offices, and then comparing her to the smiling, confident, chatty woman posing for a selfie in front of a giant Chihuly glass sculpture, it was clear to me that she was in a much better position in her life. Gone were her hesitations and second thoughts about staying in the US. The frustrating and humiliating steps of the asylum process were receding into the background. In place of quiet Suad was a self-assured woman, certain that there was nowhere else she would rather be: America is the best. But the selfie is a posed image; the insecurity of Suad's position had not entirely disappeared. She continued to tread carefully, to be a model immigrant. She told me she never threw trash on the street, she always drove slowly into an intersection despite the green light, and she never let her temper get the better of her in any public setting. She had four more years to go to be eligible for full US citizenship. Would Trump, or whoever would come after him, change the rules in the meantime? "Pray for me, Rhoda," she often asked.

2

"My life is a Bollywood film"

FATIMA AND I AGREED TO MEET IN FRONT OF A DUNKIN' DONUTS SHOP in the Port Authority Bus Terminal in midtown Manhattan. She wanted me to help her sort through her mail, which she could not read. She knew the bus terminal well (at different periods, she had slept there for days at a time). But, when I arrived at our meeting, the Dunkin' Donuts was wrapped in construction material and closed for renovations. I called Fatima on her small flip cell phone and asked her where she was. She insisted that she was standing in front of Dunkin' Donuts, but I couldn't see her anywhere. I found an information desk and asked if there was another Dunkin' Donuts in the bus station. There was not. After several more phone calls where Fatima described her surroundings to me, I eventually found her. She exclaimed, "See, I told you I was at Dunkin' Donuts," pointing to a large "Au Bon Pain" sign above her head. The fact that, despite her illiteracy, Fatima managed to apply for asylum and has accomplished so much in her life in New York still amazes me.

Fatima was carrying a pile of mail in a plastic drugstore bag. As I sorted through it, I advised her to throw away many items, from credit card solicitations to notices that she had won a cruise to the Bahamas or that her health insurance would not cover contraceptives. When I translated to her the last item, she burst out laughing. She had thought the notice was important because she knew from the logo that it had to do with her medical care, but when I translated its forbidding tone, it struck her as funny because of its irrelevance. As a single, postmenopausal abuse survivor, the risk of pregnancy was far from her mind. The pile of mail also included important items such as a bank statement, a doctor's appointment reminder, and a mistakenly issued jury duty summons.

Fatima had only gone to school until the fourth grade in Egypt. She could not read or write very well in her native language, Arabic. She had not studied English at all, but had learned some words during her time in the United States. She signed her name slowly in shaky English block letters. The combination of language barriers and illiteracy threw daily hurdles in Fatima's path. When her lawyer wanted to give Fatima the address of a doctor's office over the phone, she slowly spelled the street name where the doctor was located, and I tried to translate into Arabic. After several attempts, Fatima still did not understand the name of the street. She said not to worry: she would come to the lawyer's office in person, which was over ninety minutes away by public transportation, in order to pick up the written address. She took the opportunity to also drop a small gift of food to her lawyer, who did not want to accept presents. Once Fatima got the piece of paper with the address, she showed it to people on the subway and asked them for directions in her basic English, and she eventually found her way. Fatima in fact boasted of her ability to find any location in New York that was written for her, relying on the kindness of strangers to point her in the right direction and on her indefatigable will.

On another occasion, Fatima was asked to fax a copy of a document to a government agency. She said she did not know how to fax and preferred to hand-deliver the form herself. I suggested I could find a shop near her that could send the fax for less money than the subway fare, but she insisted that she preferred to deliver the document by hand. In the end, her personal appearance at the office may have worked in her favor, since she refused to leave—or, supposedly, understand—what the staff member was telling her until she received an affirmative answer. Fatima compensated for her lack of knowledge in some areas with amazing resilience. This is not to glamorize her interactions with state agencies or nonprofit organizations. Clearly, her inability to read or write in English or to use basic technology added tremendous stress to her daily life. But, given those limitations, she managed to get a lot done.

Of the dozens of asylum seekers I met over the last decade, I have probably learned the most from Fatima. She used her patience and persistence to overcome incredible obstacles and to compensate for numerous disadvantages—not the least of which was her history of suffering, which was the basis for her asylum. She managed eventually to find her way, just as she did on the sprawling public transportation system in New York, traveling complex routes through asylum and beyond, with courage, resourcefulness, and the help of people "God put in my path." Though she put great effort into securing her asylum and it took years, it was only a small step along her difficult journey. Fatima's experiences are an important reminder that asylum seekers, even those fortunate enough to eventually be granted the legal status of asylee, must also seek much more.

At every meeting over the four-year span during which we saw each other, Fatima thanked me profusely for my help. She would almost always start and end our meetings by saying with dramatic flair that I was like a daughter to her, though I am only a few years younger than she is. She insisted on thanking me even though I was often powerless to help her. Sometimes, Fatima seemed just to want someone to talk to. Years after we first met, when I asked Fatima for permission to write about her experiences, she became excited because this would mean more time for us to talk. She quickly chastised me for not bringing a recorder and for not taking more notes: "I will tell you everything from when I was a young school girl. It will be the best book, and you will be the first in your class." At another point, when I remarked at how incredible her experiences were, she exclaimed, "Yes, of course. My life is a Bollywood film. No, it's like three Bollywood films together!"

INTENSE INTRODUCTIONS

The first time I met Fatima in early 2012, I had responded to an email her lawyer, Lucy, had sent to a listserv when looking for a volunteer Arabic interpreter. "Preferably a female interpreter given the issues involved," the email specified. Lucy explained that her client, Fatima, had suffered extensive domestic violence at the hands of her husband in Egypt. I was to meet her a few days later at the office of a psychologist who would write, pro bono, an evaluation to support her asylum case before immigration court.

My introduction to Fatima was intense, to say the least. She arrived at the psychologist's office with two plastic bags. One was full of papers from her stays at a mental hospital—a jumble of discharge documents, bills, appointment reminders, and medication instructions she had accumulated. The other bag was full of bunches of her own hair, which she had cut off when "the turn comes," her term for what the doctor later called a panic attack. For three hours, I translated as she recounted details of years of abuse, nightmares, panic attacks, and, more recently, immigration arrest and hospitalizations. She described how and where her husband beat her in the past for the smallest of what he saw as infractions, and how, more recently, she sometimes felt a fiery heat rising from the top of her head and imagined a man was pinning her down, sitting on top of her and choking her during her panic attacks. She was in tears for most of the interview, and I could not help crying as well.

Dr. Miller had kind eyes, a soft goatee, and a nice office. He had volunteered to attend workshops at a nonprofit organization that trained health professionals to write effective evaluations for asylum cases. And he provided these evaluations for free as a service to the community. On the day of Fatima's appointment, she was essentially asked to recount her trauma for him so he could formulate his expert testimony. Like Suad in the last chapter, Fatima would be asked to retell her painful memories again and again as part of her asylum application process—and, again, I was complicit in this traumatizing process as an interpreter.

Fatima's tears were still rolling down her cheeks when the doctor announced that our time together that day had ended. But Fatima had more to tell him and many questions to ask. She hated men so much, would she ever be cured of this fear? She asked if she could die from the panic attacks. Dr. Miller answered with a question: "What strategies did your doctors at the hospital give you to use when you feel yourself getting upset?" They discussed counting slowly to ten: "one, two, three, four. . ." Even on the first day I met her, I was struck by the overwhelming odds stacked against Fatima. When we were finally ushered out by Dr. Miller, who was now late for his next appointment, she asked me to walk her to the nearby subway station. She wanted help finding the correct platform where she could catch a subway train to an address she stayed at occasionally, and we walked there slowly because of one of her old injuries inflicted by her husband many years earlier. As we inched along with New Yorkers rushing past us, she told me she would take a four-and-a-half-hour bus ride the next day back to Worcester, Massachusetts, where she worked as a live-in nanny and housekeeper at the home of a Saudi doctor and her family. Having just heard about her multiple breakdowns and panic attacks, I was surprised that Fatima was in that line of work. But as I would later learn, she was well regarded by her employer and beloved by the children. They also happened to pay her very little for what was basically around-the-clock labor.

SIMPLIFIED STORIES

Over the course of a few meetings with Fatima and her lawyer, I translated as she told her dramatic life story. It overflowed with suffering, easily providing for a compelling asylum narrative. Fatima had come to the

Unites States on a tourist visa to visit her brothers many years earlier. She had vowed never to return to Egypt, where her husband literally kept his boot on her neck. When she refused to return to her husband, her family in New York abandoned her. She found work cleaning hotels in Miami and providing childcare in Massachusetts, Connecticut, and New York. Years later, she was arrested in an immigration raid on her building in an Arab part of Brooklyn. She would have been swiftly deported had she not had a mental break while being interviewed by government agents. When she heard she was being sent back to Egypt, she now says with some humor, "I went kookoo." She was transferred to a mental hospital, where she remained for several months until the fires rising from her head subsided.

At the hospital, a social worker was eventually able to connect Fatima with a nonprofit organization that provided her with an attorney free of charge. That attorney advised Fatima that she was eligible to apply for asylum. The previous two decades, this option had been carved out by feminist legal reformers, who pushed to expand definitions of persecution.[1] Fatima remarked, "I had never heard of asylum. What's asylum? I had never heard of it before at all. I just knew that I would rather face death itself than go back to Egypt." Fatima would not have known about the possibility of asylum or her eligibility for it had it not been for her mental breakdown.[2] So, in a twist of fate, Fatima's continued presence in the US was made possible by her earlier misfortune.

Lucy was one of several hardworking attorneys at a small nonprofit serving immigrant families. The organization's offices were very modest, a sharp contrast to the flashy law offices of Suad's pro bono lawyers described earlier in this book. The walls of the nonprofit were decorated with colorful posters, many in Spanish, depicting empowered women from around the world. A corner of the reception area had a donated play kitchen and gently used toys for clients' children. There was a colorful rug one of the staff had picked up while volunteering in Central America. It was homey and comfortable and warm. Good food smells often permeated the entrance, emanating from the packed lunches of the staff being heated in the kitchenette in the back. Lucy had gone to a top law school (just as Suad's lawyers had) and had chosen to take this job, which paid a substantially lower salary than other positions she could pursue. She did so because she was committed to ideals of social justice and wanted to do "meaningful work," as she put it. She was patient and empathetic and seemed wise and experienced beyond her thirty-one years.

Over the course of three very long meetings, Lucy met with Fatima to put together a personal statement for the asylum application. I have noticed that attorneys tend to schedule multiple shorter meetings with asylum seekers at this stage—clients tend to tire after a couple of hours of retelling intense memories. But Fatima lived far away in Massachusetts and had to ask for two days off from work and take a four-and-half-hour bus ride to come to see her lawyer. Lucy made the meetings fewer and longer, so as not to burden Fatima with too many trips away from the family she cared for in Worcester.

During the first few months after I met her, and over the course of three meetings where I volunteered as an interpreter, Fatima relayed to her lawyer her complex and multilayered life story in Egypt. "I know this is upsetting to talk about, but tell me as much as you can remember about what happened in Egypt," Lucy prompted her. While all life accounts meander and loop, Fatima was particularly prone to telling long side stories, dwelling on particularly painful episodes and repeating them, and reminiscing at length about her long-lost youthful beauty. For example, she talked about her sister and her sister's suffering when her husband died. Though this was important to Fatima and her sense of the injustice of her life and the lives of women in her family, it was not central to her asylum narrative. Lucy tried to help Fatima refocus her outpouring of information, though it took a while for Fatima to do so.

From the complex multitude of information Fatima offered, Lucy was able to skillfully distill a concise and powerful affidavit. In two pages, the final statement laid out the key points relevant to the asylum application in rapid, tight, and brutal succession. Fatima was forced to marry her maternal cousin, and her father beat her when she objected. Her husband raped and beat her. She lost her front teeth during one beating and was hospitalized for others that left scars and a limp in one leg. She sought help from her family and from her father, who was a police officer, but they sent her back to her husband, telling her that her place was with him and, later, that she needed to care for her children, who arrived in quick succession. The affidavit explains that she could not seek help from the police and was not aware of any organization or place she could escape to in Egypt. Her husband took a second wife, and Fatima was treated as a servant and continued to be abused. It concluded: "I am terrified of returning to Egypt. I am afraid that I would be forced to return to my husband. . . . My husband will beat me and possibly kill me. The police also will not help protect me from him."

Lucy astutely extracted this from much longer, more dramatic, emotional, and nonlinear tellings that digressed, stopped for tears, and dwelled on issues that were, from a legal perspective, "tangential" to the case. Removed were the morbid descriptions of the hospitals, the questioning of the moral character of her parents, Fatima's long and graphic descriptions of her injuries, her yearnings for her children and grandchildren, and much else. Also edited out were her reflections on happy moments with her family and, perhaps most importantly, Fatima's outrage at the deportation of her two sons from the United States. As a skilled and responsible attorney, Lucy shortened and condensed the story to seventeen numbered points to maximize its legal impact.

This was not unique to Fatima's case. Throughout my research I witnessed the role of legal expertise in shaping strong personal narratives for asylum applications. I saw how attorneys and law students worked toward narratives that, among other things, reduced nuance and eliminated uncertainties. Unsurprisingly, this process sidelined positive experiences and brought into sharp focus particular dangers considered common to the region—and in the case of gender and sexuality asylum cases, male dangers considered common to the region. In Fatima's narrative, this male danger took the form of spousal abuse framed by its social acceptability as well as the absence of governmental protection from it.

This was confirmed by hundreds of pages of "supporting documents" included in Fatima's application. Her attorney assembled reports by the US State Department, human rights organizations, and news media as well as experts such as the psychologist and a medical doctor. They all corroborated that Fatima's fear of spousal abuse was well founded in the context of Egypt. State Department annual reports in the three years leading up to Fatima's application identified domestic violence and societal discrimination against women as significant problems in Egypt. Like Suad's file, Fatima's was very bulky. Indeed the hallmark of a good application is the thick folder full of documents that lawyers know will not *all* be read by the judges and government attorneys. The physical weight of the binder on its own lends strength to the application—though Fatima had little knowledge or understanding of what it contained.

Lucy adroitly conveyed Fatima's complicated story in a concise, impactful narrative submitted to the United States government. To be clear, this framing and crafting of narratives is not a matter of fraud but rather a necessary part of the process of preparing all claims that are fortunate enough to have a responsible attorney involved. Attorney and activist Jessica Mayo argues that asylum stories "have incredible power, but that power emerges only after the narrative passes a certain threshold of coherence, fidelity, and conformity to the listener's perception of the world."[3]

Fatima's strong and lean affidavit is effective for immigration proceedings and suggests she had a good lawyer and that her application was likely to succeed. Yet it required the flattening of her stories into a neat, black and white scenario. Because of the way in which asylum narratives, especially ones that revolve around gender or sexuality, often spread out and encompass entire life stories, this flattening effect is striking. Fatima was all victim, Egypt was villain, and the United States was savior. I wanted Fatima to be granted asylum, and, had I been her attorney, I would have probably presented her case in a similar fashion.

Samir, an asylum advocate I met, explained that, when he is asked to give expert testimony for asylum cases for LGBTQI+ applicants from Arab countries, he focuses on stereotypical depictions of their countries of origin: "I have to play on [the immigration officer's] Islamophobia. I often will mention the framework of honor killing and, for example, if it is a Shia case from Lebanon, I will make sure to mention Hezbollah. I play up the word Hezbollah repeatedly, so that the officer is afraid and wants to save the applicant. 'Hezbollah, Hezbollah, Hezbollah.' You know, whatever it takes."

On the other hand, Randa, a lawyer in a large, prominent New York law firm who worked several pro bono asylum cases, told me: "Some of these cases really appeal to the judge's racism. I turned down a case from Gaza because I just couldn't find my way to going into a court and arguing how horrible all Palestinians are in order to help just one person. Someone was going to do it, but it wasn't going to be me."

The attitudes of Samir and Randa could be seen as polar opposites, yet they both speak to the power of stereotypical narratives within the asylum system. They speak to asylum applications' strategic use of essentialism—the purposeful evocation of a stereotypical Middle East characterized by male dangers and the victimization of women and LGBTQI+ folks. In the wider American cultural milieu, the purported treatment of women and, more recently, gays is commonly represented in simplistic terms and used to demonstrate that Islam and the Middle East are oppressive and that the United States is superior.[4] This is also true within the immigration system and accounts for two trends in the past two decades: increased hostility to Islam and to Muslim immigration,[5] accompanied by a simultaneous rise, minor in number as it may be, in asylum for those perceived as the victims of Islam. To be sure, an asylum affidavit is the place neither to highlight Fatima's agency or resilience nor to talk about shades of gray in both Egypt and the United States. Also, as an interpreter, I participated in this systematic flattening. Yet, as an anthropologist retelling Fatima's story, I can't help but find the absence of any nuance deeply unsettling. I can't ignore the connection between the stereotypes that helped her stay in the US and the stereotypes that support the ongoing exclusion of many others, such as her own sons.

While attending many practice sessions arranged by attorneys, I was able to witness the morphing of clients' testimonies from messy, rambling, nonlinear, contradictory, and complex narratives into more skeletal, neat, and tight accounts. With that, cultural complexity was often edited out and gray areas were erased, leaving a simple, black and white picture. Successful narratives stick to a core story that is directed and monovocal. Indeed, more complicated stories rarely make it through the asylum system.

However, unlike Suad, Fatima was unable to learn some of the intricacies of asylum, and she had difficulty adopting the legally impactful language the court favored. For example, she could not learn to say, "I am seeking asylum to escape persecution at the hands of my abusive husband, and my government offers no relief." But, when Lucy asked why she did not want to return to Egypt, Fatima said: "Eeeeeeee! I'd rather be chained and beheaded right here than face one minute of the humiliation that that possessed man rained down on me for years. I'd rather see death than see him. What a black day! I would never go back to Egypt!" She was a dramatic narrator. Fatima used hand gestures and facial expressions. She inflected her tone and used vocal changes, like deepening her voice to a growl when quoting her husband. While she did not adopt the specialized vocabulary of persecution, her vivid rendering gave her dark story extra punch.

Fatima was unable to memorize dates, addresses, and sequences as Suad could. Lucy quickly realized this and only asked Fatima to practice memorizing her date of birth, but even that was a struggle. She had never celebrated her birthday, and the numbers did not have much significance to her. It is common in rural parts of Egypt for people from Fatima's generation to have had their birth dates roughly estimated and retroactively assigned by a bureaucrat. But it was important in immigration court for Fatima to remember this official date—it was regarded as basic required evidence that the person before a judge or asylum officer was indeed the person in the documents, rather than an imposter using someone else's identity papers. Fatima struggled and sometimes failed to remember her birth date—she confused it with the birth dates of her children, especially under the pressure of an impending court hearing. Finally, Lucy settled on Fatima saying that she did not remember the day and month but only the year of her birthday, and Fatima added later in court: "Please forgive me, judge. I'm a simple woman."

Fatima had difficulty accepting the limited view of the court. Lucy had requested that Fatima ask her sons to write an affidavit about what they remembered of their father's violence and the treatment of their mother. On one phone call I interpreted for, Lucy asked Fatima if she had been able to discuss this with her sons and whether they had agreed to write letters. As we spoke, the voices of the young children Fatima cared for could be heard in the background, at times crying for her to get off the phone. Fatima said that only Aziz, her older son, would remember and that she was sure that he could tell all the things he witnessed. But she had not asked him to write a letter yet. Fatima said, "Next time I'm in your office we can call him and he will tell you everything." Lucy explained that Aziz had to write a letter, not tell us by phone. Fatima asked why and suggested that it would be better to hear it straight from the horse's mouth. Lucy replied: "Those are the rules of the court; the judge needs it in writing." Fatima relented but maintained that it would have been better for the judge to speak to her son directly—in part, I suspect, because she thought she could appeal to the judge to also let her son back into the United States, as she often told Lucy she wanted to do. Lucy had to be very firm that Fatima could not do this.

EDITED OUT

Some elements of the messy, raw version of Fatima's story played only a limited role in the formal, orderly version. One element edited out was Fatima's relative wealth in Egypt. Her mother was the daughter of an *'omda* or chief—which is to say, he was, among other things, a large landowner. Less fortunate farmers worked her family's properties in a sort of sharecropping arrangement. The problem was that Fatima's husband was also a member of that extended landowning family. She once remarked: "I owned land and two buildings in Egypt. We used to own two houses that are now inside Cairo, worth so much money today. Do you see what time has done to me?" On another occasion she told me she had lots of gold jewelry before she came to the United States. Her husband used to buy her gold "whenever he did something wrong. He was a big name and was in the newspapers and television and wanted his reputation protected." Fatima had sold some of the jewelry in order to be able to travel to America. In the official asylum version, these elements were missing. The fact that Fatima had on paper been a member of the landowning class would be a complication, though certainly not disqualifying or diminishing of the severity of her abuse. The land and the gold did not easily fit into a simple version that depicted her as a powerless victim.

Another edited element was Fatima's mental illness. It made it into her asylum application in the form of the psychologist's expert testimony and his assessment, which stated that she suffered from post-traumatic stress disorder (PTSD) as a result of the history of abuse by her husband. It thus served as corroborating evidence. But Fatima also continued to struggle with mental illness before, during, and after her asylum case. Her hospitalization in between two court hearings was of course not brought up, and I am not sure even her lawyer knew the extent of it. This raises the question of whether too much mental illness would transform the asylum system's perception of Fatima from a victim worthy of rescue to a burden to the state. Though asylum is supposed to be for those who need it most, the presumed cost to American society is not entirely irrelevant for decision-makers in the system. For all these reasons, Fatima's mental suffering had to be packaged as PTSD and as something for which she had received expert care and treatment.

Many of Fatima's retellings of her brutalization at the hands of her husband in Egypt highlighted the fact that she had given him two sons (in addition to three daughters) and that his second wife only had a daughter. To Fatima, her husband's violence and mistreatment was made even more unjust in light of this fact (that she bore the ungrateful bastard his only sons). The asylum narrative prepared by Lucy does not dwell on this patriarchal point, though it is prominent in Fatima's accounts. These sexist opinions could potentially undermine Fatima's appeal for protection by women's rights in the United States. The application only mentions Fatima's children briefly and in two contexts: as products of her forced marriage and as reasons her parents returned her repeatedly to her abusive husband.

Finally, neither the presence of Fatima's two sons in the United States nor their subsequent deportation was mentioned—though these are perhaps the most important elements of Fatima's asylum story in her own mind and in her continued struggles. Fatima saw her own asylum as a first step toward getting her sons back to the US, something that, as Lucy tried repeatedly to explain, would be very difficult. During the immigration raid on Fatima's apartment in Brooklyn, she was picked up together with her two sons. Although all three of them had long overstayed their tourist visas, the sons were swiftly deported to Egypt while she was hospitalized for a mental breakdown following her arrest. Her hospitalization put in motion a series of contacts that led her to asylum. In that sense, her unfortunate PTSD made her more fortunate than her sons when it came to immigration. It is not clear if the sons could have received legal reprieve from deportation, but they were not given the opportunity to investigate this. Fatima was potentially rescuable as a victim of Islam, but her sons—young Muslim men—were not.

HEARINGS: FIRE ALARMS AND VIDEO SCREENS

The month before Fatima's hearing date, the government made her an offer to administratively close her case. Lucy told Fatima that if she accepted the offer, she would have to continue to report to immigration as she was already doing, but the government would not move to deport her. Lucy tried to explain that there were a number of domestic violence–based asylum cases that were then at the Board of Immigration Appeals and that, if Fatima accepted the offer and applied for asylum at a later date, it might be beneficial due to the possibility of "more guidance" from those cases.[6] Fatima sounded confused: "What?" Lucy said, "Fatima, you have a very strong case and my advice is to go forward." Lucy explained that, if Fatima received asylum, she would have access to benefits and would be able to eventually apply for a green card. Fatima wondered: "Then why would I accept this offer? I want to be legal here and not be threatened. Everyone threatens me that they will call immigration." Lucy reminded her, "While your case is in court, no one can deport you, no one can call immigration on you." (This was theoretically true, but only as long as she was not accused of committing any crime.) But Fatima insisted: "I want to get a green card and feel safe here." Lucy responsibly added that, by going forward with the trial, there was always some risk that the judge would rule negatively, though Fatima could then go through an appeal process. But if at the end she lost, Fatima would have to return to Egypt. Fatima became alarmed: "That would be black death. There is no way I can go back to Egypt." Lucy responded, "Yes, I think your case is very strong." Fatima launched into praise of Lucy and all the help she had given Fatima, "You are like my own daughter."

I attended two practice sessions where Lucy prepped Fatima for her hearing. Fatima had to take time off from her job again and make the long trip to New York for each of these meetings. She did not take direction as easily as some other asylum seekers did; she could not adopt the framings and terms that would traditionally be considered helpful for her case. But she could tell her story passionately. Lucy simply encouraged Fatima to be concise and not to digress. She explained that the time they would have with the judge was limited. She also explained that there would be a court-appointed interpreter and that "Rhoda will try to come, but she cannot be your interpreter during the hearing. So, remember to speak slowly and clearly so the interpreter can understand you." Fatima asked if the interpreter would be Egyptian and whether they would be a man; she really hoped the court-appointed interpreter would be neither. Lucy explained that there was some chance it would be an Egyptian man, but anything Fatima said at the hearing would be absolutely confidential, and the interpreter could not talk about the case to anyone else. Fatima nodded her head but seemed skeptical.

When the long-awaited hearing date finally arrived, Fatima was understandably jittery. Rather than give her the address of the courthouse, Lucy asked her to come to her office two hours beforehand, to make sure Fatima was not delayed or did not get lost. We all traveled together from the office to the courthouse. We went through a security inspection and checked in. We were informed that the cases were running behind schedule and that we needed to wait. Fatima and I went to the cafeteria as neither of us had eaten yet that day. Lucy had arranged for the expert witnesses to be on call by phone, and she worried that the delay in the start time would mean that the experts might no longer be available. We eventually were called back to the courtroom and the interpreter appeared, a tall man with an Egyptian accent, after all. The government attorney seemed jovial, though tired, his shaved head shining in the fluorescent lighting. I realized that Lucy had not explained to Fatima that there would be an opposing attorney at the hearing—to Fatima, the government lawyer and the judge were all "the government." Finally, the judge in his robes entered at the front of the room, and we all fell silent. He started the proceedings. Shortly after, the loud ringing of a fire alarm went off. We all looked at each other, unsure what to do. Lucy said, "I hope it stops." The fire alarm continued to sound. An unrushed security guard opened the courtroom door and calmly informed us that we had to evacuate the building. And so Fatima's fate was put on hold.

It was cold outdoors, and Fatima was crying, upset at her terrible luck. Though we could not smell any smoke, security guards told us to move away from the building and that all hearings had been canceled for the remainder of the day. Lucy apologized and said that this meant Fatima's hearing would have to be rescheduled, and she was not sure for when. She told Fatima that she would contact her as soon as she had any new information.

She didn't have any updates for weeks. During this time, Fatima had another mental breakdown. As she recounts it, one evening she had gone to her room after the children were asleep and locked the door. She began crying and could not stop. She could not sleep and was still crying the following morning. Her employer, Dr. Haneen, called an ambulance, and Fatima was taken to the hospital. She said they gave her medication and she fell asleep. A few days later, her employer came and collected her and told her everything would be fine. When Fatima's hearing finally got back on the schedule, her spirits were lifted, allowing her to wait for those painfully long months to pass.

We made the trip again from Lucy's office to the court, through security, and to the courtroom. The judge that day was based in another state and was videoconferencing into the hearing. This made communication strained—everyone had to speak up extra loudly, and the judge could see only the camera's angle on the courtroom. Lucy asked the judge to temporarily forgo the services of the court-appointed interpreter in the interest of time. A key witness she was calling, psychologist Dr. Miller, was only available to testify for a short time period. This suspension of time-consuming interpretation made sense, especially given that, if the proceedings did not conclude that day, the next hearing might be scheduled for months or years later.

When the judge made his closing statement and announced his decision, Fatima did not at first realize what had happened because she did not understand what he had said. The judge announced in English that he was granting Ms. Fatima Hassan asylum, noting that he found the medical and psychological documentation persuasive and that, in light of "country conditions" and given "recent political developments," the government in her country was not able to provide relief to Ms. Hassan. The fact that Mohamed Morsi of the Muslim Brotherhood had recently been elected as president of Egypt and was frequently in the news may have helped Fatima's case. Regardless of Morsi's actual record on gender relative to that of his predecessor Mubarak, the judge likely shared the general stereotypical perception that an Islamic party in power would be worse for women like Fatima. According to my speculative interpretation of the judge citing "recent political developments," one of the first democratic elections in Egypt meant to him that Fatima was even more in need of rescuing.

ASYLUM FOR ONE, EXCLUSION FOR MANY

Up to that point, the judge's decision and explanation had not been translated to Fatima, so she was still unaware that she had been granted asylum. The judge on the video screen eventually addressed her by name and asked the interpreter to start interpreting. He told Fatima that he was granting her asylum and that he wished her well. And finally, in what was surely meant as a kind gesture, he said that she should remember that "in America, there is always help." To me, the judge's comment likely referred to the fact that United States law offers some formal protections to women from domestic abuse. Fatima smiled while tears streamed down her cheeks. She interpreted his comment differently: "No, no, judge, I work, I've never taken any public assistance." The interpreter grimaced a bit as he interpreted Fatima's response to the judge on the screen. The judge smiled and nodded and shook his head all at the same time. And on that confusing note, the hearing ended.

Lucy and I congratulated Fatima and hugged her as she wept for joy. Within minutes Fatima told Lucy she now wanted her help to apply for her sons to join her. This is similar to many asylum seekers I met: their immediate concern, once granted asylum, is to unite with family members. Lucy explained that bringing Aziz and Ihab would be difficult—the adult sons had been "removed" to Egypt a few years earlier under complicated circumstances and were probably not eligible for derivative asylum. Fatima's tears of happiness very quickly became tears of sorrow: "I'm afraid I will die before I see them again."

Fatima could not understand why she could not apply for her sons to return, since "they had done nothing wrong." She saw this as a profound injustice. She refused to understand her lawyer's explanations and would not take no for an answer (in what I learned was an often effective style). Fatima continues today to ask and pressure and pursue the option of "family reunification"—a term she had heard from fellow Arab Americans and was sure she qualified for. She insisted that, surely, the boys were sent away by accident, as one son was a hard worker and had operated a halal lunch cart in the city, and the other had been an excellent student who was in his final year of school. Among the many papers Fatima carried with her was her younger son's honors certificate from school, a paper fraying at the edges that she showed to me on many occasions and had obviously shown to many others as well. Fatima's sense of isolation in the United States, during and post-asylum, crystallized around the absence of her sons. "I am number one and number two and number three and number four . . . I am all on my own and no one is there to help me or do anything for me. If my sons were here, they would take care of me—do you think I would be suffering like this?" she insisted. Despite her need for help, the rest of her family members in New York continued to cut her off for the transgression of leaving her husband. Though I celebrated with Fatima and other successful asylees the legalization of their lives in the United States, it was impossible to ignore that the system was premised on the exclusion of others deemed non-rescuable, Fatima's sons included. "I am number one and number two and number three . . ."—*this* slow counting had the opposite effect of the psychiatrist's advice to count slowly to ten in order to calm the fire rising from the top of Fatima's head.

It is for this reason, among others, that the simple story of Fatima as victim, Egypt and its men as villains, and the United States as savior rings hollow. Sadly, asylum in Fatima's case did not offer the closure and dramatic life improvement it was supposed to, but rather coincided with a period of increased despair in her life—loss of work, homelessness, and a spike in depression. Jessica, a lawyer responsible for directing and supervising pro bono lawyers in asylum cases, noted that "being granted asylum is often just a clearing of one hurdle among many for a lot of our clients. Asylum applicants often face multiple challenges and this just solves part of one of them. I tell our lawyers this but they are often surprised that their clients are not happier when they win their cases." Though Fatima had often exclaimed that "America is like heaven compared to Egypt," she would later say to me in a homeless shelter, "What is this hell I am in?" adding another shade of gray to a momentarily black-and-white story.

A few weeks before Fatima's final asylum hearing, she had suffered another breakdown at the home of the family she was living with and working for. According to Fatima, when she came to New York for her hearing, her boss told her to take a few additional days off before returning to work. Fatima waited four days after her hearing and called her boss to ask when she wanted her back. Dr. Haneen told her she no longer needed her. This was a big problem for Fatima; the family paid her an undeniably exploitative hourly rate, but they also gave her a place to live most of the month in addition to the small income. She had few other employment options.

Fatima had been paying rent to a friend in New York in order to sleep at her apartment on her occasional days off from her live-in nanny job. A short time after her boss told her not to come back, the friend with the apartment told Fatima that her husband and children would soon be arriving in the country to live with her, and she asked Fatima to pack her things and leave. Fatima was soon hospitalized again with another breakdown and was then sent to a series of homeless shelters. So, within a three-month period, she was granted asylum but also lost both her job and her home.

Fatima was probably the most disadvantaged of the asylum seekers I met over the course of ten years, in terms of education and language as well as her psychological difficulties. But, in some ways, she was also the most resilient and forceful. That Fatima managed to work her way to asylum is impressive; given the arduousness of this path, there are likely many others in similar positions who have been deported. Nonetheless, the system she faced while trying to get herself back on her feet at this point would push anyone to their limits.

ASYLEE BENEFITS, BUREAUCRATIC TORTURE

Though I expected that my role as interpreter would taper off when Fatima's asylum case was decided, she continued to call to ask for my help for weeks that turned into months and years. I wound up spending many more hours interpreting for her after asylum than I did before. At the time, I did not think I would be writing about this portion of her experiences. I had conceived of my research as more narrowly focused on asylum narratives. But I could not turn my back on Fatima once she was granted asylum, especially since her life had then taken a downward turn. Moreover, I increasingly recognized that asylum was a step along a steeper climb, not the apex of asylum seekers' struggles.

Fatima's first task after being granted asylum was to figure out the meager refugee assistance she was entitled to. This poses a bureaucratic puzzle for any person, but even more so for someone with limited English and who is barely literate in Arabic. Lucy explained to Fatima that she was entitled to four months of refugee assistance. She gave her the names of two different agencies she could visit to obtain this. After it became clear that Fatima's boss would not be asking her back to work as a live-in nanny, she needed whatever help she could get.

Lucy was able to easily make an appointment for Fatima at one of the two agencies, the Refugee Resettlement section of Catholic Charities, and Fatima asked me to accompany her. When we arrived for the appointment, we were quickly ushered in to meet Anna, a kind and soft-spoken gray-haired woman. She explained that her organization offered job training and placement. With my interpretation help, Fatima inquired about urgent items like food and housing. Anna explained that they did not provide much in this area and could only offer minimal financial support of $289/month for four months. Anyone familiar with prices in New York City would recognize how insignificant that amount was. Anna advised Fatima to inquire at the second organization her lawyer had told her about, a governmental office called the Refugee and Immigrant Job Center in Brooklyn, since they might be able to offer her more financial help.

While Fatima was eager to receive urgently needed food and housing assistance, she was also interested in Catholic Charities' job placement services. We requested more information on the elderly care certification course, and Fatima asked to be placed on the waiting list for the training. But Anna said Fatima had to first choose between the two organizations offering refugee assistance: "The difference is that this is a gentle, small organization and the other place is a huge, impersonal bureaucracy. Here, we are an employment office, but you might get more financial payments at the other place." She was patient and encouraging but insisted that Fatima had to choose one of the two organizations and could not access the services of both.

Fatima and I later discovered, after multiple time-consuming visits to both organizations, that this was simply not true. Fatima insisted on applying for both the financial assistance from the Brooklyn-based agency as well as for the job training from Catholic Charities, even though she was told she could not do both. And sure, enough, Anna eventually relented. She arranged for Fatima to speak to her colleague, Monika, who specialized in elderly care employment. Monika was very grumpy. She huffed impatiently throughout our short meeting and rolled her eyes. "What do you want?" was her opening line. She seemed hostile from the get-go, and I couldn't help wondering why. Fatima's sense that she didn't like Muslims may have had some truth to it, but it is hard to be sure. In any case, Fatima was entirely unintimidated and asked many astute questions: If she were to complete the training course, would they guarantee her a job? How much would it pay? Can it be in an institution or only in private homes? Monika quipped that Fatima was "being very picky. She has no certification and no English. What kind of job is she expecting to get? In this economy? I won't play games with you, she is not ready." I interpreted to Monika that Fatima's preference to not work in homes is related to her history of abuse. This softened her ever so slightly, but she quickly pointed out that "mental health issues are a liability." To Fatima's disappointment, she learned after several visits that she could not pass the initial test to register for the elderly care training, as it required sixth-grade English. The course was sometimes offered in other languages, such as Russian, but there supposedly was no demand for it in Arabic.

Fatima also visited the second organization, the Brooklyn-based Job Center, to see what assistance she could get there. On her first attempt, she got lost on the subway, going over an hour in the wrong direction. On the second try, she found her way. I did not accompany her that day, because Anna had advised that Fatima should go on her own: "They will provide her with an interpreter; they are obligated to do so by law. And they will do the work that they would otherwise try to push onto you, Rhoda." Both Fatima and I had assumed that my interpretation help, as well as my education and relative privilege, might help protect her from bureaucratic neglect. But Anna suggested my presence could trigger neglect in this case. Fatima's lawyer, Lucy, had already given her cards that stated, "I require an interpreter," and had Arabic checked off on a list of languages. Elizabeth gave Fatima more of these, and Fatima added them to the stack in her purse.

However, the Job Center did not provide Fatima with an interpreter—card or no card, law or no law. Fatima told me she waited a long time and eventually saw a woman who was very gruff with her. She not only didn't get her an interpreter, but asked her to sign all kinds of papers in English.[7] When Fatima objected that she did not know what she was signing, the woman laughed and mockingly asked, "Are you afraid you are going to sign away your inheritance?" She said she could only offer her $250 for housing in her friend's apartment. She did get her emergency food stamps, though, which Fatima was grateful to have. She then gave her a series of verbal instructions that Fatima did not understand.

Fatima told me that she had mentioned to this difficult woman that she knew a very good interpreter who could work for her. She often praised me to the various agents we encountered in different organizations, in an effort to open employment opportunities for me. Regardless of how many times I explained to Fatima that I was not looking for a paid interpreter position, she kindly never gave up on trying to secure such a job for me. I did not succeed in conveying to her the odd nature of my work. My anthropological endeavor seemed only to make sense to her as an act of love ("You have done more for me than my own daughters would"—which is unlikely), as a student project ("Why aren't you recording more of what I'm telling you? Don't you want to be first in your class?"), or as a paid position, as in the interpretation jobs she tried to help me get. In a sense, some combination of all of these would in fact be a generous assessment of my research: it ideally could have some societal benefits in humanizing asylum seekers, while also advancing my career and livelihood (such as they were). When Fatima thanked me profusely for my help post-asylum, as she often did, I reminded her that she was helping me, too, by sharing her experiences. But she continued to insist on trying to secure interpretation jobs for me.

After visiting the Brooklyn Center, Fatima did not know how to proceed. She asked me to call them to inquire on her behalf. I dialed the number but kept on getting transferred to a voice recording. A young, upbeat woman's voice asked callers to leave a message and said, "We will get back to you as *soon* as possible," with a strong emphasis on soon. I left several messages over several days but never received a call back. Finally, after calling several more times, someone answered the phone. She looked Fatima up on the computer system and told me her case had been rejected because of missing documents. She said Fatima had to go back to their center in person and reapply. She recommended that we arrive early to get a number and wait to be called.

I accompanied Fatima the following week to the Brooklyn Refugee and Immigrant Job Center Center. We arrived at 9:30 a.m. to an already crowded waiting room—just as Anna had warned, this was a large and impersonal place. We signed in and waited, along with many other people, until a clerk called out Fatima's name. We approached the thick plexiglass barrier that he sat behind: "What are you here for?" he asked. We explained and he gave Fatima a number in order to see one of the clerks positioned across the hall from him. We waited again and, when our number was called, the second clerk asked Fatima the same question. He then gave her a second number that allowed her to wait again and then see a third person on another floor who—yes, I kid you not—then gave her another number, this time finally to see a caseworker. By then, it was afternoon. The caseworker, Celeste, looked tired but had a soothing lilt to her voice. She proceeded to give Fatima a number to go to another floor in the building to stand in more lines for fingerprinting and to get a free MetroCard for her two rides that day to and from the Center! Fatima could return on another day, she explained, to make an appointment with Celeste to discuss her needs.

When I emailed Lucy to ask for her advice on how to proceed and which organization to follow up with, she was "astounded by how difficult it is, by the barriers built into absorbing refugees." She had not been aware that there was a difference between the two agencies she had told Fatima about. Lucy and I, both educated and fluent in English, were stumped by the complexity of the system. On Fatima's next visit to the Brooklyn office, it took hours to get in to see Celeste. When we finally made it to her desk, she worked very slowly, confusing Fatima's papers with those of other clients (and accidently giving Fatima a document belonging to someone else). Her typing was painfully slow. The appointment took the entire day, but Fatima was able to apply for and receive more emergency food stamps on the spot.

However, these were then canceled two weeks later because Fatima did not respond to a letter that had been mailed to her listed address, an address she was forced to move out of in the interim. Fatima asked me to call Celeste on her behalf to ask why the food stamps had been cut off. When I finally reached her, Celeste seemed unsurprised and said she could not issue more emergency food stamps that day (it was February 28th) because Fatima had already been issued them in February. But if I called back the following day, March 1st, she could issue them to her then. When I called the following day, however, Celeste asked me for something new. Could Fatima call her former employer and ask her to write a letter that stated that she had let her go because of her breakdown and when? When I explained to Fatima Celeste's request, she asked, "Why is she treating me badly? I already showed her my hospital papers. There's no way my boss will admit to this; she won't even admit that she had employed me in the first place." Fatima said she would go back in to talk to Celeste in person and explain.

I called Fatima the following week, but her phone gave a busy signal that day and for many weeks after. I worried about her, as it was unlike her not to call me for so long. I asked Lucy if she had heard from Fatima. She hadn't. I called the hospital I knew she had been to before, but because of legal restrictions they could not give me any information. Inspired by Fatima's persistence, I didn't just hang up. I explained that Fatima was recently granted asylum and had limited English and had lost her job; the staff person asked, "What is asylum?" He told me Fatima's lawyer could send a written inquiry to the hospital. Lucy did so, to no avail. I didn't hear from Fatima till four months later. She was calling from a homeless shelter.

SEEKING SHELTER

It turned out that Fatima had checked herself into a different hospital. After several weeks, the social worker there placed her in a homeless shelter in East New York. Fatima was eventually able to buy more prepaid minutes on her phone and called me. I offered to come see her but she refused: "This is an ugly place and it's far away. I don't want you to come here." She insisted she was in the wrong kind of shelter, complaining that the people there were, in her opinion, all drug addicts and prostitutes.

Instead, Fatima wanted me to meet her near Port Authority to help her sort through old mail and voice messages: "I don't trust the people at the shelter to read my papers." She complained bitterly about the requirement that she wake up at 7:00 every morning and leave the shelter for the entire day, regardless of how bad the weather was outside. She said she was old and tired and needed to rest. She requested an appointment with the shelter's doctor, and he gave her special permission to stay in bed the following day because she was not feeling well. Having done so during her first appointment with him, he then refused to do it again. "Look at me, I'm in my sixties and I am working," he told her on a subsequent visit, "You are young. You can do it." Soon she wasn't given appointments to see him at all; she was told that he was in high demand by other residents at the shelter. So, every day she had to leave the shelter and could not return till evening. The staff would then thoroughly search her and all the other clients before allowing them to reenter, in order to prevent them from bringing in certain items, from sharp objects to bread. "Is this a prison or a shelter?" she remarked.

Fatima refused to eat much of the food at the shelter, since she didn't eat pork and only ate halal meat.[8] She had bought her own peanut butter, bread, and honey with her food stamps so she could eat those instead of the meat at the canteen, but the security guards did not allow her to bring those items in. Fatima did not give up easily. One day she threw a fit, and the security guards gathered around her until, finally, the director of the shelter was called and gave Fatima special permission to bring her own food in because "me eat kosher," as Fatima explained to her. Fatima seemed pleased at this minor triumph and noted that she was the only person in the shelter allowed to bring her own food in.

When I met Fatima after she had been staying at the shelter, she looked like she had lost some weight. She kept her eyes on her long-term goal of bringing her sons to live with her again in New York, but in the short term she was unsure what to do next. She did not want to stay in that miserable shelter, but her employer did not want her back. She asked me to help her look for live-in nanny jobs online, and I said I might be able to find requests for Arabic-speaking nannies, but she insisted: "Oh no, I can speak English well enough to talk about food and cooking and sleeping. I could do any job." I admired Fatima's tenacity but had my doubts about a non-Arabic-speaking family hiring her. I was later (again) proved wrong.

Many months earlier, Fatima had asked me if I had someone to pick up my daughter from school. Within Fatima's question was the implicit suggestion that she could do that job. I ignored her hint and steered the conversation in a different direction. I honestly was uncomfortable with Fatima taking care of my children, given that she suffered from PTSD. Moreover, I felt I needed to maintain a bit of distance between us. This was true of the majority of asylum seekers I worked with—though I spent long hours with many of them, befriended most, and became emotionally attached, I did maintain certain boundaries. In particular, I hesitated introducing my children, though most asylum seekers did have occasion to meet my parents, Fatima included. Fatima never asked me outright for anything except interpretation and language help. She never asked me for money and indeed often tried to give *me* gifts for my children (baby powder, baby shampoo, and other drugstore products), which I did not accept. When we met at coffee shops, she never wanted to order anything, so I would buy an extra cup of tea or a pastry for her, which she only occasionally consumed. Fatima was independent and proud. But she was in a tough position. "You should write your book about me Rhoda, so everyone will read it and cry over me," she said. Though I hope my writing on asylum goes beyond this kind of condescending pity, the conditions of Fatima's life at this point were very difficult indeed.

The person Fatima dealt with most at the shelter was named Johnson. At our first meeting after she was placed in the shelter, she talked about him quite a bit. She was mad at Johnson for refusing to make additional appointments for her with the shelter doctor. She later softened toward him when he helped her take care of mistaken jury summonses that were being sent to her with an increasingly threatening tone. Johnson got the summons withdrawn due to Fatima's homeless status. I am not sure how Fatima received the jury summons in the first place, given that she was not a citizen, but regardless of the bureaucratic glitch that caused the error, it nonetheless gave Johnson the mistaken impression that Fatima was an American citizen. And Fatima did not disabuse him of this assumption. What distinguishes Fatima's experience from that of many other New Yorkers who have used the city's homeless shelters are the language barrier she faced and her status as an asylee. This immigration status was often an enigma to many of the people she encountered in the bureaucracies—the vast majority had never heard of it before. It placed a big question mark over Fatima's head and, whenever it was noticed, threw into question her right to access basic services and at the very least caused uncertainty and significant delays. She quickly learned not to mention it unless necessary.

At the shelter, Fatima watched with horror news reports she didn't fully understand about a bombing incident during the Boston Marathon. She said she immediately felt that everyone at the shelter, especially the security staff, was mad at her because she was Muslim, but she did not fully understand what had happened. Unlike Suad, Fatima wore a headscarf and was therefore visibly identifiable as Muslim and often felt the sting of Islamophobia. She called me to ask what the news reports were about, and I explained that three people had been killed and hundreds were injured, many of them losing legs. "*Ya lahwi*, that's so terrible. And the bombers were Arab?" I explained that the suspects were Muslim but not Arab, and this confused her—Fatima's contact with Muslims in New York was limited by her Arabic. She later told me that, after our phone conversation, she confronted Johnson: "Why do you hate me? Because me Muslim? Those two boys, they do something bad, not me. Why you hate me?" She said Johnson laughed really hard and was kinder to her after that.

Johnson gave Fatima the name and phone number of Brianna Davis, who worked at a nonprofit organization that provided long-term housing. Brianna's organization was located far from the shelter, but she scheduled time to come to meet Fatima there two weeks later. We would subsequently learn that Brianna had just recently started her job and that her visit to Fatima would be her first visit to a homeless shelter ever. When we finally spoke with Brianna, she said she guessed that the housing application would take a day or two to complete, and then we would have the answer two or three weeks later. This turned out to be a radical underestimation, with the process taking closer to half a year, but we wouldn't learn that for a while longer. To begin with, Brianna explained, she couldn't start the application right away because it was the end of the month and she had a lot of other paperwork due. But she said she would start to work on Fatima's application the following week.

A few days later, Fatima called and left me an excited message, though her voice sounded extra tired. She had been transferred to a "nice shelter in Manhattan." Fatima wanted to meet so I could help her follow up on her application with Brianna, and she asked me to come to the shelter—this one she was not embarrassed by. She later told me that Johnson had refused to give her another turn to see the doctor at the first shelter, even though "I was the first to sign up." So Fatima got upset and started a small rebellion. The doctor then was forced to see her and took her to the shelter director to argue that Fatima didn't belong there: "She is sick and needs to stay in bed," Fatima said he told the director. She had earlier been upset with the doctor for not giving her permission to stay in the shelter during the day, but she said he turned out to be sweet "as honey." Johnson drove Fatima to the door of the new shelter; he, too, turned out to be "a prince," after all.

As far as I could make out, the new facility was smaller, cleaner, had less strict security measures, and was centrally located in a relatively affluent part of New York. I am not sure Fatima ever understood that it was a special shelter for homeless women with mental health needs. During my next several visits with her, Fatima's eyes drooped and she spoke slowly like she had just been woken up from a deep sleep. It was clear to me that she was heavily medicated. She was relieved to be out of the first shelter but certainly did not want to stay in the new one very long either. She had yet another social worker there, Susie, who told her that it would probably take six months to obtain housing. "Six months!?" Fatima was disappointed and upset about this. She was suspicious of Susie and speculated that she wanted to make more money off her and therefore did not want to help her quickly. Though, structurally, this is not an unreasonable analysis, I noticed an increase in Fatima's paranoia during this period. She spoke in a low voice that day and complained about feeling lethargic. I mentioned the marked lethargy to Susie before I left, and she seemed unsurprised. She said, "We will have the doctor adjust her medications at her next appointment," which was scheduled for several days later since he had no availability before then.

The day after Fatima moved to the new shelter happened to be the day of her much-anticipated housing appointment with Brianna Davis. As soon as I found out about Fatima's move, I called Brianna several times and left two voice messages letting her know that Fatima had been transferred to a different shelter and giving her the new address. Brianna apparently did not get my messages. She drove to the old shelter in East New York. By the time she figured out what had happened, she said, it was too late to come into Manhattan that day. Fatima was again disappointed and anxious to have Brianna complete her housing application as soon as possible, since Brianna's time estimate for securing housing was much shorter than Susie's. I would have guessed that there were regulations that prevented applicants from making two simultaneous housing applications through these parallel systems, but Fatima assumed otherwise and she was correct. She wanted to pursue both processes in order to select the best option offered to her.

Fatima continued to call and ask me to interpret meetings for her. Sometimes I would not hear from her for weeks, but then, every so often, she wanted me to spend many hours with her at a time, sometimes multiple times a week. This was beyond what I had envisioned as my role, but I found it difficult to say no, even though it was not always clear that my presence was in fact helpful. Moreover, with Fatima's mental illness, I often felt in over my head and poorly equipped to handle certain situations. But, given that she had so few allies who spoke her language, I did not feel I could just bow out.

Brianna finally came to meet Fatima. She seemed inexperienced, as though she was learning as she went along, but genuinely caring. Fatima asked me to call her several more times to inquire whether she had completed the forms. In the end, it took Brianna twelve weeks, not two to three days, just to submit the application for Fatima. Susie, the second shelter's social worker, had at least been explicit about having other priorities. She knew Fatima hated living in the shelter and was eager to find her own place but told us that, to her, Fatima's mental health and other benefits needed to come first. Susie did not seem to consider that Fatima's mental health was additionally stressed by being in the shelter. To Susie, the best place for Fatima was in the institution she worked for.

At one point, Susie questioned whether Fatima would be eligible to apply for housing at all because of her status as an asylee. This upset Fatima a great deal; she told Susie that her lawyer had assured her that her asylee status was just like having a green card. Susie's supervisor eventually intervened and later was able to confirm that Fatima was indeed eligible to apply for housing. This was yet another example of how Fatima's asylum status frequently threw uncertainty and delays in her path.

In addition to her illiteracy, Fatima's eyesight was weak and she had cataracts. As she went through the asylum process and then tried to access assistance afterwards, various government agencies came to play major roles in her life. All of them relied heavily on mailing her documents—documents of the kind that anthropologist Smadar Lavie calls "implements of torture."[9] Fatima's poor eyesight, together with her illiteracy, made these pieces of paper a source of great anxiety. Her loss of her home and difficulty keeping track of her belongings added to this stress. The intimidating barrage of mail she received in relation to her immigration status, her healthcare, her finances, and more was difficult to keep track of, all the more so when she was homeless. When she had her purse stolen on the street, it took considerable time and money, as well as help from her lawyer, to replace some of the documents she lost. Fatima was very guarded about her papers—but her inability to read her own mail, and her need to ask other people to help her do so, meant she had no privacy about her personal matters.

Such documents seemed to have great power over Fatima's life, yet she attempted to exert some control over them. Like many other asylum seekers I met, she often carried around scores of documents that were vital to her. For one thing, because of her deep fear of deportation to Egypt, she carried evidence of her legal status on her person at all times in one separate special bundle. She did so in order to prove her legal status in the US, should this be questioned. But she also did so later for another reason: the separated bundle helped her to avoid disclosing her noncitizen status by accidentally handing someone an asylum document. She wanted to prevent service providers in New York from questioning her access, because she had already encountered difficulties and delays of this kind at the shelter, where caseworkers did not know what asylum was, not to mention what kind of benefits an asylee was entitled to. They frequently assumed it was none, and it was left up to Fatima with her limited English to prove otherwise. Despite her inability to read and write, she tried to circumvent such bureaucratic speed bumps and literally held some of her documents close to her chest.

I hesitated to include this detail in my account of Fatima's struggles. There is a strong preference for depicting asylum seekers as victims and not as strategizing to improve their positions. Anthropologist Miriam Ticktin notes that humanitarianism "requires the suffering person to be represented in the *passivity* of their suffering, not in the action they take to confront and escape it"—performances that are too active and strategic become unconvincing.[10] But, of course, asylum seekers need to strategize—at the risk of being stigmatized as manipulative and therefore undeserving of asylum—because the systems they must navigate absolutely require copious maneuvering by anyone who wishes to get through.

In all of her dealings with nonprofit organizations and governmental agencies after asylum, Fatima was presented with one conundrum after another. These systems sometimes seemed to operate as forms of what Lavie calls "bureaucratic torture":[11] they were painfully ineffective and could drive anyone to despair. Yet, Fatima, despite her slow and painful gait, her difficulty navigating the city, her weak English, and her illiteracy, did not despair—or perhaps she could not afford to. But the absurdity of the system is hard to convey in full. It is compounded by often underpaid, undertrained, or overworked employees. The precise roles, responsibilities, and powers of the numerous workers Fatima was introduced to were not always clear. Some of them were experienced, efficient, and helpful, but others clearly were not. Like Lucy, some had chosen jobs in this field, despite the low pay, because of a commitment to social ideals. Some were sweet, patient, and gentle—and did their utmost to help Fatima. Others were rude, dismissive, or racist. One I met was downright disdainful. A friend who works as a health advocate for New York City argued, "A lot of people in city social services have good intentions, but the bureaucracy oppresses them too. It is such a layered labyrinth that it creates dysfunctional workplaces, the stress of which gets transferred to people seeking benefits."

Regardless, the system threw up obstacle after obstacle in Fatima's path. The agents with their various demeanors and levels of competence can hardly be held responsible for systems seemingly designed to work badly. From refugee benefits to homeless shelters to public housing, these systems seemed magically illogical and dysfunctional. The bureaucratic hurdles Fatima had to overcome after being granted asylum cast dark shadows over the expected highs of freedom and opportunity.

Successful asylum stories are supposed to have happy endings. Most asylum personal statements end on a hopeful note along the lines of: "If I am granted asylum, I will pursue my education/work/family life in the United States." Fatima could not realistically pursue an education, and her children had been deported. Her work—and she worked extremely hard—was never mentioned in her application. The type of work she did as a hotel cleaner, household laborer, and caregiver, was never discussed. The hopefulness of her asylum was built on escaping the abuse of her husband and not necessarily on her bright future in the United States. After her ordeal of many months to pick the pieces of her life back up again, the judge's final words to her at her asylum hearing—"Remember, in America, there is always help"—seemed misleading.

MAMA HAS A HOUSE

Of course Fatima was very fortunate to have been granted asylum and for being able to access the many social service agencies available in a state like New York. Yet the housing eventually offered to Fatima through

Brianna Davis's agency was more than two hours out of the city, in an area Fatima said was as terrible as it was inaccessible. Susie's housing application yielded a room in a supervised housing arrangement, with shared bathrooms and kitchens and a security booth at the front that enforced a curfew and prevented nonresidents from entering. It was basically a nicer shelter that involved similar limitations and surveillance of daily life. Fatima was thoroughly disappointed with both options and felt like, after over a year of struggle, she was back to zero.

During this time, Fatima's elderly mother, who had been brought to the United States by her brothers, became severely ill. Although the family had cut Fatima off years earlier, one of Fatima's nephews contacted her to tell her that her mother was in her final days. Fatima went, with Susie in tow, to visit her dying mother in the hospital. The mother refused to see her and kicked her out. Fatima was sad and humiliated: "I felt very embarrassed that Susie had to witness that. They kicked me out of the hospital, and all of them were there—all of my brothers are garbage. . . . I feel very bad because my mother died while she did not approve of me. To them, I am just a whore. Just a whore. I am sorry I am telling you all these things, but there is no one else I can tell it to. I have friends, of course, but I have to tell them that everything is fine." All of Fatima's brothers living in the United States were *zift* (terrible), she said, except maybe for one, Subhi: "He saw me at the hospital, and he tried to console me after my mother humiliated me and kicked me out." Fatima eventually reconciled with Subhi. She speculated that he might have felt guilty because Fatima was homeless, while he and the rest of her brothers had inherited their mother's landholdings and split them up among them, leaving the sisters out.

Many months later, this reconciliation opened another housing option for Fatima: to share a subsidized apartment in Queens with Subhi and his Dominican wife and adult children and their partners. This description is the short version of a very long and convoluted process— but after many setbacks and a long struggle, Fatima did eventually make her way out of the shelter system. But the arrangement with her brother was not ideal, as Fatima had ongoing heated disagreements with him and particularly with her sister-in-law and their extended family. Miraculously, Fatima eventually found another live-in caregiver job, this time with an Indian family in Chicago. This eased the tension as she only lived in the house a few days a month during her time off from work. When she next called me, I could again hear children's voices and a television on in the background. It still astonishes me that Fatima was able to accomplish all this given the obstacles she faced. Her employer flew Fatima back to

New York once every forty days for a four-day break. Fatima proudly said I should bring my family for a meal at her house in Queens next time she is off from work, because "Mama has a house now." She was pleased with this, but also sad, as she wished she could fill this new home with her sons and their families.

GREEN CARD

Fatima was technically eligible to apply for her permanent residency, or a green card, one year after she had been granted asylum. But it took significantly longer for her to make her way to applying. By then, her lawyer, Lucy, had left her job at the nonprofit and could no longer help Fatima with her application. When Fatima reached out to the organization, she was connected with Joanne, a new lawyer there, who told Fatima that, because her address had changed, the nonprofit could no longer help her. Fatima objected that Lucy had already vetted and accepted her case. Joanne repeated that their policy was that they would not be able to help her if she had moved: "Your residence is outside the area we serve." Fatima did not accept this unequivocal "you cannot use the services here" answer. She pushed back. She explained that she had used the services in the past, the organization had all her records, and it would be very difficult and time-consuming for her to start over with a new organization. She cried and pleaded and, in the end, Joanne relented. Whereas my instinct was to accept Joanne's answer and to quickly proceed to the "correct" office, Fatima was able to cut out that long detour with her persistence. But other hurdles remained.

Fatima needed a current medical exam from a doctor who was certified to provide it to the government. Such exams were usually costly, but Joanne located a medical office that provided them for free. However, when Fatima went for this free medical exam, she was told that she required a number of immunizations that she had to pay for. Fatima had called me from the doctor's office so that I could speak to the staff person to clarify the situation. The doctor's office explained that Fatima might be able to get reimbursed for these costs later from Medicaid, but she had to pay for them that day. Fatima said she could get these immunizations for free from her regular doctor, and she would do so and come back later to get the medical report for the green card. Given that she did all this in bits and pieces in between her forty-day work stints in Chicago, it took a significant amount of time.

The next obstacle was paying for her green card application fee—this, too, was costly, running over a thousand dollars. Joanne explained that Fatima could apply for an exemption from these fees but needed extensive paperwork from the social security office to do so. Joanne warned that, even with the correct paperwork, this exemption was rarely granted. Fatima made several visits to the social security office and finally was able to get the correct paperwork. However, by the time she obtained these, her medical report had already expired.

NOT A HAPPY ENDING

Fatima did eventually get her green card after much delay. She also never gave up on bringing her sons to the United States. She had reconciled with one of her brothers, but that relationship had its ups and downs. She continued to find work—last I heard, as a live-in caregiver for the elderly grandmother of another family in Chicago. But her mental health also continued to ebb and flow, with periods of improvement and then deterioration and hospitalization.

Fatima's story is complicated and does not necessarily point toward a happy ending or an upward trajectory—she has zigzagged her way through her difficult life. Some friends who read early drafts of this chapter wondered whether I should include it in my book—to put it mildly, Fatima is not a poster child for asylum. One reader was surprised that Fatima was granted asylum at all, given the possible burden on government services she represented. But Fatima's story is a reminder that asylum—narrow as its definition may be—is not only about saving famous scientists and ballerinas. It is supposed to be about providing refuge to those who need it. Given the extremely volatile status of asylum under the Trump administration and beyond, I certainly sympathize with the desire for uplifting asylum stories demonstrating the triumph of the human spirit, with stellar asylees who excel in their fields. I enjoy accounts of asylum seekers who become soccer stars, successful restaurateurs, or famous fashion designers just as much as the next person. But such politics place an undue burden on asylum. It was, after all, enshrined as a right for those fleeing persecution, to provide freedom from fear, and not built on the merits of an applicant's resume.

Fatima liked to remind me that her life is like a Bollywood film; it was certainly full of dramatic highs and lows. She kept a keychain in her purse—sometimes with no functioning keys on it—with an old photo of her as a beautiful young woman in the heart-shaped key holder. She would lift it up next to her face and say: "See how far I have fallen? I was once young and beautiful." Inside her purse were pictures of her sons and daughters and grandchildren in Egypt. She was saved by asylum, but they were excluded. She had to traverse the torturous bureaucracies of asylum, refugee aid, homelessness, and much more, on her own with only a smattering of English words, squinting through her cataracts at document after document sent her way, and relying on her beat-up old flip phone to call on people to help. She is anything if not resilient, battling her way through subway stations, waiting rooms, invasive caseworker meetings, and yet another required fingerprinting. And, of course, her story goes on, even as this chapter ends. Her ability, as a domestic abuse survivor who has struggled with ongoing mental health challenges, to make any progress in these relentlessly demanding systems is, for me, testament enough to the human spirit—and to one human in particular who managed to squeeze through the narrow opening asylum provides.

3

"I wish it was a happier ending"

WHEN FADI ARRIVED IN THE UNITED STATES, he stayed for a few weeks in Los Angeles with Bassem, a childhood friend from Amman. For years now, Bassem had been urging Fadi to come to LA, promising that he would hook him up with work through his family's business. Like many Jordanians, Fadi envisioned America as a land of economic opportunity and social freedom. If Bassem's family helped him to get off the ground, perhaps with hard work and diligence Fadi could eventually find someone to sponsor him for a green card. After the excitement of his initial arrival, Fadi said he waited for Bassem to approach his dad about hiring him. Two weeks went by, and Bassem had still not done so. Fadi didn't want to be rude to his host, but the $10,000 he had saved up in Amman and brought with him was being rapidly depleted. He knew those savings wouldn't last long, and he was eager to start working. He soon learned that, in fact, Bassem had not been on speaking terms with his father for over two years! Fadi's hopes of being hired by that family quickly evaporated. And he learned that Bassem's telephonic descriptions of life in America were misleading in more ways than one.

He stayed in Bassem's apartment and tried to figure out what to do next. There was no way he would go back to Jordan. Every day, Bassem would leave to go to work, and Fadi would stay in his apartment alone, waiting, worrying, trying to figure out how he would cope. Up to that point, Fadi's exciting new American life had not shaped up the way he had hoped. Sometimes, Fadi logged onto gay chat rooms. He was lonely and hoped he would meet someone online. Maybe even someone who could help him get a job. As a recently arrived Jordanian man, how else could he hope to find work except through a friend? One day, Bassem returned home early and saw Fadi's computer open to a gay dating website. He became enraged and kicked Fadi out: "He shouted at me 'I don't need a faggot in my house.'"[1] Fadi asked, "Did this faggot ever bother you or do something wrong to you?" Bassem cursed and said, "Our culture and our religion don't allow that." Fadi called Bassem a hypocrite, pointing out that, by the same token, "our culture" doesn't allow Bassem to have a fiancée in Amman and then sleep around with "every kind of woman" in LA either.

Fadi wasn't sure where to turn next. He called Khalil, Bassem's younger brother. Fadi had been closer to Khalil in their childhood, as they were the same age, and Khalil had lived with Fadi's family in Amman for several months before following his parents to the US. Fadi explained what had happened, and Khalil came and picked him up. He made Fadi welcome in his run-down apartment in East Los Angeles, but he "had all kinds of drama going on," including drug addiction. Fadi was thankful to Khalil for taking him in, "but I hated my life."

The day after he kicked Fadi out of his house, Bassem contacted Fadi's older brother, Nihad, who was his age-mate. He telephoned him in Jordan and outed Fadi to him: "Your brother is homo." The next day Nihad called Fadi to ask if it was true, and Fadi admitted that it was. Fadi recounts that his brother replied: "'Ok. Well, I can't change you. It's your life. You should try to make it work in America. Try not to come back here, because the family won't be happy if you are known to be gay here.'[2] 'Let's hope,' he told me, 'that Bassem is not going to tell anybody else in the family.'" Fadi was relieved that Nihad did not take it too badly.

He stayed with Khalil but was miserable. He didn't know how he would manage to remain in the US longer or whether he would be able to find work. He continued to try to meet people online, and some nights he borrowed Khalil's car and went out to gay bars and clubs in hopes of meeting Americans. Fadi was interested in hooking up, but beyond sex or romance, he also wanted to build a community for himself. He was accustomed to having many friends and worried that "if I don't meet people and make contacts, I am not going to get a job." In fact, he met his first American boyfriend, Jack, a few weeks later. They met at a bar, where Jack was celebrating with friends his upcoming move to San Francisco for a new job. Fadi and Jack hung out together for two weeks, and when Jack was about to relocate, he suggested that Fadi come with him: "He told me 'You don't know anybody here. Why don't you come to San Francisco with me, just to visit and see if you like it?'" Fadi had nothing keeping him in LA. He agreed.

Though Khalil had taken him in, Fadi's preexisting small network of family and friends from Amman would not get him very far in the US, especially since he did not want to continue to hide the fact that he was gay. He had to make new friends—and fast. Soon after going to San Francisco with Jack, Fadi met Camille, a French woman, at a birthday party for Jack's friend. They immediately clicked. Fadi liked practicing his French, and Camille enjoyed his sense of humor. She invited Fadi and Jack to a barbecue at her house in the Pacifica neighborhood the next week and then generously suggested that they leave the cheap hotel where they were crashing and stay in her guest room until they found a place to rent.

For years, Fadi would struggle to afford rents in the Bay Area and often relied on partners or friends to help with housing. For many months in San Francisco, he didn't have full-time work, but his friends and friends-of-friends offered him odd jobs, such as cleaning houses and doing basic office tasks. The pay was not great and certainly not steady, but with no work permit, no postsecondary education, and a reluctance to approach Arab businesses, this was the best he could manage that first year. He had left a well-paying job in Amman, and he increasingly doubted he would ever be able to earn a similar living in the US. Though he soon was enjoying new freedoms in San Francisco, he was also experiencing new levels of economic despair and dependency that would last for almost a decade.

Even though Fadi was willing to work without a permit, he couldn't find a steady job. By contrast, Nasser, a Palestinian asylum seeker I also interviewed, was too nervous to even try. He told me: "The government is in the process of doing a background check on me. I'm obsessed that they are watching me. I know that there are, like, tens of thousands of applicants, and they are not going to watch every single one. I know that a lot of people, regardless of whether they are LGBT asylum seekers or whatever, work under the table. But I don't know, maybe I'm too much of a rule follower. I'm afraid to do it." Other asylum seekers I have met have managed to find jobs without a permit, though these are ripe for exploitation, as demonstrated, for example, by Fatima's years of work as a poorly paid 24/7 live-in nanny. Asylum seekers survive the difficult period before they receive work permits using a variety of strategies, none of them ideal.

However, Fadi's new connections to friends in the Bay Area proved crucial. His networks not only enabled him to survive financially, but helped at many other levels as well, including finding a legal solution to his immigration status and connecting him to a therapist to help him ride out the emotional challenges. He managed to tap into a number of support organizations that became key to his navigation of his first years in America. It was through these contacts that he found a free therapist, who became "like a mother" to him. And it was through the therapist that he discovered he could apply for asylum and get connected to a pro bono lawyer. His path to legalizing his life in the US and beyond was significantly facilitated by these networks. And he was fortunate that this path to asylum was relatively short—his case was decided in just over a year after he arrived in the US, a much shorter period than the great majority of the asylum seekers I met. But his financial struggles were long. His economic journey was bumpy and winding and placed a damper on his otherwise relatively smooth legal immigration journey. Despite his "best case scenario" asylum experience, he was bogged down by a decade of ongoing financial struggle.

When I met Fadi through his network of gay Arab friends, he had already been granted asylum seven years earlier and could work legally. But he was still struggling to find a decent job. He had recently started a position at a national chain hardware store but was only given twenty hours of work per week. He was waiting and hoping to be promoted to full time, but "these things take a while," he said. The job was okay since he liked the work, but the hourly pay was low. Given his education level, his other employment opportunities were limited. His part-time work schedule made it easy for us to speak: "I would be more than happy to help with your book. . . . I like talking about these things; it helps me work through stuff."

COMING TO AMERICA

At a young age, Fadi decided that he wanted to "get the hell out of Jordan." As a teenager, he focused on building up his English and later studied French as well. He kept up pen pal friendships with foreigners and tried to meet Europeans and Americans who visited or lived in Jordan. "Since I was 17, I've always been thinking about how to get out," he told me. Like many immigrants who hail from poorer countries, Fadi held some version of the American dream; his version was contoured with visions of gay liberation. And his desire to leave was in part born out of a traumatic experience in Jordan. This was of course quite unfortunate, but in the American immigration system, that trauma gave him a pathway that he would otherwise not have had.

Fadi was arrested in Amman when he was seventeen after having sex in a government-owned office building with a man he had been seeing.

Fadi and the other man were apprehended by undercover policemen, who accused them of having had sex. They both denied it. Though there were no laws against homosexuality in Jordan, the authorities behaved otherwise. Fadi, a descendent of Palestinians who had fled to Jordan before he was born, was held by the authorities for ten days and tortured and humiliated. The man he had been with was full Jordanian, older, and wealthier. He had connections to influential people in the Jordanian government and was quickly released.

The police took Fadi to a doctor to supposedly determine whether he had had anal sex. Such forced anal exams have been medically discredited and are in themselves a form of torture.[3] Fadi described the humiliation: "It was awful, just awful. It was so dehumanizing. I wished I could just disappear into thin air, but there was no way out." His sexual partner managed to avoid this examination, thanks to his Jordanian ethnicity and political connections. At one point, the policemen shoved a filthy slipper in Fadi's mouth: "They told me, 'Suck this slipper the way you suck dick.'"

As Fadi narrates it, he naturally wanted to get out of Jordan after that: "I hated the way I was treated. And I began trying to figure out how to leave ever since. . . . The undercover cops were lurking everywhere, and you never know when you will get in trouble." Having already experienced arrest and torture, Fadi said this lurking threat felt very real. He had a small circle of gay friends, and there were known cruising areas in Amman, but he constantly worried about getting caught or found out.

In addition to the ever-present threat of police harassment, Fadi also worried about his family and wider community shunning him should they discover he was gay. He came under increasing pressure by his family to get married—to a woman, of course. The older he got, the harder it was to find excuses. All three of his brothers—both older and younger—had already married, and his parents insisted it was his turn now. This type of pressure was a common complaint among other gay asylees I met. Nasser, a Palestinian asylum seeker, also told me that the escalation of his family's demands that he get married was part of the impetus for him to leave. His unmarried status raised his family's suspicions that something may be "wrong" with him: "My father wanted to take me to a doctor to see why I was resisting marriage. He wanted to check to see if I have any sexual problems, to find out why my brothers had married at age twenty-two and twenty-three and I was in my thirties and didn't want to get married. He wanted to figure out why I was so delayed." For both Fadi and Nasser, this was hardly the primary reason for leaving, but the family demands felt unrelenting. Though the pressure to marry grew out of their families' heteronormative hopes that their sons would live happy lives, its effect was suffocating and oppressive to those sons, especially given the unknown reaction of families to discovering the real reason they were resisting marriage.

To get away from mounting family pressure, police harassment, and more, Fadi applied for a tourist visa to the United States as soon as he could afford to. Such a visa is not easy to come by for Jordanians: at a minimum they must prove substantial income and savings, just as Suad had to do in Sudan. Though this alone is far from a guarantee of visa approval, it is a minimum condition that must be met. And it was out of Fadi's reach for years; it was not until his late twenties that he managed to save some money. In 2003, he finally applied for a US visa but, despite his presumed financial eligibility, he was denied. He did not give up. He applied two more times that year, but both applications were also denied without any explanation. He did, however, manage to get a European visa and traveled to France, Spain, and Portugal with an eye to evaluating them as possible places to immigrate to. But as he explained it, he did not have contacts in those countries to help him, and so he returned to Jordan before his visa expired.

At that time, Fadi was working at an American company with an office in Amman, and, after a promotion, his boss proposed to send him for a training workshop in the United States. Fadi applied again for a US visa in 2005. This time, during his interview at the embassy, he was able to point to his American employer's desire to send him for training. He also showed that he had traveled to Europe and returned to Jordan in a timely fashion. Finally, on this fourth try, the embassy granted him a visa, valid for six months.

As soon as the visa arrived, Fadi quit his job. He got rid of his apartment and sold all of his furniture. He knew he did not want to come back. His family thought he was foolish for leaving a well-paying job for an uncertain future far away. His brothers urged him to visit America first and see how he fared there, before giving up his position in Amman. But Fadi did not care to hold on to a possible retreat path; he took the plunge and dove ahead.

Though it had taken four tries, Fadi was fortunate to have eventually gotten a six-month visa to visit the US. He was less lucky with his entry to the country. Agents of the immigration system are given vast discretion in their decisions, especially at the border, and immigrants' fates are shaped by the luck of the draw—and by the disposition or even mood of the officers they happen to encounter.[4] When Fadi landed in New York, the agent he met flagged him. He was taken aside and questioned for two hours. Another agent thoroughly searched all of his luggage. He asked Fadi why he had brought so much clothing—he had in fact brought his whole wardrobe. Fadi gave the excuse that he had transited through France for ten days and that he was going to visit his aunt for two weeks so he needed clothing to cover that whole period. The agent seemed skeptical: "Haven't you heard of laundromats?" Fadi said he didn't want to spend his vacation washing clothes. The agents opened his cameras and looked through his photos and videos.

Fadi told me that he had felt he was being treated like a criminal. Tired after his flight and then the long delay, he had wearily pointed out that he had already gone through an extensive security background check when he applied for the visa in Amman. But this was 2005, and the shadow of 9/11/2001 undoubtedly hung thick in the air. Fadi named the elephant in the arrivals hall: "I'm not one of those terrorists." Fadi said the agent replied, "I'm just doing my job." He noted suspiciously that Fadi spoke English quite well for someone who had only finished high school. Fadi repeated that he had been working for an American company. In the end, the agent decided to allow him into the country but reduced the length of time he would be allowed to stay. Though the embassy had approved six months, the agent told Fadi that, since he wanted to visit his aunt for two weeks, he was changing the length of time Fadi was allowed to stay in the country to exactly that long. He warned Fadi to leave at the end of that period. Otherwise, he threatened, agents would come to his aunt's house and pick him up and deport him. Fadi told me he pretended that was fine by him: "I told him, 'No problem, that would be nice actually. We can have a cup of tea there, and I'll show the agents our Arab hospitality. It will save me the taxi fare to the airport.'" He was allowed in, despite his sass.

When Fadi arrived at his aunt's in Michigan, he stayed for only two days, then quickly made his way to Los Angeles to Bassem's. With his savings and Bassem's connections, Fadi paid a lawyer to help him apply to extend his visa to six months. With documents that the lawyer provided, Fadi could now legally stay longer, but not much. After Bassem kicked him out and he left Khalil's place and went with his new boyfriend to San Francisco, that six-month deadline loomed near. Fadi was thankful for the help of his new friends, Jack and Camille, but he was still not working. New Arab arrivals in the area might normally search for employment at

Arab-run businesses, possibly using networks from back home to connect them, but Fadi was hesitant after his experience with Bassem. He didn't want to "deal with Arabs after what happened in LA." Jack went to work every day, and Fadi was home alone in foggy Pacifica. He was running out of money. He hadn't found a job. His visa would soon expire. He didn't know where his life was headed. He went "into a deep funk."

GETTING CONNECTED

Fadi struggled with depression and anxiety because of the uncertainty of his future. Jack suggested that they go to Magnet, an AIDS health justice organization with a wide range of services based in the Castro district of San Francisco. At a minimum, they could get STI testing, and they could also "see if they have other things to offer." Luckily, the organization had a social worker on staff, and Fadi told her a bit about his story and the depression and anxiety he was experiencing. The social worker said she would help him find a therapist who understands his culture to work with him. Fadi balked at the idea. He explained that he did not want to deal with Arabs. After his humiliating experience with an Arab friend in LA, he was reluctant to interact with other non-gay Arabs after he moved to the Bay Area, not to mention pour his heart out to one. But the social worker insisted she would find a professional who would understand his language *and* his sexuality. Fadi said he would think about it.

Less than a week later, the social worker called to tell Fadi that a therapist named Ghada, who was also Palestinian, had agreed to work with him, and, since he was unemployed, she would do so pro bono. The social worker reassured him that Ghada was well qualified and experienced and had dealt with issues of sexuality regularly as part of her work. Fadi was hesitant but decided to give it a try. Ghada turned out to be "nothing short of wonderful—she was a huge influence in my life." She had almost legendary status in San Francisco, and several other gay Arab men living in the region also mentioned Ghada to me separately and discussed how important her care was in their lives. She has helped many Arabic speakers over the years, gay and otherwise, and was instrumental in creating numerous community programs post–9/11 that flourished well beyond her retirement.

Fadi recognizes that, in American culture, therapists are not supposed to become personal friends with their patients, but both he and Ghada were Palestinian: "We can't entirely shake our customs and traditions." He adored Ghada and, in her warmth, guidance, and generosity, she became "like a second mother to me." Ghada explained that, having come to the field of therapy late in life, she pushed back against the traditional western rules of boundary setting between clients and therapists. Speaking about her many gay, lesbian, and transgender Arab clients over the years, she described how "we would go for walks, go to lunch, honestly I treated them like my sons and daughters.... I let them text me, like a mom. This was a no-no for western therapists, but my understanding of Arab culture empowered me to follow my instincts for what was best for them."

Years after he had stopped seeing her for therapy, Fadi stayed in touch and spent time with Ghada. She loved gardening and invited Fadi to help in her yard. Ghada calls her garden "Little Palestine"—it had a loquat tree, za'atar herbs, and many other botanical reminders of home. Fadi told me: "She worked me hard there [he used the Arabic term *harthat 'alay*, meaning "she hitched me to a plough"], and I loved it. It brought me so much joy and comfort to be in her garden with her." He made sure to check in on Ghada regularly: "She means so much to me. She taught me so much. She explained to me many things about life in the US . . . how to navigate this society. She was a huge influence."

Ghada was in fact the one who told Fadi about asylum. He had been desperate to stay in the US but wasn't sure how he would be able to do so. He had hoped to find a job that would sponsor him, but that had not materialized. When Fadi told Ghada during therapy about all the difficulties he had faced in Jordan, including his imprisonment and torture, she asked him if he had heard about asylum: "I said, 'what is that?' I didn't know about it. I knew about refugees and refugee camps—my family are Palestinian refugees. But Ghada said, 'This is like a refugee but you have to be in the country to apply. . . . Since you're gay and Muslim and from the Middle East, I'm sure you will get it! And you have gone through so much, so your case will be strong.'"

In my years of research, I have encountered many people like Fadi who knew they wanted to change the conditions of their lives and build new ones in the United States but were unaware of the legal option of asylum until after they managed to enter the country. Of course, not all asylum seekers chance upon asylum that way. Nasser, for example, knew about asylum in detail before embarking upon his journey. While living in Palestine, he had researched online how gays and lesbians were treated in different countries and learned about asylum from various websites. In fact, he found the detailed how-to YouTube videos of two Arab lesbians who had applied for asylum themselves and settled in California:

I saw their videos online, and then I contacted them. I asked them about the process. Actually, before that, I was planning to immigrate to Australia, but I didn't know anyone there. I was going to go do the whole process by myself, knowing no one. And then when I saw the YouTube videos, I was like, their story sounds interesting; maybe I can follow the same scenario. They were nice. They replied to my email, and they explained the process and everything, and I went to the same lawyer they used. They even met me at the airport when I arrived.[5]

Nasser initially considered immigrating to Australia, not as an asylum seeker but as an internet technology worker. The fact that he *chose* instead to apply for asylum, and in the US rather than Australia, does not mean he was undeserving of it, for he in fact had suffered extensive persecution. Similarly, Fadi had initially hoped to get a work visa through family connections and found his way to asylum when the job route fell through. This frames asylum as one of a number of possible immigration pathways. It also reveals the false premise that migration has a singular motivation and that forced migration to flee from persecution can be neatly separated from voluntary movement in pursuit of better economic opportunities—the two are almost always intertwined. And asylum becomes more important when other pathways are narrowed or blocked, as they increasingly have been for Arabs hoping to come to the United States. In a related vein, Yasmin Nair states that the emphasis during the 2000s in the gay rights movement on the Uniting American Families Act, which would allow US citizens to sponsor their same-sex partners, "provides the illusion that the entrance of queers/LGBTs into the United States has been determined entirely by their status *as* queers/LGBTs, but in fact queer immigration has always been interlinked with the history of immigrant labor and has always been affected by the gendering of that labor."[6]

A LAWYER

Fadi stumbled upon asylum several months after arriving in California, thanks to Ghada's help. And, like Suad and Fatima, it embodied something close to what he in fact wanted, though initially he didn't know its name or rules. The next hurdle he faced was finding a lawyer to assist him in the complex process. Friends connected him to an experienced private attorney who had won many asylum cases, but Fadi could not afford his retainer (not to mention his full fee). Ghada came to the rescue yet again! She put him in touch with a nonprofit called Lawyer's Committee for Civil Rights, which provides free legal aid to asylum seekers. The Lawyer's Committee found Fadi a pro bono attorney. The AIDS health justice organization offering free services and connecting him to Ghada, Ghada offering therapy pro bono and connecting him to the legal nonprofit, and the legal nonprofit connecting him with a lawyer he didn't have to pay—all of these organizations and individuals' services were essential to Fadi's path to stabilizing his life in the US. I became well acquainted with many similar NGOs, often based similarly in coastal urban centers. Such organizations carry the increasingly heavy weight of aiding immigrants and asylum seekers, queer and otherwise, whom the US government—in the very best of cases—abandons to find their paths on their own through the complicated and burdensome asylum system.

Tawfiq from Egypt noted that, in the United States, "through the whole asylum process, you are completely on your own. Finding an attorney, paying for that, organizing and developing your case, and going to your asylum interview—you are just completely by yourself without any government help. This is not the case everywhere. In Holland, for example, from the moment you say you are in need of asylum, the government supports you. I have a friend who went through this [around 2000], and even when you get asylum they continue to support you by providing classes to help integrate you into Dutch society. And they help you find a place to live. Here the government doesn't do any of that. There are nonprofit organizations that do some of it, but you have to find them." Indeed, other wealthy countries have historically provided more support to asylum seekers than the United States does,[7] though that support has waned and varied in recent years in Europe. But, all along, applicants in the US, even children, have not had even the basic right to legal counsel.

Thanks to the work of NGOs, Fadi's path toward asylum became possible. Many asylum seekers who attempt to navigate the system on their own (because they have no other choice) face difficult odds. Taking account of all other barriers, having a lawyer on an asylum case has been found to make it 400 percent more likely for that case to be successful.[8] Other studies estimate that chances are improved five-fold,[9] others eleven-fold.[10] Even when asylum seekers have enough money to hire an attorney themselves, they are vulnerable to poor-quality representation or outright exploitation. Sharif, a Palestinian asylum seeker I met, initially hired a private immigration attorney in New York who then proceeded to sexually harass him, offering to help him only if Sharif provided him sexual favors. Sharif was able eventually to switch his case to a larger nonprofit, but his experience demonstrates that legal assistance is not a simple matter. Yet the great majority of asylum seekers go to court without any lawyer at all.[11] Fadi was in a lucky minority.

Only three days after his initial interview at the legal aid organization, a staff member called Fadi with the news that they had found him a pro bono lawyer. The caller explained that the attorney's name was Angela and that she was "African American and also a lesbian." She was originally from Chicago and worked at a prominent law firm in San Francisco. Like many pro bono lawyers I met, Angela did not have prior experience doing asylum cases, but she was capable and dedicated. Fadi was extremely lucky for the speed at which these connections were made.

"YOU DON'T LOOK GAY"

A few days after the call from the legal aid organization, Fadi was already introducing himself at Angela's office at a prestigious law firm. At their first meeting, Angela looked at him and said, "You don't look gay. That's a problem." Fadi told me, "What the hell was I supposed to say to that? I told her, 'Well, when you hear my story you will know I'm gay.'" Of course, there is no universal way to "look gay," but Fadi did not fit the mold Angela had in mind. As he explains it, he is relatively masculine and was not dressed in a fashion that signaled to Angela his homosexuality. Angela legitimately worried that this could be an issue for the asylum officer. The organization Immigration Equality warns lawyers never to "take for granted that the [adjudicator] accepts that your client actually is LGBTQ/H."[12] Though Angela was perhaps overly blunt, her observation that gay men are expected to look a particular way in the US was not unique. In the landmark case of Jorge Soto Vega, a young man from Mexico, his asylum application was initially denied because the immigration judge found that he didn't "appear gay" and could therefore hide his sexuality if he wanted to.[13]

Preconceived notions of what gay men look like, how they dress, or how they behave are often used by adjudicators as part of their credibility determinations. These decision-makers are asked to decide whether they believe a person claiming to be gay is in fact gay and, unsurprisingly, they often use what is commonly considered "intuition," which is formed by deeply ingrained cultural assumptions, to make this determination.

The bogus requirement of "looking gay" is one that anthropology scholars love to pick apart. To start with, they widely agree there are no universal categories of sexuality, since these vary across cultures and time. And it follows that there is no universal form of being gay, or for that matter, being masculine. Even within a given culture, those markers can be fluid and shift over time. However, this basic understanding of cultural differences is not always recognized in immigration courts. Adjudicators in the system regularly decide whether they believe an applicant's representation of their sexuality or not, based on their own culturally specific, often narrow, understandings, which they take to be universal. In one ridiculous illustration of this from Austria, an adjudicator rejected an eighteen-year-old Afghan asylum seeker because he was unfamiliar with old Bee Gees lyrics![14] Legal scholar Senthorun Sunil Raj argues that, to date, asylum law "anxiously maintains ethnocentric assumptions about popular culture consumption, public visibility, gender expressions, sexual practices, and social marginalisation."[15] Even pro-LGBT actors in this sphere regard more "queer" intimacies or fluidity as downright threatening to the asylum system.[16]

Though Angela did not tell Fadi to dress a particular way, he says she advised him that "you might be inclined to dress more conservatively for the official interview because you think this is what is expected, but I encourage you to just be yourself." A training module for asylum officers issued during the Obama years states: "Some applicants with LGBTI-related claims will not 'look' or 'act' gay. If an applicant provides detailed testimony about his or her experiences . . . it would be inappropriate for you [to] hold against the applicant the fact that he or she does not fit your notion for how LGBTI people should look or behave."[17] The training module actually lists a number of cases in which such faulty assumptions led to decisions that were later overturned. In one example, an immigration judge "improperly relied on his own stereotypes and found an Albanian applicant's claim to be gay not credible because he did not exhibit gay 'mannerisms', 'dress' or 'speech.'"

Despite this guidance issued in late 2011, asylum officers often continue to rely on their own understanding of sexuality in adjudicating cases. Lawyer Kimberly Topel argues that, regardless of whether an immigration judge is empathetic or hostile to gay issues, "they can find themselves asking questions that are . . . reliant on Western stereotypes in order to determine whether the refugee seated in front of them is actually gay."[18] Aaron Morris of Immigration Equality has been quoted in Vogler explaining that "'stereotypes are my best friend and my worst enemy. If you walk in and you are like a male dancer hair stylist who is especially effeminate and meets the expectation of what a gay guy might look like, probably they're not going to be that concerned about your sexual orientation.' Conversely, he continues, 'If you are more of a linebacker with a wife and two kids who has either naturally developed almost no stereotyped sexual orientation aspect or attribute or has tried very hard not to do those things, then it's harder.'"[19] Also, lawyers and advocacy organizations "risk reproducing decision-makers' disputable stereotypical assumptions" in their efforts to maximize applicants' chances of succeeding in asylum.[20] This is another area in which the fate of asylum seekers in the end depends on the luck of the draw and on something as far out of their control as, for example, whether their adjudicator has ever encountered a masculine gay man before.

BUILDING THE FILE

Since 1996, the law has required asylum seekers to submit their applications within one year of arriving in the United States. At the point that Fadi met his pro bono asylum lawyer, he had only six months remaining till that deadline. He went every few weeks to the law firm to meet with Angela and her assistant. These sessions were stressful and draining, but, as more information for his case was assembled, they eventually gave Fadi some sense of progress. His narrative began with his involvement in his late teens with a group of young gay men in Amman and detailed how undercover policemen there would harass them. Fadi asked friends from his former circle in Amman to send supporting statements that had to be translated, reviewed by Angela, then notarized in Jordan by a lawyer they could trust with this information, and finally mailed. Adding to the stress of the preparation, Fadi had to be delicate about whom he asked for help, as he had not told his parents or some of his siblings that he was gay, nor had he mentioned that he was using sexuality as a basis for his asylum. Fadi found this stressful, just as Suad had been stressed in collecting her supporting statements from female relatives in Khartoum.

And like many LGBTQI+ asylum seekers, Fadi also collected casual photos of himself in Amman with boyfriends as part of his proof of his gay identity. But, like personal appearance, what photos are accepted as proof is another level at which narrow assumptions about sexuality can operate. Anthropologist Elif Sari found herself "browsing hundreds of personal photos and brainstorming with people about which images could make their identities legible to [Canadian NGOs that could facilitate resettlement], my eyes became trained to notice the elements that would count as 'proof' of non-normative sexuality and gender. During those acts of curation, I often became complicit in the reproduction of universalizing identity categories and White, visible, middle-class gay and lesbian aesthetic."[21] It is unsurprising that Fadi went through a similar process.

Angela was concerned that the asylum officer would fixate on the fact that there were no longer laws against homosexuality in Jordan. While the earlier British Mandate Criminal Code there had banned same-sex activity, Jordan's penal code adopted in 1951 did not. It is generally more difficult to argue for asylum from a country where there are no explicit laws that criminalize homosexuality, even when, in reality, LGBTQI+ people face persecution.

Signs of gay life in Amman are not difficult to find. Fadi indeed described having a significant circle of gay friends there. Hashimiyya square is a well-known area for gay men to meet each other. There is a gay-friendly café whose owner is open about his sexuality—but Fadi explained that the proprietor was a friend of the royal family and therefore enjoyed special protection that Fadi and his friends without political connections did not have. But these signs of public gay life could be used to argue that Fadi's fear of persecution was unfounded.

Despite the lack of laws criminalizing homosexuality in Jordan, Fadi could point to the problem of the undercover policemen who frequently harassed him and other men suspected of having sex with each other. Fadi's arrest, imprisonment, and torture were a prime example of this. His narrative dwelled extensively on his ten-day imprisonment and torture: "The strongest part of my case was spending time in jail." Moreover, the social stigma that would result from being discovered could range from shunning to threats of harm. Fadi's narrative highlighted the case of his friend, Rashid, who died soon after his family found out he was involved with another man, apparently having been pushed out of the fourth floor of his building. Fadi asked his friends back home to find newspaper articles about Rashid's death, which were then translated to English and added to his file.

EXOTIC HOMOPHOBIA

Fadi explained to me that his asylum narrative argued that "although there is no law in Jordan that would condemn a gay person to death, people achieve the same goal with honor killing," and he used the English words "honor killing" in our Arabic conversation. I think it is not a coincidence that Fadi switches to English here; the term is intended for a western audience. The language of "honor killing" grew as part of an NGO vocabulary with a complicated history in which it was increasingly taken up by LGBTQI+ rights organizations, especially western ones.

The term began to be used by many Arab feminist organizations in the 1990s, often in the form of "so-called honor killing" to signal that such acts were indeed not honorable. The term commonly referred to violence against women who were seen to violate society's sexual mores, usually by being suspected of having sexual relations outside of marriage. In English and in the western imagination, the term became shorthand for Muslim violence against women, and donor organizations prioritized fighting it, though such framings have had questionable results.[22] More recently, Arab feminist organizations have become more wary of the term and instead simply refer to "violence against women," but international organizations have been slower to move away from it.

Men who have sex with men may be ostracized, considered an embarrassment to their families, and subjected to threats and violence, but the Arabic term "honor killing" is rarely used to refer to such violence within Arab societies or among Arab NGOs. One of the organizers of a hotline for LGBTQI+ Palestinians told me that callers who reach out to the hotline do not use that vocabulary: "We hear 'my family found out and they want to kill me,' or 'my family threatened me because I'm homo' [using the English term] or 'my father threatened me when he found out' and so on." The organizer explained that "gays don't use the 'honor' language at all when they call, even transgender women. . . . I've never heard this language in all the years I've worked in this field. . . . It is my impression that this is the language of certain institutions and it is used in order to simplify explanations." One Palestinian gay asylee explained to me in Arabic that "family honor is the girl. For a gay man, people say, 'so and so was killed because he was gay and being gay is forbidden.'[23] The English term 'honor killing' is a kind of western translation of this that helps asylum seekers." In essence, the term "honor killing" is often used by those with a stake in exoticizing the violence.

Many Arab gay asylum seekers in the United States use the term, in my opinion, because it likely resonates with the stereotypical image decision-makers have of their countries of origin. The use of this specific term is important, as it marks the violence as exotic and therefore lends itself to asylum rescue narratives. This is part of a larger tendency in gender and sexuality asylum, in which applicants are pushed to "package" violence "as traditional and cultural."[24] I point this out, not to diminish the violence or fear that Fadi and other men have experienced, nor to imply that notions of family honor are not part of the system that produces this violence, but to point to the cultural abbreviations and distortions that using the term "honor killing" relies upon. Anthropologist Lila Abu-Lughod argues that the category "stigmatizes not a particular act but entire cultures or ethnic communities"[25] and also that it characterizes the violence as ethnically specific and somehow unrelated to violence against women and LGBTQI+ persons in the United States.

Rendering this violence exotic and "other" makes it easier to argue for asylum in the United States, where it is considered nonexistent. If the violence were simply called homophobic violence, then the argument for America as savior becomes more complicated, since homophobic violence certainly does occur in America as well (and one would then have to prove a subtler argument that it occurs at lower rates). Asylum narratives function by definition as rescue narratives—and often appeal to the self-congratulatory western impulse to, in Gayatri Spivak's famous words, "save brown women from brown men,"[26] or, in Arab gay asylum cases, save brown, supposedly gay men from brown, supposedly straight men. For this reason, they often lean heavily on stereotypical and hegemonic understandings of other cultures.

Legal scholar Anita Sinha argues that successful gender-based asylum cases more generally tend to be granted when the persecution is seen as cultural in nature.[27] Anthropologist Kamala Visweswaran similarly observes that an ethnically Tajik woman in Afghanistan, for example, is more likely to have asylum granted as an Afghan woman facing "repressive social norms" than as a member of an ethnic minority persecuted by the Taliban.[28] There is in fact a marked preference for granting gender and sexual orientation asylum cases under the "social group" category rather than the "political opinion" category, as the US prefers "asylees who are cultural victims, rather than political dissidents."[29] One asylum advocate I met, Samir, said he was well aware of this bias and used it to help asylum seekers. A sample letter of support he shared with me stated: "Approving Mr. X's case will mean giving him a new chance at life. He has been persecuted *by his culture* long enough to know and appreciate the value of freedom that you may grant him" (emphasis added).

Karen Musalo and Stephen Knight suggest that there are regional patterns in gender asylum. In their review of 443 gender-based asylum cases, they found that, among applicants from the Middle East, there were relatively few domestic violence cases and even fewer rape-based cases. The majority of claims were rooted in "Restrictive Social Mores."[30] Asylum scholars have argued that US asylum law has moved toward establishing "exoticized harms like genital cutting" as a basis for asylum protection, while remaining "inconsistent" or "schizophrenic" on its treatment of "quotidian harms like domestic violence."[31] And, according to sociologist Connie Oxford, the more exotic forms of harm get highlighted in asylum cases, which "decreases the visibility of less exotic practices such as political activism [and] torture . . ."[32] "Honor killing" fits well into this framework and, given that it has proven successful in winning over adjudicators, it is unsurprising that some queer Arab men use that language in their applications.

In Arab gay asylum cases, exotic forms and names of harm float to the top, and stereotypes are evoked to inspire adjudicators to rescue the applicant. Sharif from Gaza told me he repeatedly mentioned "Hamas, Hamas, every other sentence" in his application. Fadi's therapist, Ghada, encouraged him to apply for asylum by explaining: "Since you're gay and Muslim and from the Middle East, I'm sure you will get it!" Though Ghada knew the details of Fadi's experience and the likely strength of his legal case, her recognition of the equation in which "gay" plus "Muslim" plus "Middle East" equals asylum points to the significance of stereotypes.

In fact, it would have been difficult to provide any account at all (of Fadi's social persecution and the threats of violence he faced) to westerners without them seeing stereotype confirmation. I don't have a simple solution for how gay asylum seekers can frame their cases without evoking and benefiting from distorted preconceived notions. Moreover, it would be unfair to single out this vulnerable group as responsible for offering a more complex understanding of their countries of origin. Gay asylum seekers cannot shoulder the burden of undoing such widespread and longstanding historical biases. And, in any case, any single carefully worded account is unlikely to change this larger framework.

The use of this sort of strategic essentialism in individual cases is certainly understandable, and had I been Fadi's lawyer, I would have probably encouraged him to use "honor killing" too. However, such asylum accounts wind up reinforcing powerful stereotypes that continue to feed oppressive politics and foreign policies. In other words, it is unreasonable to look to asylum narratives to contest widespread stereotypes about the asylee's country of origin, but the use of these stereotypes to some extent props up geopolitical systems that produce the inequalities and conditions that, among other results, create asylum seekers. At some level, rescuing Fadi in this way is built on a system that creates more Fadis in Jordan. This is not unique to him as a person but rather reflects the impossible structural position Arab LGBTQI+ asylum seekers find themselves in.

The description of Fadi's experiences in Amman that he shared with me included some positives, such as his close friends and the café, the love of his family, a comfortable income, as well as negatives: harassment, imprisonment, fear, and violence. His asylum narrative of course emphasized the latter (the negatives), because the former would complicate his claim and hurt his chances of success. The high bar of persecution in asylum makes this a problem more generally for asylum advocacy organizations as well.

The former head of a large gay asylum organization in the US told me: "There is this ghoulish aspect to our work, where when you hear a report that things are improving for LGBT people in x country, you think, damn, that's too bad. Because it makes our [asylum] work harder." There is an inherent tension between LGBTQI+ advocacy within a given country on the one hand, and advocacy for LGBTQI+ asylum seekers from that country applying in the US on the other. This tension is evident in the history of one of the larger organizations in the field. The International Gay and Lesbian Human Rights Commission (IGLHRC) used to include two branches of work, in-country rights advocacy and asylum advocacy in the US, but soon found these two at odds with one another. For example, I was told that leading members of a Jamaican gay rights organization (who themselves sought and received asylum in the United States) were allegedly unwilling to write reports for IGLHRC that described Jamaica as a place where no self-respecting gay or lesbian could continue to live. As a result of this form of tension, IGLHRC closed its asylum documentation program in mid-2007.[33]

The flip side of this is that LGBTQI+ rights organizations in the region seek to highlight the positive and fulfilling lives that many of their members lead in their home countries. One advocate in Palestine told me in 2015 that, while it was important to help people, such as one young man who "clearly had PTSD symptoms and we helped him find a therapist and offered to help him as he sought asylum," asylum was nonetheless not a solution they generally wanted to promote. She emphasized that many other members of the community stay and make important changes in society.

In contrast, the American embassy in nearby Jordan quickly provided

Angela with a letter that confirmed Fadi's description of the frequent harassment of gay men there by undercover police despite the absence of laws criminalizing homosexuality. The letter also highlighted a number of "honor killings" involving gay men, thereby supporting Fadi's claim. As with the other fortunate cases I was connected to where strong lawyers were involved, Fadi's case file grew thick and heavy, containing almost five hundred pages of documents, pictures, and support letters.

THE BIG DAY

Fadi was fortunate to receive an interview date within a few weeks of submitting his application. He noted that "it was the first year that they changed the rules. Before that you would have to wait five years, six years, seven years until you got an interview. So I was very lucky." Fadi was indeed fortunate, and had he applied a few years later, his wait time after the interview would have likely been longer as well. The arduousness of the asylum process has been in flux, just as the opportunity for someone like Fadi to even step foot in the United States has changed, having narrowed in the years following 9/11 and then narrowing further as a result of Trump's Muslim bans and anti-immigrant policies. This fluctuation was far beyond Fadi's control, of course, and had little to do with the merits of Fadi's individual case.

Historically, American immigration law has explicitly excluded so-called sexually deviant foreign nationals.[34] The Immigration Act of 1917 banned gay people seeking to enter the United States as "aliens afflicted with psychopathic personalities, sexual deviation, or a mental defect."[35] The 1952 Immigration and Nationality Act excluded them as mentally defective, per the psychiatric standards of that time. That act was voided as vague in 1963, but Congress moved quickly to explicitly exclude persons with "sexual deviation" in 1965.[36] Despite changes made by the American Psychiatric Association in the 1970s that removed homosexuality from its list of disorders, the Department of Justice announced in 1980 that it had "a legal obligation to exclude homosexuals from entering the United States."[37] It was not until the Immigration Act of 1990 that "lesbians and gay men were no longer automatically barred from entering or immigrating to the United States."[38] However, they were still vulnerable to exclusion "based on convictions for sodomy or public morality offenses under the 'crimes involving moral turpitude' or 'good moral character' exclusions still enshrined in immigration laws."[39]

1990 was also the year in which Toboso-Alfonso, who had applied for asylum because of his persecution as a gay man in Cuba, was granted withholding of deportation (a provision similar to asylum). In 1994, then Attorney General Janet Reno declared the Toboso-Alfonso case as precedent, allowing sexual orientation as a basis for asylum.[40] By then, there were already forty other asylum cases pending that used sexual orientation.[41] Within two years of Reno's order, the International Gay and Lesbian Human Rights Commission had won asylum for at least sixty applicants.[42] In 2000, the Lesbian and Gay Immigration Rights Task Force (now known as Immigration Equality) estimated that two thousand sexual orientation–based asylum claims had been filed.[43] And by 2003, IGLHRC reported, approximately six hundred people had received asylum based on sexual orientation.[44]

Attorney Victoria Neilsen argued in 2005 that "lesbians, like many women, are more likely to face persecution in the private rather than the public sphere. As a result, they have greater difficulties than gay men in proving eligibility for asylum."[45] In their review of almost two hundred cases of asylum decisions for cisgender sexual minorities, Roxana Akbari and Stefan Vogler determined that men fared significantly better than women.[46] Lesbian applicants also tended to suffer from additional gender and class discrimination and, therefore, increased barriers to asylum. IGLHRC estimates that only eighty-seven of the aforementioned six hundred asylees were women, "illustrating a severe gender disparity in the asylum process."[47] In August 2000, another groundbreaking case was decided in which "sexual identity," not orientation, constituted membership in a protected social group, thereby making it easier for transgender applicants to win asylum.[48] There are no governmental statistics showing the number of cases using particular bases for asylum over the years, but estimates suggest that the number of LGBTQI+ cases has increased gradually ever since.[49] A small portion of these, perhaps close to 5 percent, have been from the Middle East.[50] There was an uptick in the number of detained gay Muslims requesting aid from IGLHRC's asylum program after the introduction of the post–9/11 National Security Entry-Exit Registration System (which imposed special registration requirements on males aged sixteen years and older who were nationals of twenty-five countries, twenty-four of which were majority Arab or Muslim).[51]

The paths of asylees to citizenship have been subject to many changes, reflecting larger social shifts, political trends, and legal transformations—having nothing to do with Fadi or other asylum seekers who were often at the mercy of these ebbs and flows. These changes can greatly impact the kind of hand an asylum seeker is dealt. Beyond such historical shifts, asylum in any given year is like a roulette game—there are huge disparities in the grant rates of particular judges and cities that are beyond the control of asylum seekers and independent of the merits of their cases.[52] For example, according to one study, "Colombians had an 88 percent chance of winning asylum from one judge in the Miami immigration court and a 5 percent chance from another judge in the same court."[53] An immigrant advocacy lawyer in Florida told a reporter: "It's heartbreaking. . . . How do you explain to people asking for refuge that even in the United States of America we can't assure them they will receive due process and justice?"[54]

But Fadi was ready to throw his dice. When the day of his interview finally arrived, he was, unsurprisingly, extremely nervous. The agent assigned to his case turned out to be a woman in her fifties whom Fadi considered "so calm that it was scary." He said it was difficult for him to get a read off her; she seemed detached and just looked from her computer screen to the documents, then back to the screen. She avoided eye contact with him and hardly looked up at all.

A key part of the unpredictable gamble of asylum is the agent or judge assigned to a case. Tawfiq from Egypt told me: "Your fate is in the hands of the asylum officer. It all depends on the person you get, on the kind of officer assigned to you. Not on how strong your case is. The decision is, in the end, subjective." Nasser similarly noted that "in the end, a human being will interview you. The immigration officer is a human being, not a computer. I reasoned that the mentality of the officers in San Francisco is probably more sympathetic than the officers in Texas, which is partly why I chose SF."

FINAL QUESTION

Fadi was told to prepare for an approximately two-hour meeting, but his interview only lasted fifty minutes. Toward the end, the agent asked Fadi why he was afraid to return to Jordan: "'Why can't you return to Jordan? There are no laws in your country against homosexuality. You are just scared. Nothing happened to you. Your parents have not found out. Your cousin didn't find out. You just *feel* scared.' I said 'Yes, but why should I spend the rest of my life in fear? I don't want to do that.'"

Fadi remembered that the very last question the immigration officer asked him at his interview was whether he had ever slept with a woman.

I tried to speculate with Fadi as to why the officer would ask this, and whether ever having had sex with a woman would put Fadi's gayness in question. Her query seemed premised on an all-or-nothing, neatly compartmentalized notion of sexuality. In another case I interpreted for, Haitham presented a challenge to his lawyers since he had had many relationships with women and boasted about his skill at having sex with them. Yet, he also had sex with men and had a strong preference for them, identifying himself most definitely as "gay." The lawyers seemed to want to tell a clear, black-and-white story as preferred by the system, even though Haitham's experiences were not easily simplified that way. This is another example of how culturally narrow understandings of sexuality make their way into asylum. Deborah Morgan observes that "the construction of homosexual identity as a basis for asylum arose from a historical context" that essentially "presumes clarity of boundaries between heterosexual and homosexual identity."[55] Kate Sheill argues that human rights discourse "requires stable categories" that emphasize the "'normality' of lesbian, gay, bisexual and transgender" people.[56]

Fadi told me: "I don't know why the officer asked me [whether I had ever slept with a woman]. And I don't know why I answered the way that I did. I was so nervous, I wasn't thinking straight. . . . I said, 'With all due respect, I don't like fish; I like the beach.'" I did not quite understand what Fadi meant: I had heard the derogatory reference to women's vaginas as "fishy," but had not heard the word "beach" used in this way before. He explained: "What I meant is that I'm attracted to the anatomy of men, not women." Fadi said that the officer laughed nervously and then ended the interview. His lawyer Angela later asked him, "'Why did you say that?' I said I didn't know. I was just so nervous. I know it was not a polite thing to say. But I was so afraid, my heart was beating so hard, you can't imagine, and that's what came out."

Since Fadi's hearing, Justice Department guidance has told asylum officers that "the applicant's specific sexual practices are not relevant to the claim for asylum or refugee status. Therefore, asking questions about 'what he or she does in bed' is never appropriate." It also instructs officers that, "if the applicant begins to volunteer such information, you should politely tell him or her that you do not need to hear these intimate details in order to fairly evaluate the claim." Yet, despite these guidelines, in many of the cases involving gay men I have learned about, aspects of sexual practice—including details of who penetrated whom, where, and how frequently—have most definitely been a subject of interest and consideration.[57]

A HAPPY-ISH ENDING

Fadi returned to the asylum office two weeks later to receive the decision on his application. He was accompanied by his lawyer, Angela, and her assistant Gina. Fadi remembers his name being called and the intense anxiety he felt: "It was one of the scariest moments of my life. Because either I am going to be denied and asked to leave, or I'm going to be changing my life for good." Of course, if Fadi had not been granted asylum at that point, he would still have had the option of taking his case to immigration court. Despite his awareness of that option, like many asylum seekers I met, he felt the significance of this first decision on his application. Given the difficulty of the court process and the lengthy time it requires, this initial verdict is certainly weighty. He described how he was asked questions about his date of birth and dates of entry. "Then they told me to come and do fingerprinting," he continued. "I put down my fingers while I was shaking, and my lawyers stood one on the right and one on the left. They were holding my shoulders, and my knees felt weak. Then they gave me the answer. The woman said to me, 'Congratulations, you've been granted asylum, welcome to the United States of America.'"

Fadi and his lawyers exchanged hugs as they all cried: "I was just so relieved." Toying with everyone's fears, Fadi wanted to play a joke on his boyfriend Jack and asked Angela to call him and tell him that Fadi had been deported. Such a scenario had been a source of great anxiety for Fadi and his friends. Angela and Gina declined to be so cruel. Fadi and Jack celebrated that evening: "We had a party, Ghada came, and friends from the network joined, and it was a very nice feeling."

A dramatic rendition of Fadi's story could juxtapose his torture and humiliation in an Amman jail with his work organizing a group to march in an American gay pride parade a few years later. And the change in his life was dramatic, but that story of liberation is complicated by, among other things, Fadi's financial difficulties. At one point during our Skype meetings, I remarked that his case had a happy ending. He replied, "but I wish it was a happier ending." Indeed his account of his asylum case goes straight from the dramatic grant of asylum and celebration to: "I then started the hard process of finding a job. For someone with only a high school education, you quickly learn that your options are very limited."

Fadi did not receive his work permit until he received his asylum decision. It took him two months to find his first official job. Though his English was "perfect" (as he liked to say), he had experience working for an American company in Amman, and he mobilized his network of friends and allies in his job search, the results were minimum-wage and part-time jobs that meant he couldn't afford rent in the greater Bay Area. Even after years of struggle, Fadi was unable to come anywhere near the income level he had enjoyed at his job in Amman.

His first position was at a chain furniture store he loved. He started part-time but worked hard and within six months was promoted to department head—with a slightly higher hourly salary, but still not enough to get by. However, he was let go soon after, because the work permit he had submitted at the start of his employment with the company was about to expire. Fadi explained to the Human Resources staff that he was an asylee and did not need a separate work permit. He gave them his lawyer's contact information for them to verify. They did not know what asylee meant and did not seem interested in learning. Like Fatima's experiences at the homeless shelter, the people in charge had not heard about asylees and were quick to deny them what they were legally entitled to. The manager at the furniture store refused to listen and Fadi was out of a job. At that point, he found himself "back to Ghada again." He felt defeated and depressed: "I was still adjusting to life in America." Ghada connected Fadi to another lawyer from a nonprofit that specialized in illegal termination. He eventually received several months' pay in compensation, but he was back to the drawing board as far as employment went.

Fadi kept hunting for a good job and eventually applied for a position with an airline as a customer service agent. He had to go through several months of training in another city a two-hour flight away. Two months into this new job, Fadi was dealing with a difficult breakup with Jack, ongoing economic insecurity, and a long-distance weekly commute. During one argument on a Friday night, a friend of Jack's got involved and insulted Fadi: "He said to me, 'You Middle Eastern piece of shit. If you're not happy, go back and throw rocks at the people in Palestine.' I punched him in the face. He called the police and pressed charges. I ended up in jail for twenty-four hours." As an asylee and a recent hire, Fadi had a lot to lose as a result of this physical outburst; he immediately regretted it.

When Fadi was released from jail, he called Jack and begged him to ask his friend to drop the charges: "If [the airline] finds out, I will lose my position. Finally I found a decent job. Please!" This could also have potentially jeopardized his immigration status. The Clinton-era Immigration Bill of 1996 had increased penalties on immigrants and made deportation a "constant and plausible threat to millions of immigrants," while radically expanding the list of "which crimes made an immigrant eligible for deportation."[58] Punching someone could be charged as battery, which for immigration purposes is an aggravated felony and therefore a "removable offense."[59] Meaning, Fadi could be deported.

Luckily, Jack's friend agreed to drop the charges, but Fadi had to go to court on Monday morning in order for them to be formally dropped. He had to delay his required commute that Monday: "The airline was not happy, but they agreed. I went to the court in the morning, and then I *ran* to the airport and caught my flight." All this travel was for a temporary twenty-hours-per-week position. It took Fadi ten whole months to make it to full time and the salary was not great. However, he eventually received the key perk of being able to fly for free—that, together with his green card, significantly increased his mobility.

GOING HOME AGAIN

Fadi continued to struggle financially. He was thankful for his new life in the United States but desperately missed his family in Jordan. He received his permanent residency and flight benefits from his airline job. These set him on a path to eventually travel home again, a trip that could be considered a challenge to the asylum and border regime. When Fadi began thinking about going back to Jordan, he knew he would be taking a risk by doing so. His lawyer advised him against it—she warned that there was some chance he might not be allowed to reenter the United States. He could potentially lose his green card and asylum. According to the USCIS policy manual, it "may terminate asylum if [it] determines that the applicant . . . has voluntarily availed himself or herself of the protection of the country of nationality or last habitual residence by returning to such country . . . ."[60] Along with accounts of asylees who had traveled home and back to the US without a problem, he had also heard cautionary tales of some who ran into problems reentering. But Fadi's yearning for his family didn't go away. It was so strong that he eventually decided to take the risk. Four years after he had left his family in Jordan, he made up his mind to travel back.

Fadi had no desire to live in Jordan: "I hate Jordan. I still do. There's nothing for me there. . . . And I know the undercover cops could make my life hell." Fadi could hardly have forgotten his imprisonment and torture, but he still wanted to visit his siblings and parents. He told me: "Despite all the bad experiences associated with the place, I still want to go to visit. I hate Jordan. I certainly don't want to live there, but I want to see the people I love." The complicated relationship Fadi had with Jordan was not exceptional; many asylum seekers I met expressed similarly mixed sentiments, a combination of yearning and antipathy. Yet the asylum system allows for only simple, black-and-white stories in which an asylee would never so much as step foot back in his or her country. Otherwise, he or she would be deemed undeserving of asylum. Former immigration attorney Jawzia Zaman explains that asylum obscures "the possibility that an immigrant's relationship with the country of her birth might be complicated . . . that she could loathe it and long for it at the same time."[61]

Fadi had already had his green card for several years when he decided to visit his family. And because he was working for an airline and had flight privileges, a trip to Jordan had become financially feasible. He managed to get three weeks of vacation from his job and arranged for his then boyfriend Joe to join him for part of his trip. Joe was from Southern California and had never traveled outside of the United States before. Fadi introduced Joe to his parents as a friend and roommate. He was excited to reunite with his parents and siblings, and the trip turned out to be healing for him. During his visit, he bonded with one brother to whom he had been outed soon after he had left for the United States. And he came out to and was warmly accepted by his oldest brother.

BRING JOE TO RAMADAN DINNER

The model of "coming out" has been criticized by some LGBTQI+ activists in the Middle East. Visibility is not necessarily an appropriate strategy, nor is it a priority for everyone.[62] In anthropologist Jason Ritchie's analysis, queer Palestinian activists, for example, reject "the language of the closet altogether."[63] They do not seek to make visible to the nation a kind of intelligible queer subject, as is often the case for many queer western activists.[64] Rather, they try to create space for "bodies, desires and identifications . . . in all their perverse and incoherent glory" outside the "state's regulatory gaze and beyond the reach of its checkpoints."[65] Anthropologist Sa'ed Atshan describes a process of "inviting in," whereby "LGBTQ Palestinians reveal aspects of themselves and their sexuality in a methodical, patient, and individual fashion and only with those with whom they have established trust and a sense of security,"[66] a description that resonates with what Fadi described slowly doing in relation to his friends and family in Jordan. Atshan relates queer Palestinian accounts of engaging in a series of "dances" where "the boundaries of disclosure and nondisclosure and between legibility and nonrecognition require constant vigilance, recalibration, and flexibility."[67]

"Coming out of the closet" has also been criticized for being built on an understanding of same-sex practices as being foundational to individual identity, rather than a behavior or desire. It is modeled on the western presumption that someone who has sex with a person of the same sex has a distinct identity, which is then made public. But this assumption of a separate gay identity should not be taken for granted.[68] Moreover, asylum adjudicators often rely on a "'pre-understanding' of sexual identity development as a uniform and linear trajectory," with coming out as an essential necessary stage.[69]

But Sharif, another asylum seeker I met, rejected the assumption of American friends that he should seek to "come out" to his family; he said, "they had enough on their hands living in Gaza. In any case, I don't need any particular label for me personally." Yet, he was punished by an LGBTQI+ organization in the US for not conforming to the strategy of visibility: Sharif tried to apply for a scholarship for queer students, but when he contacted the granting organization to explain that he did not want his name and photo on their website, he was told that he was ineligible to apply because visibility was at the core of that program. That Sharif was considered simply unsuitable for refusing to be out on the internet is an example of the ethnocentrism operating in some US LGBTQI+ circles.

Nonetheless, Fadi, as an individual, self-identified as gay and subscribed to the ideal of coming out. He said it was personally significant for him to tell his siblings, to whom he is very close, that he was gay. Their responses and ongoing affection for him afterwards made him very happy. Fadi related that some of his friends in Amman had no interest in coming out, while others shared information only with a select group. Still others had had bad experiences when they were accidentally discovered having sex with men. However, Fadi was clear that he wanted to come out to select members of his family and friends. And when he did, he felt it was positive, even therapeutic, and counteracted some of the emotional harm done by his earlier experiences of persecution by undercover cops and rejection by friends both in Jordan and the US.

Fadi had initially been forcibly outed to his brother, Nihad, by Bassem soon after arriving in Los Angeles. When Nihad then spoke to Fadi about this, he seemed, in Fadi's estimation, to be "accepting." Fadi said his brother told him: "'It's your life. You should try to make it work in America.'" Though Nihad was not a textbook ally, he did tell Fadi that he loved him. Not long before that, Fadi had also told his brother Marwan, who had lived in Eastern Europe since the 1980s. When Fadi called Marwan and told him that he was gay, Marwan started to cry: "He told me, if you want my life, I'll give it to you. You are my brother. I understand this is not a choice; this is who you are.'" Fadi concluded: "Thank god I have such supportive brothers."

And finally, during Fadi's trip back to Amman after he received asylum, he decided to come out to his oldest brother Nazih: "I was afraid. There was a moment when I was getting ready to get into a taxicab one evening. And I said to myself, I'll tell him on my way out, so if it goes badly, I can jump in the cab and leave. So I told him the story: 1, 2, 3. I told him 'Joe, the guy who is with me, we've been dating since June.' My brother said, 'Okay, make sure to bring him tomorrow to the Ramadan *iftar* [breaking of the fast] dinner with us.'" Fadi smiled brightly as he recounted this to me: "So I brought Joe to the iftar and he was like part of the family. I was sitting in the middle between my brother Nazih and Joe and, because Nazih doesn't speak English, I was translating between them. Nazih was talking politics. They had a good talk. And it was just so nice." Later that week, Fadi and Joe went to the Dead Sea for a couple of days and Nazih, who worked nearby, met them: "He hung out with us at a coffee shop, giggling and laughing." Fadi said that made him feel "just so good."

Yes, he had been imprisoned and beaten and humiliated in Jordan on the suspicion that he was having sex with another man, and one of his friends had probably been pushed from a fourth floor window when his family learned he was having sex with a man. But Fadi's brothers were loving and accepting. Jordan, like most places, is complex. Asylum narratives leave no room for this. The system is built on painting an entire society with one brushstroke and presenting asylees as entirely renouncing their home countries.

That Fadi broke that asylum mold and traveled back to Jordan did worry him. When it was time for him to fly back from Jordan to the US, he called Joe, who had left earlier, and made sure he had his lawyer's number: "I told him, if anything happens, if they hold me or something, call Angela and see what she can do. But it actually was the smoothest time I ever had entering the United States! The agent asked me 'Why did you travel to Jordan?' 'Because my dad was ill and I went to check on him.' 'Well I hope your dad is good. Welcome back to the United States'! That was it!" Again demonstrating the unpredictable luck of the draw, Fadi was fortunate with his entry that time. He noted that, ironically, "Joe actually got held at the airport longer than I was. I had given him all the cheese and za'atar to take back to California. I said, 'You take this with you. You are a white boy, they are not going to bother you.' They did ask him, 'Why do you have so much luggage?' And he said, 'Oh, I like shoes. I have to have my shoes,' and they let him through. So anyway, that entry was easy for me."

That trip hung over his head for a while longer though. He worried it would come back to haunt him, especially when he applied for citizenship two years later. Angela's former assistant, Gina, who had gone on to work for another law firm, helped Fadi apply for his citizenship at no cost. She told Fadi: "It should be fine. If they did not want you, they would have stopped you from coming back in from Jordan."

Fadi's asylum application had asserted that gay men in his country had to live in secret for their own safety, as supported by State Department country reports and an embassy letter.[70] The file's necessary focus on widespread public condemnation and cases of discrimination and persecution leaves little room for possible positive individual experiences, such as the ones Fadi himself later had. This provides another argument against taking asylum narratives, produced under particular legal conditions, and uncritically circulating them beyond the immigration adjudication context. They are, by design, narrow and erase contradictions. I asked Fadi if he agreed that he had been unlucky by being imprisoned and tortured, but lucky with his family. Fadi said, "Yes, and the second part is more important to me now. I have nothing for me in Jordan. I hate it there. The only thing is that I miss my family. You know how our culture is: we are so close. I miss that *bond* from back home." He said he often wishes that someone from his family lived near him in the United States, but quickly qualified that: "Then again, I have my aunt's family in Michigan, and they are nuts and I stay far away from them."

SIMPLE ACCOUNTS ARE MESSY

In the monochromatic stories asylum applicants must present, their countries and cultures often become the antagonist. At the risk of being deemed "not credible," asylum seekers are encouraged to represent their native countries as evil and, in lawyer Jessica Mayo's words, "perhaps irredeemable." They are pushed to "abandon all allegiance to national practices or, often, cultural practices."[71] According to law professor Michelle McKinley, the system does not allow for "ambivalent attachments" and is premised on extending protection in exchange for cultural repudiation.[72]

Suad's attorneys, for example, insisted she could not equivocate on whether she would live in another country or whether she would travel back to Sudan. They told her she had to emphasize: "I have no right to stay in Saudi Arabia, and I will absolutely never go back to Sudan for any reason." Yet, in many cases I have encountered, asylum seekers have taken risks (both to their safety and to their immigration status) and traveled back to their countries, often through indirect routes, to visit loved ones.

Walid is a gay asylum seeker from Egypt. He had been imprisoned, tortured, and beaten to "within an inch of my life" back home, yet he traveled there despite his intense fears in order to see his dying father:

> I breached the rules and went back when my father got very sick. He didn't know I was gay, and I think it's best that way because it would have killed him to find out. But I know he loved me so much. When I found out he was dying, it was a difficult decision for me. I knew I could never forgive myself if I didn't go to see him. But I had a lot of fear and paranoia. There were times I was so scared I couldn't even breathe. But I made the trip. I got there in time, thank god, and saw him before he passed and was there to bury him. I couldn't not go back. . . . If it wasn't for the imprisonment, I was actually so happy back home, I would have never left in the first place. I was a manager at a big company. I had a good life, good friends, we partied all night. I never thought of leaving before I was arrested.

The complicated relationship Walid had to both his family and his country could not have been part of his asylum application. Asylum seekers are under pressure by the system to tell a simplified, unqualified story, framing themselves as cultural victims who seek emancipation in the discrimination-free United States of America and promising to repudiate their connections to the countries they were born in. But this simple-stories-only standard makes a mess—it invalidates asylum seekers' frequently complicated relationships to their countries and potentially destabilizes their legal status.

SHORT AND SENSATIONAL

Narratives that are strategic in asylum proceedings make their way beyond the confines of the immigration offices and courts. In the wider world, they reinforce simplistic common understandings about other countries. They get used in public discourse for fundraising campaigns, legislative lobbying, policy papers, even movies. But it is important to remember that they are products of a narrow system. An account that is suitable for a legal adjudication is just that.

I have already mentioned how the websites of organizations such as the Tahirih Justice Center have provided short descriptions of successful asylees that lend themselves to a stereotypical reading. Tahirih's lobbying efforts also rely on similar accounts: at a congressional briefing in 2008, the organization screened a promotional video featuring asylum seekers who speak on camera to make the "life-saving hope that the United States can offer to women and girls fleeing violence, real and immediate for the audience."[73] At the fundraisers of similar organizations, "former clients" are regularly featured. Often on the stages of lavish banquet halls, they are asked to quickly describe their life stories with the expected trajectory of oppression in country of origin, followed by rescue and freedom in America. Featured clients usually only speak for a few minutes and commonly highlight the transformations they experienced thanks to the help of the organization. Their presentations are often met by standing ovations by inspired crowds of donors who then proceed to write their checks. This format lends itself to cut-and-dried versions of asylees' lives.

In the 2016 film *Out of Iraq*, Btoo, a young Iraqi soldier struggling to leave Iraq and follow his gay lover to the West, explains in Arabic: "My feeling is that the possibility that I would end up killed was 70 percent, I mean more than half."[74] The film's subtitles translate this as: "and I had a feeling that I would end up being killed if I stayed in Iraq." Though "70 percent" or "more than half" are terrible odds that no one should be forced to face, the translation eliminates the 30 percent chance that Btoo would not be killed. Though there is no disputing that Btoo was in danger, the absolutist English rendering is strategically stronger in an asylum or refugee application. The subtitles, among other aspects of the film, unfortunately bleach out this nuance.

Among all of his siblings, it was his sister Nida that Fadi had the hardest time telling that he was gay. When he finally did so over the phone from California, Nida started to cry and said, "'Oh my god, this is a sin,' and all this bullshit." Fadi said to her, "I want you to think about it. I love you. You're my only sister. I don't want to lose you." Through her tears, Nida asked, "'Didn't you go to doctors to help you?' I told her, 'I went to everybody. I went to a sheikh, and actually I had sex with him. Even the sheikh who was praying five times a day and all that stuff, I did it with him, in his room, full of books about religion.'" Two weeks later, Nida called Fadi to tell him how much she loved him. She asked him cheerfully, "Are you seeing anyone new?" He told her about a dermatologist he was dating, and "she said, 'I wish you happiness.'" This complicated scenario was also precluded by Fadi's asylum narrative. The bar for asylum is such that he had to express fear so generalized and ubiquitous that he worried that his sister, along with the rest of his family, might harm him or want him dead if they were to find out that he was having sex with men, or that they might even call for his "honor killing." Though Fadi did face violence and could have faced more had he stayed in Jordan, the asylum system narrowed his narrative and allowed no room for this experience. It required him to fear violence from everyone. Just as the filmmakers edited Btoo's likelihood of death, asylum advocates would edit out the shades of gray in Fadi's family relationships.

GAY, BUT STILL BROWN

While some asylum cases may get a boost from racist stereotypes, those same stereotypes can ricochet back onto applicants themselves. Asylum seekers from Muslim-majority countries are sometimes singled out for extra security checks before their asylum decisions are returned. In the last decade, the standard applied to most asylum applicants in the United States at the initial stage of application has been to receive decisions within a two-week period after the interview.[75] However, some Arab asylum seekers post–9/11 have been subjected to extensive secret security checks that can take an indefinite amount of time. The applicant and lawyer (if there is one) have no access to the content or progress of a background check, and there is no formal recourse to redress extensive delays.

In four of the cases I am familiar with, the asylum seekers—three men and one woman—have been subject to this security check and the longer waits. For example, Nasser explained that, after his much-anticipated asylum interview, he was given a form to fill out in order to come collect the decision two weeks later. But this routine expectation soon evaporated: "My lawyer sent me an email a few days later, saying the immigration officer informed her not to come on that date because they are doing a background check and it will take more time. That was seven months ago and I'm still waiting. We don't have any information about how much longer. This is very painful but my lawyer says there is nothing to do but wait."

Nasser's lawyer explained to him that his travel to Saudi Arabia had likely triggered the security check. During his interview, Nasser was asked why he had traveled there, since "it's like a hell for gay people. Why leave the Palestinian Territories and go there?" Nasser had already explained that he had gone there for a one-year work contract with an American company:

> I had an offer to work in Saudi Arabia from the year before, but I hadn't taken it. Then an officer in the Palestinian intelligence set me up and started blackmailing me. He threatened me and said I had to give him names of other gay boys or he will make problems for me or put me in jail. So I immediately decided to take that job offer to get away. I was given that offer six months earlier, so I quickly contacted the company and told them that I would take it. I'm not staying in Palestine. I wanted to get away as quickly as possible, and the job offer in Saudi was a way to do so. I told the asylum interviewer all of that and I thought he understood it. But apparently not.

Did Nasser's travel to Saudi Arabia, an American ally country, to work for an American company place him under suspicion of terrorism? It is impossible to know for sure. Nasser was certainly not responsible for creating the bogeyman stereotype that caused the painful delay in his asylum case, nor was he in a position to challenge it. Yet the stories told in and around asylum about having to rescue Arab gays from dangerous Arabs (shorthand for brown straight men) do add logs, marginal as they may be, to the racist fire.

Jaafar, a Palestinian man from the West Bank, applied for asylum, not in relation to his sexuality but because of "persecution by religious extremists." He had attempted several years earlier to live in Jordan, where his wife was from. During his time there, he was forced to renew his visa to Jordan every three months by crossing the border back into the West Bank and then turning around and reentering Jordan with a new three-month visa. Since the process of crossing the border and returning back to Jordan was expensive, time-consuming, and unpredictable, especially on the Israeli-controlled side of the bridge with the West Bank, he tried a border crossing to Iraq, which he had been advised by other noncitizens was a cheaper and faster way to get an entry stamp to Jordan. As he explained to the asylum officer, he had technically exited Jordan and passed through the Jordanian passport control at the border, but he did not enter the Iraqi passport control area and instead simply turned around and reentered Jordan to receive a new visa that would allow him to stay in Jordan another three months. This disclosure of crossing the border to Iraq became an important line of questioning for the immigration officer, even though it was not directly related to Jaafar's asylum claim: "How many times did you go to Iraq? Why did you decide on Iraq? Did you meet anyone in Iraq? Do you know anyone from Iraq?" Jaafar's lawyer intervened to say, "I think my client has already provided a clear answer to these questions," at which point the officer repeated more Iraq-related questions. Smoking a cigarette after the interview, Jaafar complained to me that he felt humiliated by the questions and their antagonistic tone: "Am I on trial here just because I'm an Arab and a Muslim?" It seems the asylum officer suspected Jaafar of having ties to religious extremist groups not unlike the ones he said he was trying to flee from. While awaiting his decision, Jaafar relayed rumors of a Palestinian from Gaza who had been waiting thirteen years for his asylum claim to be decided. Jaafar's security check delayed his (eventually positive) decision by six months.

The injustice of these delays hits home especially hard for me personally since my own application to sponsor my father for a green card was subjected to a similarly humiliating suspicion, a totally opaque process, and an unknown wait time. My father is educated and middle class—a traditionally desirable candidate for that immigration status. He is a graduate of Harvard Medical School, a husband of over fifty years to an American spouse, and the father of two American children, with five American grandchildren—all features that should have eased his immigration path. My brother and I encouraged my father to apply for a green card in order to ease his travels and extensive stays with us. Yet his application, which was supposed to be processed in six to eight months, took fifty-four months. It required seemingly endless waiting, with no information or time frame for a decision, thousands of dollars in lawyers' fees, and expensive and time-consuming applications for interim travel documents. My father was inclined to abandon the application, though my brother and I encouraged him to stick with it, given the uncertain future of American immigration policies. From this family experience, I know viscerally that to be under unspecified and secret investigation for undisclosed security reasons, to be racially profiled, is humiliating and burdensome, to say the least.

But asylum seekers are in a much more vulnerable position than my father was. Most have no other option and are forced to wait out the delays of unknown length caused by background security checks. Their attempts to gain asylum shift "the forms of surveillance, discipline, normalizations and exploitation" to which they are subject.[76] One asylum seeker I translated for waited for almost three years for his background security check to be completed before deciding to abandon his asylum case altogether. He left to Canada to start from zero all over again and submitted an asylum application there, which fortunately was granted within a few months. Though Fadi had to ask, essentially, to be rescued from brown men in Jordan, he was still scary to many Americans as a brown man himself. His very entry into the United States took place in the shadow of this fear and suspicion, with his first few hours on US soil spent under interrogation and baggage search and his six-month visa reduced to two weeks.

This suspicion followed him as he made his way in the United States. He was fortunate that his asylum decision was not delayed by a security background check, as it was for Nasser and Jaafar. But the suspicion hovered over his early job prospects: "Who is going to give me work? I'm an Arab Muslim without a work permit!" It also affected some of his personal relationships. His boyfriend Joe's mom spelled it out clearly when her son started dating Fadi; she told him: "'If he's Muslim, those are the people who killed us on September 11.' Joe told her, 'Mom! He is gay. Who cares about all that stuff? He's a nice guy.'" Throughout their relationship, the mom worried that Fadi was brainwashing her son. Though the son was more liberal, "he knew very little about the Palestinians and Israelis. When I was explaining to him about it, he says to me, 'Oh, so you hate Jews?' I said, 'No I don't hate Jews. . . . If I'm going to hate Jews, then I'm being like your mom, hating every Muslim because of 9/11.'"

But it is by presenting themselves as victims of this scary Islamic or Arab culture that asylum seekers, like Fadi, who are Arab Muslims themselves, gain a path toward citizenship in the United States. Recall the refrain, "Hezbollah, Hezbollah, Hezbollah." Fadi and other gay male asylees have gained asylum in the midst of decades of narrowing pathways for most Muslim Arabs wishing to enter the US, crowned recently by the Muslim travel ban. Many other folks from the Middle East have been turned down, even for non-immigrant visas, as was evident in Fadi's own difficulty obtaining a tourist visa in the first place. In addition, the queue of refugees wanting to come to the US is long indeed, and being "gay and Muslim and from the Middle East," as Ghada put it, has helped refugee applicants skip to the front of the line.[77] According to US policy under Obama, the applications of gay Iraqis or Syrians, for example, were given priority over other refugees from those countries.[78] (This priority was reassigned under Trump to religious minorities, mostly Christians.) The overall number of refugees who have resettled in the US is small, making this jump in the queue all the more significant.[79] Though Fadi applied for asylum, not refugee resettlement, the logic of these priorities is relevant. Moving LGBTQI+ folks to the front of the line demonstrates an American preference for those deemed to be cultural victims of Islam over those deemed to be victims of more a banal sort—of war and poverty. Indeed, anthropologist Fadi Saleh argues that applicants are only intelligible and admissible through a "performative splitting" of sexual identity from any other aspects of identity linking them to countries such as Syria and through the presentation of curated narratives of injury focused exclusively on sexuality.[80]

This also fits into a larger US strategy, initiated in the Obama years, of using the fight for LGBTQI+ rights to pinkwash its foreign policies. Just as the claim of rescuing Muslim women has a long history of being used as a colonial tool,[81] (recently illustrated by Senator Mitch McConnell's call to continue the American war in Afghanistan in order to allegedly protect women there[82]), the claim of rescuing gays and lesbians from their oppressive cultures now plays a similar role in justifying American policies abroad. As Ratna Kapur argues, while the conferral of humanity on sexual minorities is certainly cause for celebration, it is important to note when these shifts are dangerously framed within the logic of security.[83]

FREE (AND POOR) AT LAST

When it finally came time for Fadi to apply for his citizenship, he was nervous about his interview—would they ask about his travel back to Jordan? They didn't. Soon after, he went to his swearing-in ceremony. He invited his ex-boyfriends, Ghada his therapist, and several other friends. They had all helped him during his long struggle, and he wanted them to be there to help him celebrate. There were five hundred and sixty new citizens at the event, and they were asked to stand up when the name of their country was called out. He was the only one from Jordan. He said he became emotional because it felt like he was "finally free": "I stood there and as they started to sing the American national anthem, the whole last seven and a half years rushed through my head, and I started to cry. The whole process, the struggle, the jail, the airline, everything went through my mind. And I thought to myself: 'I did it!'" Asylum and his immigration efforts were part of that struggle, but so were work, frugality, and his ongoing uphill financial fight. Fadi was thirty-seven, and his dream to leave Jordan had started at seventeen. He told me: "After eight years, I am a citizen, free. I can go wherever I want." And, without losing a beat, he immediately added: "But the financial situation is hard."

Fadi noted that the Bay Area is "super expensive" and that he has continued to struggle. Gaining US citizenship was a huge milestone, but it did not solve his ongoing money problems. He explained that, currently, he was living with a new boyfriend he had met a few months before: "He asked me to stay with him. I don't pay rent, because I can't afford this area. For what I am making at Home Depot, I can't afford a closet. But I applied for department supervisor. Last week, I had my interview, so I am hoping to get that position."

I was hardly the only person to find Fadi's story compelling. He has a vibrant personality and seems to relish talking about his experiences: "Talking is my kind of therapy, it's really nice for me." His accounts reflect this desire to speak and are powerful to hear. "My friend who is a professor at Berkeley told me I should write a book about my life," Fadi tells me. "There's definitely lots of drama," he adds half-jokingly. I noted that his story seemed to have a happy ending. "It *is* a happy ending," he told me, "but I wish it was a happier ending." Though asylum and, later, citizenship were certainly significant for Fadi, as they were for other asylum seekers, there was that familiar sense of anticlimax. Other significant struggles, often economic, persisted and dampened the triumph often expected around asylum. Having luckily survived the "brutal math" of the asylum process,[84] Fadi and others certainly felt empowered by the legalization of their lives in the US. Yet, the financial difficulties of staying afloat—the different brutal math of US urban economies—tempered that sense of freedom and diluted "triumph" into something more humble.

POSTSCRIPT: A LOT OF HARD WORK AND A STROKE OR TWO OF LUCK

Following up with Fadi six years later and sharing drafts with him of this chapter, which ends with his financial troubles, he was eager to update me on his improved circumstances. To get out of his fiscal rut, and on the advice of friends, he had enrolled at Corinthian Colleges for a two-year associate's degree in business administration. He managed to complete that program while holding down a full-time job at the hardware chain *and* a part-time job driving, first for Postmates and then for Uber: "It was very tough. I left at 6:00 a.m. and didn't get home till 10:00 p.m. The days I didn't have school, I did Postmates, and I did homework during lunch breaks at Home Depot." Fadi was fatigued and burning out. During his last term at Corinthian, he even considered spending the semester with his family in Jordan, since his classes were online and he would have lower expenses in Amman, but he didn't go through with that. Soon after Fadi completed his degree, the college shut down under pressure from the US government, as it was found to have misled students by deliberately inflating its job-placement rates.[85] To Fadi's great fortune, not only had he already finished his degree before the college was shut down by authorities, but the $28,000 in student loans he had taken out was also forgiven![86] With this degree and, miraculously, no student debt, Fadi was able to secure better-paying positions in the tech industry.

He also built himself a new family. Fadi fell in love with Alex, and they decided to marry. They now have two dogs, Casper and Tala. Combining his income with Alex's, Fadi is now "more comfortable than I've been since I left Jordan." The newlyweds hope to move to a cheaper city in Southern California where they may be able to afford to buy a home. However, there are fewer jobs there, so they are struggling to convert their positions to remote ones while also experimenting with starting an online business. Despite the lack of job security and the ongoing challenges, Fadi is more optimistic about his future. Back in Jordan, he had dreamt of an American life of economic prosperity in addition to the freedom to be openly gay. His American reality has been more complicated, with unexpected setbacks as well as long and steady, grinding economic pressure. But his ability to create a family with Alex (guaranteed by a 2015 supreme court decision, *Obergefell v. Hodges*) is something he could not have done openly in Jordan. That privilege has also come with tax advantages, allowing him to join the ranks of struggling American families.

"Many reasons to leave"

SITTING IN A CIRCLE IN A UNIVERSITY CLASSROOM IN 2017, I could not help noticing the young woman sitting two chairs away, who introduced herself as Marwa. As her infant twin boys played on the floor in front of her (to the delight of the other workshop attendees), Marwa quickly arrived at a question that had crystallized in my mind through years of research: "How do we not perpetuate stereotypes in asylum?" She spoke loudly and clearly: "I am Lebanese. I am Shia. I am queer. I am a feminist. I am an environmentalist. But my asylum lawyer pushed me to choose only some of these, to simplify who I am." She had a clear assessment of her asylum: she desperately needed it, but it came at the expense of "many other things."

In the months and years that followed, I learned from Marwa about some of those other things with which she paid — her ability to shape her own identity without boxes, her mental well-being, and her relationship to her family. I also learned how she struggled to undo that harm. As an activist and student of law, she was outspoken and irreverently blunt about asylum in a way I had not encountered from other asylees. In another forum, she explained that she had "survived six wars and more than twelve displacements in [her] life"; you could hear in her voice that she was not going to take any more shit from anyone. When I discussed my book with Marwa, she was excited to offer a complex perspective on asylum: "When most people hear that I am Lebanese and that I sought asylum in the US, they just think 'Of course, your country is bad,' and that is the end of the story for them. But reality is more complicated. I experienced a lot of freedom in the US, but I also experienced a lot of Islamophobia and xenophobia." And, on another occasion, she explained: "There is a lot of messed-up stuff in Lebanon, but there are also many things and people I love." Marwa has thought long and hard about asylum, and I was fortunate that she was willing to share some of her sophisticated insights.

FIGHTING ON MANY FRONTS: QUEER FEMINIST ENVIRONMENTALIST

Marwa was steeped in a long history of activism and community-building. Starting in her teens in Lebanon, she had worked with a group of activists there under the umbrella of IndyAct, initially focusing on environmental issues. With the central motto of "you cannot be complacent," the group carried out high-profile direct protest actions. They wore diving suits and unfurled banners reading "You Can't Drink Oil" to challenge the Arab state's environmentally destructive pro-petroleum policies. They strung blue do-not-enter tape across the city that read "seawater level" to bring attention to the impact of global warming. Through this activism, Marwa met many like-minded young women who soon felt collectively the need to carve additional organizing spaces for themselves.

While she continued her work with IndyAct, Marwa helped found two other organizations, including Meem, a queer women's group whose work remained largely underground, and Nasawiyya, a feminist organization. Meem sought to "create a safe space in Lebanon where lesbians can meet, talk, discuss issues, share experiences, and work on improving their lives and themselves." They offered legal support, psychological counseling, social events, and "the opportunity to work on social change."

IndyAct's environmental protest actions were receiving growing media attention, and this irked the Lebanese government. Marwa said that she and her fellow activists soon became convinced that state authorities were monitoring their emails: "The armed forces and police met us at a protest meeting-point way before the protest itself. They knew exactly what parking lot we were meeting at and what time we were planning to do our action, even before we did it." These police interceptions were menacing, and on several occasions Marwa and her fellow activists were cornered at gunpoint and even detained in the back of police trucks. In addition to disrupting their protest plans, Marwa worried about what else the authorities were learning from her emails: "I was doing environmental work *and* LGBTQ work.... The government was spying on my environmental work, but because of my underground involvement with

Meem, I was scared for the three hundred other women I worked with." Many of those women, like Marwa at that point, were not public about their membership in the group.

At the same time, Marwa was coming under mounting pressure in her personal life as well. Her father became furious when she cut her hair short, when she got piercings, and when she got a tattoo. Both he and her mother were increasingly alarmed by her growing social and political militancy and tried to curtail her behaviors. They were emotionally and, in the case of her mother, physically abusive in their attempts to control Marwa. Her family refused to continue paying her university tuition, putting Marwa under considerable financial strain. She explained: "My reality was just impossible. I had to make a change. There was no single reason I wanted to leave. Many things happened at the same time." Marwa had traveled to the United States previously to attend a conference advocating for renewable energy. She still had a valid visa from that trip, and she was in a relationship then with a woman living in Michigan.

She had no concrete plans or long-term vision of what she would do. She just decided to leave Lebanon and go to Michigan to stay with her girlfriend. When I asked Marwa if her girlfriend knew that she was going to stay long-term, she explained: "*I* didn't even know, to be honest. I just knew I was leaving Lebanon at a time that was really, really not good for me for many reasons, but I didn't know what I would do after that. I just knew I had to leave." Marwa quickly plugged into a network of friends and activists, many of them queer and Arab, in the Detroit area. It did not take her long to begin carving a new organizing space there, starting a collective modeled on her work with Meem in Lebanon. She considered enrolling in college in Michigan, but the tuition was expensive and she knew her father would refuse to help her pay for it. Though she had swiftly become rooted in activist circles, she was also adrift, with no solid path to stabilizing her life in the long term. A friend Marwa met through activist circles told her about asylum, and she started to read about it. She explained: "Asylum laws are actually very inaccessible, so I didn't even know that that was an option at first. I just thought I would go to the US and be with my girlfriend for a bit until I figured things out. As I did more research, I then started to see, oh, maybe asylum could apply to me. At the time, I barely understood English. I remember reading a lot and stressing and googling what this term means and what that term means and whether my experience in Lebanon would amount to enough to qualify for asylum. The more I read, the more I thought that it did."

GETTING BY WITH A LITTLE HELP FROM MY FRIENDS

Marwa had arrived with only $1,000 to her name. She was young, and her family was not assisting her financially—even if they had wanted to, they were not wealthy. But the community she connected with in Michigan—mostly feminist, queer, and Arab American activists—helped her a great deal: "They looked after me *a lot*, from feeding me to making sure I had a ride, checking in on me, all those things. They were really there for me." It was during this time that she began to search for a lawyer to help her apply for asylum. Like all other asylum seekers, as a noncitizen, Marwa did not have the right to a government-paid attorney. Her options were: find an organization that could provide her with legal assistance or connect her to a pro bono attorney, or try to somehow come up with the fees for an immigration attorney she found on her own.

A friend advised Marwa about a local legal aid organization, and she was able to schedule a meeting to see if they could assist her with her asylum application. Like many intake interviews, this was an uncomfortable, draining encounter. Marwa had to disclose a lot of personal information with the organization's representative. This included confiding in them about parts of her experiences in Lebanon that revolved around her sexuality, something she had only shared with a small circle of friends. Since the legal aid organization was linked to interconnected orbits of Arab, Muslim, and feminist activism that Marwa was also a part of, she was concerned about being able to maintain her privacy: "I was first worried about them judging my choices. Then, if it became known that I was gay (I was not out at the time), people would assume that my girlfriend is gay too, and she wasn't out. So it was complicated." Rachel Lewis notes that, for women who have been persecuted because of their sexuality, or who perceive it "as a private and deeply intimate aspect of their lives, proving their sexual orientation in the context of the political asylum process is incredibly challenging."[1] This is part of the increase in barriers queer women face in asylum and contributes to the gender disparity discussed in the previous chapter.

Though the legal aid organization did offer to help Marwa apply for asylum at a subsidized rate of several hundred dollars, she said it did not feel right: "The legal representatives there were really shitty about me being gay and Muslim. They were like, 'How can you really be gay *and* Muslim?'" That skepticism scared Marwa off. She said she did not feel safe there: "My identity wasn't welcome." She decided not to use that organization's attorneys. She was disappointed and increasingly desperate.

She became excited again when she came across another organization online that specifically worked with LGBTQ asylum seekers. Marwa thought they would be the ideal organization to help her. She reached out to them via their website, briefly explaining her situation. She did not anticipate their less-than-enthusiastic response: "I don't remember their exact language, but their email reply basically was 'Oh, you're from Lebanon. Being gay there is fine.' Then when I pushed back, they basically let me know that they don't do that kind of case." Lebanon is home to a couple of LGBTQI+ organizations, including Helem (meaning Dream), and Beirut has a number of popular gay-friendly bars and clubs—though these contested "queer spaces" are sometimes subject to raids and shutdowns.[2] Laws potentially criminalizing homosexuality as "against the order of nature" have been intermittently and (arguably) diminishingly enforced.[3] This legal loosening poses a challenge for LGBTQI+ asylum applicants who come from there, even if non-state, interpersonal discrimination is more commonplace.[4] The asylum organization Marwa turned to seemed reluctant to take on cases from Lebanon. She was again let down: "That was really hard to hear at that time. I had thought, oh they're gay, they have this LGBTQ agenda and that should match really well with me. But they just were totally dismissive."

Eventually, a fellow activist suggested that Marwa contact a prominent private lawyer in San Francisco named Amin, who worked asylum cases. Amin was gay and Muslim himself and had successfully represented several high-profile Arab gay asylum seekers in the past. Marwa spoke to him over the phone and immediately felt like he understood many things about her experience: "He just seemed to get it." She felt he would be a great attorney for her case. But Marwa was wading into a world rife with potential exploitation, from fake immigration lawyers and exploitative *notarios* to licensed lawyers who offered substandard or incompetent services.[5] Luckily, Amin turned out to be skilled and his reputation for winning cases deserved.

Amin asked to meet her in person to discuss her application and to sign an agreement to represent her. Marwa wanted to work with Amin, but the trip would be expensive. Luckily, a friend was able to book her a flight to San Francisco using his miles. She arrived in the city with her backpack and the address of a friend of a friend who had offered a couch for her to sleep on, but that arrangement did not work out. Marwa wound up sleeping that night in a factory warehouse space, on the ground, under a truck. The next day she was exhausted and stressed, but she slung her backpack on and kept going. She met with Amin and again felt he understood what she had been through. In retrospect, working with him turned out to be complicated, but at that point she had felt reassured that "at least he got the part about me being gay and Arab and Muslim."

The immediate downside of choosing Amin was that he required a $5,000 fee. This was just the basic charge for normal processing of an asylum application—clients have to cover other expenses and pay additional fees should the case proceed less than smoothly. To unemployed Marwa, the basic fee alone was exorbitant, but Amin insisted at their meeting that it was nonnegotiable. The heavy price tag demoralized Marwa, who was by then couch surfing in Detroit. She returned from California deflated, but her Michigan friends encouraged her not to give up, and eventually one even offered to loan her most of the required amount.

Like Fadi's friends, Marwa's small community suggested organizations and lawyers to her, but also booked her flights, offered her their couches to sleep on, and loaned her money for the fees. They were essential to filling the void created by the US government's lack of support to asylum seekers. And Marwa was lucky to find this generosity and personal help in her close-knit community of fellow activists, many of whom were from middle-class backgrounds.

WATCH YOUR LANGUAGE

Marwa decided to work with Amin to apply for asylum because he "accepted some of my nuances." He was strict about his payments and would not budge on any part of that. He also insisted on certain language in Marwa's application. He told her that she couldn't use the term "queer" or "gender nonconforming" in her personal statement: "He said, 'You have to be a lesbian. The asylum officers don't understand what queer is, and the laws don't understand what queer is, so it's better to be clear. Keep it simple and use the word "lesbian."' I had to agree at that time. As a lawyer now, I see that there is no room for queer in the law." Amin's advice may have been legally sound, but for Marwa the language of "lesbian" felt like an uncomfortable fit. In one of her public lectures she explained: "I worked so hard to find the word queer," only to "be told by the American government that I can't identify that way!" She noted that the term "lesbian" didn't reflect her full range of desires and caused her to worry "that I couldn't share that I have desires that are not black and white like that." She was concerned she would have to erase or edit her sexuality to fit the legal identity box of "lesbian."

Amin also wanted to represent Marwa according to assumptions common in American LGBTQI+ politics: that, since she was a queer Muslim, she could not possibly be religious. She told him that "actually, I'm not really atheist. I tried to explain the complications and my struggle with Islam. He said, 'No, no, you have to be atheist.'" Marwa now spends quite a bit of her time questioning this "forced secularization"; the stereotypical assumption that a queer Muslim could not be religious is one she in fact directly organizes against by building queer Muslim spaces "where we are not judged for being interested in the Quran, for praying, for caring about our religion." She now insists: "I am actually Muslim *and* I'm Queer." But back then she was not in a position to insist.

Amin asked Marwa to have a first go at writing her statement, the narrative core of her asylum application. Her grasp of English had been improving, but he was asking her to write her story in a language that she was just starting to get comfortable in: "It took everything out of me to write that draft. I cried nonstop. It was very traumatic." Marwa put a great deal of time, energy, and emotion into writing that initial version, but Amin took one look at it and immediately said it was no good. He told her she had to start over again. Marwa was devastated. "I was not in a good mental state. I was crying every time I sat down to write. I hated every step of it. . . . Look at me: five years later, I'm still crying," she told me, with tears wetting her face. Whenever she has had to revisit her statement, despite the passage of time, "it's always retraumatizing." Marwa talked to Amin via Skype and, step by painful step, he helped her write a narrative he thought would be legally powerful for her case—which, of course, is precisely the role of a capable attorney in this context. This involved whittling down her complicated experiences and background, from "I am Lebanese, I am Shia, I am queer, I am a feminist, I am an environmentalist" to a more stripped-down version that focused on her persecution as a lesbian in a Shia family and a Muslim-dominated society.

Amin also steered some of the politics of Marwa's narrative. He pushed her to remove references to the Israeli occupation of southern Lebanon,[6] saying they were unnecessary. He changed her mention of "'48 Arabs," a term preferred by many Palestinians who live inside Israel for referring to themselves, substituting instead the Israeli-sanctioned term "Israeli Arab." With the passage of several years, Marwa reflects that her lawyer pushed her into a position that didn't align with her politics. But he did so gently, using professionalism and the need for clarity to frame the changes he wanted made.

Discussing the details of her asylum application was still difficult for

Marwa when we met. As we chatted over tea in her New York apartment while her twins napped, she said she was eager to share her experiences, but that discussing the asylum application always triggered her. Particularly difficult was talking about the abuse she suffered from her parents. Marwa still loved them and, deep down, felt that they still loved her as well. Her relationship with her mother when she left Lebanon had been broken, but Marwa still had hope of somehow repairing it. Amin discouraged this. He told her it would be best if she did not have any contact with her family while her asylum was pending: "This really compounded my trauma. I missed them. I was building my chosen family in Michigan, but I still wanted a connection with my past. In the end, I did what my lawyer advised and didn't speak to them for two years."

WHAT DID YOU EAT FOR LUNCH LAST WEEK?

Though it felt much longer, Marwa got her asylum interview date within a few months of submitting her application. The closest asylum office to her was in Chicago, so she had to pay to travel there, as well as pay the expenses of her lawyer, who was traveling from San Francisco. Reflecting on the interview overall, Marwa described how "you are really made to continuously feel like you are guilty or you are lying, until you prove otherwise." Immigration attorney Marty Rosenbluth agrees that, in the topsy-turvy world of immigration proceedings, none of the due process safeguards officially provided in the regular court system apply—including the assumption of innocence until proven guilty.[7]

When describing the abuse she had suffered at the hands of her mother, the asylum officer who interviewed Marwa asked repeatedly for more details and for the dates of the abuse. As mentioned in describing Suad's preparation for her hearing, asylum adjudicators routinely scrutinize whether applicants can accurately repeat exact numbers and sequences of events as a measure of their credibility. Clearly, the expected exact recollection of precise dates on a range of events—both significant and not, including traumatic ones—and their perfect repetition is not an organic way of remembering. This recounting of life's events by precise dates was taken to the extreme in the case of Angel, who applied for asylum in the UK: the adjudicator in her case asked when she knew she was a lesbian, as if they expected "a date and time."[8] Even asylum seekers who can come up with precise dates are still in jeopardy. Legal scholars Laurie Berg and Jenni Millbank describe a 2004 case in Australia where an "applicant gave different ages in response to questions about when he 'realised' or 'became aware' that he was gay," offering at one point a date at which he realized when he was not attracted to girls and another for when he felt a same-sex attraction. The adjudicator assumed this was an inconsistency and impugned his credibility.[9]

What stands out most in Marwa's memory of her interview is an outburst she had when the interviewer "was really digging" and pushing her on the dates and sequence of her mother's abuse:

> I was crying a lot, and I just remember the asylum officer going back and forth with the same question. She was badgering me: she would repeat the same question in a different way to see if the sequence was the same as I told her before. And at some point she asked me again: "Can you please tell me how many times and when did your mom do this and this?" I was so upset and sobbing, I looked up at her and shouted, "Do you know what you ate last week for every day for every meal?" She was shocked. My lawyer looked at me like, what are you doing? The officer looked at me and said, "No." I said, "That's how often my mom beat me. So I don't remember exactly what time and where; I don't remember the details because it was very, very frequent. But the ones that I wrote in my narrative were the ones that were special, like the time that I almost died, I was bruised purple from head to toe, and I couldn't speak. I remember that time in detail because I really felt like I was going to die. So I put that in my asylum application. But if you want me to recall all the other times, I can't. It's impossible." The officer stopped that line of questioning there.

As Marwa recounts this interview to me, she adds a significant note: "Just for the record, my mom and I are best friends now. And the whole reason why I am today a lawyer who believes in no prisons and no police is because of my experience with my own mother."

Refugee lawyer Hilary Cameron argues that "refugee status decision-makers typically have unreasonable expectations of what and how people remember." She cites numerous psychological studies that demonstrate that memories are neither as complete nor as stable as these decision-makers assume.[10] She notes that "temporal information, such as dates, frequency, duration and sequence" are difficult to recall accurately and argues that adjudicators need to "fundamentally readjust their thinking about claimants' memories." Yet, it is precisely the recall of temporal information that remains at the core of how asylum officers typically determine the credibility of applicants. A 2016 training manual for asylum offers instructs interviewers to (1) "elicit as much detail as possible," and (2) "when appropriate, ask questions out of chronological order. If an applicant is not telling the truth, he or she may have memorized the story in sequence. If you ask questions so that the applicant is required to describe events out of chronological order, the applicant may not be able to relate the story accurately."[11]

Somehow Marwa made it through that test. As she awaited the decision on her case, she spent many weeks checking her mailbox for a notice, three or four times a day. When she finally received the approval, she remembers "screaming for joy and crying with sadness, all at once." She felt that she had somehow lost something in connection to her past, but that she was also finally getting a handle on "the basics. I can be here now, even though I don't have money and I don't have a good job. I can start building from here—I have a chance to do that."

YOU ARE GOING TO BE LONELY

Marwa is a skilled and vibrant conversationalist and has always enjoyed a large circle of friends. Yet, looking back at her early years in the United States, she remembers feeling considerable isolation and loneliness. This seems to be a hallmark of many asylum experiences, as so many asylum seekers I met related to me.

Tawfiq from Egypt reflected that asylum involves "being uprooted and leaving your family, your friends, your home, your culture, your everything and going to a new country. That in itself is incredibly traumatic and stressful. . . . That's on top of the stress and trauma of preparing your asylum case." It is not that Tawfiq had never lived outside of Egypt; quite the contrary, he had worked and traveled all over the world beforehand and had lived with his family in Europe for a while: "But it was still very hard. . . . I was homesick for *years*!" Tawfiq stayed in close touch with his family after arriving in the US, and they visited him while he was applying for asylum. But, even though they communicated regularly, he had

> major, major homesickness. It was really bad. I would say it took me two years just to be okay being here. When I've talked to other people who have gone the asylum route, some of them got over it more quickly. But for me it took a long time. I'm very comfortable talking to you right now, and I'm in good spirits, but that wasn't the case back

then. I went through phases of major depression. And anxiety. You know, it was really, really tough. And I am one of the lucky ones: I had a university degree and was fluent in English and was financially comfortable.

Tawfiq told me that, in many ways, he loved his country and wished he hadn't had to leave: "I was sad that I had to give up everything I had in Egypt." Part of the difficulty of asylum in the US for him arose from cultural differences: "It's very different in the Middle East. Over there, people are in your business way too much. And here, it's the other extreme. . . . You could be on your own for an extended period of time, and everybody is so busy, they won't notice. You will experience loneliness *for sure*." This isolation is of course exponentially compounded for many less fortunate asylum seekers who are detained. The suffering of the men and women in this book, extensive as it may be, pales in comparison to the thousands of detained asylum seekers who endure much more extreme hardship.[12]

Some NGOs seek to lessen the impact of this isolation. Nasser's contact with other queer Arab asylum seekers through support groups helped "because you see there are people who are going through similar things, or others who face even worse problems. Also, you can see to the other side. You see those who have gotten their approval, and you can see that they went through the same things you are going through now, and then at the end there is like a happy ending." Indeed, many of the queer asylees I met in New York and San Francisco volunteered with nonprofits after they had received asylum. Nasser described interpreting for an Iraqi guy "who came like a week ago and he doesn't speak any English. And at the organization that took his case, no one speaks Arabic. So the least I can do is volunteer to interpret. He has it much harder than I did." Fadi helped organize a group to march in the gay pride parade that included many Arabs; he saw this as a fun but important community service that had helped him early on to feel like he was not alone. Marwa was fortunate to quickly build her community of friends.

SLOWLY STANDING ON MY FEET

The community Marwa had built in Michigan thanks to her wealth of activist experiences again helped her navigate these difficult waters and the financial turmoil she experienced in her early years. But it wasn't easy:

"There was a lot of, how do I say it . . . just living a hard life." Based on his own experience, Tawfiq, an asylee from Egypt, offers:

> The main advice that I would give anyone who wants to apply for asylum is that you need to come with money. You have to have some kind of financial support that will last for several months at least, if not more. And it's not necessarily for attorney fees, but for a place to stay if you don't have somebody to stay with. And even if you have the money, it's still tough. . . . It's enough to go through the trauma of leaving your country; if you also don't know where to stay and don't have money either, then it becomes even more difficult. There are some people who have had to spend nights on the street. They've had to be homeless.

What Tawfiq warns about, Marwa in fact experienced. Of course, not everyone who needs asylum has this option of bringing lots of money, even if they know it is necessary. Yasmin Nair points out that cases such as that of Shirley Tan—a lesbian immigrant who had been denied asylum and who was later presented as worthy because of her bourgeois, suburban, church-attending family life and for whom Senator Diane Feinstein sponsored a private bill in Tan's name—demonstrate the ways in which class and education can significantly alleviate the experience of queer immigration and undocumented status.[13]

That there is no governmental support for asylum seekers in the United States is not coincidental; the American government wants the process to be arduous. As mentioned earlier, the government-mandated five-month waiting period for submitting work permit applications, for example, was deliberately introduced in the 1990s as a deterring barrier.[14] Then, it was extended in 2020 to a whole year by the Trump administration, while the processing time was also extended from thirty days to several months,[15] all to make the process of asylum seeking more unbearable. It is part of a larger framework that attacks various aspects of daily life, as law professor K-Sue Park argues, aiming to have people remove themselves from the country or to subordinate their labor if they stay.[16]

While Marwa relied on her community of close friends to survive during this period, she was eventually able to get a work permit with Amin's help. But even after she received the authorization, it was still not easy to find a good job. She was referred to a church group to help her find employment. She prepared a resume that included her organizing experiences and her fluency in French and Arabic. The employment expert she met with didn't even look at the resume: "He knew I was an asylum seeker and immediately assumed I would be looking for a manual labor job. There's nothing wrong with that kind of work, of course. But I was qualified for more skilled positions. I had to fight for that." The employment adviser initially suggested that Marwa apply to a nearby factory that was looking for workers to tape boxes on an assembly line. Marwa pushed back and said she was qualified to do more skilled office work. The adviser eventually suggested she contact a nearby branch of a chain hotel that was looking to hire workers who also spoke Arabic.

She wound up working at the front desk of that hotel, making less than ten dollars an hour before taxes. Though it was not manual labor, it was physically demanding. She was assigned the overnight shift and was not supposed to sit all night—she was expected to stand behind the tall reception desk ready for customers to approach at any time. In addition to all the guest check-ins, she also did auditing work for the hotel and used her French and Arabic to assist guests. She was often alone in the reception area through the night with only one other employee in another part of the hotel. Once she was threatened by a caller who told her that he had a gun and was looking at her through the sliding glass door entrance from across the street: "I was vulnerable; they provided no protection for me. *And* I was basically doing two or three people's jobs for very little pay."

Marwa had to supplement that full-time job with more work through a temp agency. She was assigned to a car company to help make recall arrangements for French Canadian clients. She often had to be on calls with an English-speaking engineer and a French-speaking client, interpreting technical terms and negotiating procedures: "I learned a lot on the job, and I got paid almost $11 an hour, which felt great at the time." She had to work other jobs during this period as well, including working at a restaurant where her pay consisted mostly of tips, but amounts left on credit cards were not always given to her. In addition to working multiple positions, Marwa also interned at a domestic violence shelter for no pay: "I can't help but do those things, even if there's no money. That's just in my blood—I have no choice. I feel I have to do them. But I paid the price with my health, to be honest. I was stretched too thin."

Standing on her own feet took a while, but not for lack of effort on Marwa's part: "I had two full-time jobs and did eventually find some consultancy stuff in addition. All that just to afford minimal basics and to pay back my debts." To be clear, her independence did not instantly follow the arrival of the work permit: "It was not easy transitioning. As you know, in America, in order to rent anything, you need credit history. And as an asylum seeker, you are fresh, you don't have any record of credit history.[17] So, even when I got my employment permit, it was really hard to find a job but also to get a car, an apartment, etc. It took a while longer till I was able to overcome those hurdles. I was able to get a used car with another loan from a friend, then I lived in that car for six months, and then I found a place to rent that I could afford. Then, the journey continued on from there."

Marwa had completed one semester of university studies in Lebanon and, after starting to stabilize her life in Michigan, she applied to continue her studies at Wayne State University. This, too, required struggle and perseverance. Even small tasks, like getting copies of her high school transcripts from Lebanon, were challenging. Once she managed that, she applied to the university but was rejected. She reapplied and was rejected again several times, but she kept on reapplying: "They sent me so many rejection letters. And I kept appealing—five times, again and again. I think at the end of the day, they were like, that's enough, we are bored of this person, let's just admit her." After she was admitted, she then discovered that she had been denied the lower in-state tuition rate, but again kept on appealing: "I had to write five or six letters fighting for it. I didn't have documents that proved I was a resident of Michigan for the required period, because I was staying with friends and didn't have my own place." Marwa had to explain repeatedly that "I'm an asylum seeker. Here's my entry date. I have been in the state for longer than the required period. The system didn't understand—it was not set up to understand my circumstances. But I just kept on appealing." She eventually succeeded in enrolling as an in-state student and attended school full-time at Wayne State, facing the challenge of studying in English head-on. She did so while also working multiple jobs and volunteering: "I was basically not sleeping for months to barely make rent, pay for school tuition, and pay my lawyer."

It is important to note here that, unlike Suad, who was frequently identified by others as Black, Fatima, who was identified as Muslim, and Fadi as Middle Eastern, Marwa's appearance could pass as white. She didn't choose to assimilate to whiteness, as some Arab Americans have historically done,[18] and she was othered in many ways, facing Islamophobia and xenophobia. However, she also seemed to be accorded some level of access or a small foothold that the other asylum seekers didn't have—and that expanded her "life chances," to use Dean Spade's language.[19] Her organizing experience gave her a vocabulary that made her intelligible and appealing in certain LGBTQI+ circles and among Arab American community activists, even as she was marginalized within these spaces and tried to push at some of their limitations. This is not to dismiss her difficult experiences of discrimination, poverty, and institutional torture. But her familiarity with activist language (even if it was initially in French and Arabic) and her light skin color may have given her quicker access to networks of support that helped in the difficult period of adjustment to life in the US.

TRIGGERING EXPERT OPINION

Marwa continues to have a visceral negative reaction at the mere sight of her immigration document folder. This is partly due to the recounting of traumatic experiences contained in her asylum application, extracted through long sessions of painful remembering and writing. But also contributing to this repulsion is the expert testimony her lawyer obtained to support her case. Amin, Marwa's lawyer, advised her to pay an academic expert to write a statement for her application. Not knowing much about this, Marwa agreed. But it was "a hot mess."

Many of my academic colleagues have been asked, as I have been, to provide expert testimony in asylum cases for applicants from the regions they study, but some find the requests difficult. The expertise required is most helpful when presented in the form of certainties and generalizations—or "emphatic statements and reductive pictures," as anthropologist Roger Lancaster puts it.[20] Such reductive pictures are precisely what many academics try to avoid in their professional writing. Anthropology, particularly in recent decades, has preferred nuance and complexity. But the expert opinions sought for asylum require the opposite: the pronouncement that the applicant, as a member of a particular social group, would be in danger of persecution anywhere in her country of origin; and its corollary, that she would be safe and free (by implication, anywhere) in the United States. Sociologist Lionel Cantú, with Eithne Luibhéid and Alexandra Minna Stern, argues that asylum relies on a model of other cultures as ahistorical, timeless, hermetically sealed, "divorced from social, economic and political variables," and organized according to strictly nationalist logics.[21] Lancaster similarly notes that when he begins "to qualify, to equivocate, and to draw exceptions to the rule . . . the lawyers with whom I have spoken decide that it would be unwise to put me on the witness stand."[22] Consequently, scholars who have given expert testimony are often reluctant to even share (not to mention publish) their reports outside the asylum system or in academic circles.

However, once an academic has given an expert opinion in one asylum case, word travels among attorneys and organizations, and they are often asked to do so again. While almost all of the colleagues I spoke to about this expressed some level of discomfort or wariness about giving such expert opinions, some outside of my circle are less reluctant. Dr. Shaul Gabbay is one example of a professor who sees his way easily to the certainties required. His website (muslimworldexpert.com) explains that the advantage of hiring him for an asylum case is that he can "present evidence in a clinical manner."[23] His website announces: "When questions about the Middle East or the Muslim Community worldwide present themselves, an expert witness like Dr. Shaul Gabbay knows how to present relevant, succinct expert testimony for the case in court."[24] "Homosexuality" and "honor killing" are two items listed among the many "predominant hardships" in Muslim countries that he can speak to,[25] reflecting the growing pseudo-feminist and what Jasbir Puar has described as the homonationalist orientation of American politics.[26] Gabbay advocates for a "forensic sociology" approach to honor killings in the Middle East and "the Muslim World" at large.[27] Dr. Gabbay's website emphasizes his ability to provide expert information on thirty-six countries, from Djibouti to Tajikistan, all in "a clinical manner"! I find Gabbay's online pages jarring, not only because of their commercial, self-promotional quality and the implausibility of a single person claiming expertise on the cultures, histories, and politics of so many different countries, but also because of the blanket statements his work promotes.

Imagine my surprise when Marwa told me, several years after I had learned of Gabbay through my online research, that her lawyer had hired an expert named Shaul Gabbay! Marwa says: "I beat myself up a lot about this, because I feel guilty that I didn't know at the time. But my lawyer should have known, he knew very well my relationship to the Israeli occupation in south Lebanon, and how I survived bombings and stuff. But I didn't know at the time that I actually paid $2000 for this so-called country expert, Shaul Gabbay. I will never forget him. I hate him!" At the time of submitting her application for asylum, Marwa had not yet read Gabbay's expert contribution to her case. This is quite common among asylum seekers: Suad, for example, did not know much about the expert testimony on "FGM in Sudan" that her pro bono lawyers had added to her application. Marwa explained: "I was too vulnerable, too busy trying to survive, trying to eat and sleep, doing all those basic things, that I didn't read." But a year and a half later, when Marwa was preparing to apply for her green card, she reviewed her asylum file and, at that point, "I could understand English better and in a more nuanced way. I actually sat and read the report. . . . Then I read that he is an expert because he was a sergeant in the Israeli Defense Forces in Lebanon! That just crushed me."[28]

Marwa regrets having given her hard-earned money to that expert, helping to set him up as "the authority that the judge should listen to, to help keep me here!" Emotionally, Marwa feels that this has compounded the trauma of her asylum: "It's to this day something that I can't live with. I feel like my lawyer should have known that that was not okay and it was actually unethical of him." The fact that this expert served with the Israeli military in its invasion of Lebanon has fed Marwa's sense that her asylum narrative may bolster anti-Arab sentiments. She is well aware that the granting of asylum and rights to a few LGBTQI+ applicants can function as a form of pinkwashing masking the US's other policies in the region or directing attention away from them. Though this expert opinion likely helped Marwa's asylum case, it was financially and emotionally costly.

Lancaster, who studies Latin America, urges scholars who write or testify in asylum cases to pay attention to caveats and equivocations, as well as to the particular historical, political, and economic contexts where repression occurs. This would make sexual asylum arguments more accurate. It would also reduce the insidious play of "the scary, dark-hued Latino bogeyman" in American politics.[29] The same of course can be said in relation to the Middle East. The simplistic accounts of sexual repression in the Middle East that are common in asylum cases also reinforce the racist images of a scary, dark-hued Arab or Muslim bogeyman that are already heavily circulating. Though this exhortation to nuance and context is a legitimate demand of academic experts in general, it would be unrealistic to place the responsibility of countering widespread stereotypes on the shoulders of asylum seekers, a group of structurally vulnerable individuals. In the absence of alternatives or more complex narratives within the legal system, simplistic stories are often seen as the only option.

BREAKING THE MOLD

Though asylum is premised on a repudiation of an asylee's country of origin, Marwa strongly resisted this scenario. The contrast between life in the old country and life after asylum in America is often not as sharp as the asylum system figures it to be. Marwa is quick to note that "nowhere is perfect!" She told a reporter in 2015 that, though she no longer had to dodge bombs and political harassment as she did in Lebanon, she now faced persecution in her new country as an American Muslim. She explained that, especially in Michigan, she was often made to feel like the "other," including within queer circles. Randazzo points out that lesbian and gay communities in the United States, though "sometimes romanticized as sites of liberation and equality, typically reproduce the same racial and gender inequalities characteristic of the US social order."[30]

In Muslim American organizations, Marwa also experienced discrimination as queer. When she did community work with an Arab American organization, her supervisors asked her not to join certain meetings because of "how she looked," referring to her short hair and piercings. Her expectation of freedom to be "whoever I want" in the US was quickly upended: "You are ridiculed for being queer by Arab Americans. Then, you're being ridiculed because you care about praying or the Quran by LGBTQ people. And you're like, wait a second, I don't belong to either this or that, and you feel like maybe you have to find a space where you can be all of those things at once. And that's how Z collective got founded in Michigan."

The collective's page on social media featured a famous quote attributed to Margaret Mead: "Never doubt that a small group of thoughtful, committed citizens can change the world; indeed, it's the only thing that ever has." The collective was focused on empowering members to do "radical political work in our respective communities." Marwa later moved to the East Coast and joined a then-small national collective called the Muslim Alliance for Sexual and Gender Diversity (the acronym "MSGD" sounds like mosque in Arabic) and has been an active member for several years. The trajectory of Marwa's work with Nasawiyya and Meem in Lebanon to Z collective and MSGD in the US is one of continuity, rather than a sharp break between pre- and post-asylum or the land of persecution versus the land of freedom. Marwa regularly introduces herself as having been involved in activism around gender and sexuality issues "in two countries . . . for about 10 years."

HEALING AS FREEDOM

Marwa is certain that the "biggest accomplishment of my social justice activism is to heal with my mom." After she arrived in the US and as she applied for asylum and awaited her decision, Marwa didn't speak to her parents: "I lost two years, completely cut off from them." She recognizes that the asylum system "really wants you to make an enemy of your own family and your country." She says she hesitated to contact her family for those years, "and my lawyer contributed to this. He said 'don't talk to them, don't contact them at all.' His concerns were valid, but 'don't contact' compounded my trauma and my fear. I really needed them." She later explained that asylum "de-roots you from the healthy parts of your system. So okay, I get it, there's a lot of fucked-up stuff in Lebanon, but you can't just deprive me from the good and the bad. It's too hard to come back from that, and I still struggle with it."

After she received her asylum decision, Marwa did contact her mother. And her mother was in fact happy to hear from her. She started a long journey of talking to her mom and "processing our experiences together." This was not always smooth going. Marwa recognized that the path to healing is "full of tumbling and learning to get back up." She enjoys her recently acquired hobby of rock climbing precisely because "failing and falling and then getting back up" is built right into it. She proudly declares: "I slowly healed. And now my friends tell me 'You are so lucky. You have the best relationship with your mom.'"

Though Marwa never thought she would want to have biological children, when she found a spiritual home in MSGD and her community there, the idea slowly grew on her. She bonded with Sharif, one of her gay Muslim male comrades at MSGD, and "something just felt like home, and I really wanted that for myself." Sharif and Marwa decided to co-parent: "You know, especially when you lose your family and you're uprooted. . . . I felt like I wanted to make my own roots. So, my two babies are my roots here and they are my home."

Late in Marwa's pregnancy with her twins, her mother was able to get a visa and came to visit and assist her in caring for the children. This was a huge help to Marwa and meant a great deal to her, reinforcing her sense of family and its significance in her life, much like the support Fadi felt from his brothers and his delight at them welcoming his boyfriend at iftar dinner. This scenario of the extended Arab Muslim family celebrating their gay or queer members was precluded within the asylum narratives that needed to represent Jordan and Lebanon as dangerous places for Fadi and Marwa.

And that framing exacted a long-term price from Marwa: though she was able to reconcile with her mother, her absence from Lebanon caused her to lose precious time with other members of her family, time that she could not get back. She explains: "The main thing that was so hard to cope with around asylum, and it really continues to destroy me, is that because of very xenophobic, Islamophobic laws, I had to stay away from people I love in Lebanon for ten years." Her sense of loss is particularly acute in relation to her grandfather, whom she was extremely close to in Lebanon. Even during the period when her parents were angry with her and punished her for disobeying them and for her activism, her grandpa stood by her. When her father kicked her out of the house after she came home with piercings and tattoos, her *jiddo* ("grandpa" in Arabic) offered her his couch and his protection. He supported her and told her he thought she was brave: "It's hard to explain how tremendous that was, how much it meant to me at the time." Though Marwa spoke to him on the phone after she received her asylum, she was never able to see him again. He passed away two years later: "He was like my father figure, and there's a hole in my heart that he used to fill." When her grandfather fell ill and doctors advised the family that he might soon die, Marwa wanted to go see him, but her lawyer insisted that she should not—traveling to Lebanon, even though she had her green card by then, could jeopardize her status. Marwa explains: "The law is not clear. There's a humanitarian exception that allows an asylum seeker to travel, but it would be a huge risk." She was not able to say a proper goodbye to her jiddo.

The death of her grandfather before she could see him is a source of pain for Marwa, "the kind of pain that you can't wrap your head around." Also, her beloved grandmother has begun to suffer from dementia and no longer recognizes Marwa. These losses are difficult, especially since the decision not to visit "was not by choice; it was forced on me. I think those losses are the price of exile. It's so hard to describe with words that kind of wound, the feeling of not belonging, and losing your roots."

Marwa strongly questions the logic behind this uprooting of asylum seekers: cutting them off from the "healthy parts" along with the "bad" is psychologically damaging and is "hard to come back from." She pushes back against the requirement that asylum seekers not travel back to their countries of origin: "I feel strongly that once you are approved as an asylum seeker, that you should be granted freedom of movement, instead of it being, 'if you go to Lebanon you are abandoning your status.' It shouldn't work that way." Marwa's framework of restorative justice led her to want to heal: "Even my dad who was so fucked up and my mom who was very physically abusive—I can work on changing my relationships with them. It's my choice! If I have struggled and worked hard to change those relationships, that shouldn't cost me my status. If the American government believes in human rights, it should afford people the chance to work on reparation and making things right!"

Instead, the rules around asylum and immigration "wind up producing a lot of additional stress and anxiety. They make you question your choices." Marwa felt that many aspects of her private life remained "under the microscope," making her feel continuously uneasy and insecure. Even several years later when Marwa applied for citizenship, the attorney she hired for this purpose suggested that she might come under scrutiny and her sexuality be thrown into question for having decided to have children. The lawyer advised that, as part of her citizenship interview, she might be asked if she was in fact lesbian, since she had given birth! Marwa was astonished at the naïveté of such a question: "I said, is that even a legitimate question? And the lawyers were like, yeah. So I was stressing that because I have the babies and Sharif is a cis man, that people are going to assume that we are together. I was like, what the fuck?"

In this situation, like many others, the state asserts its interest in who has sex with whom and how, and conditions benefits and rights on these intimate details. Just as Fadi was asked in his asylum interview whether he had ever had sex with a woman, Marwa had to anticipate the intrusion of the question of whether she had had sex with Sharif. This is problematic, not only because of its invasion of the applicant's privacy, but also because of the simplistic and narrow understanding of sexuality implied—whereby a single sex act could somehow invalidate queerness. Marwa objected: "Imagine, I had to explain that, you know guys, we did IVF, we never had sex, yes we live together, etc." The private lives of asylum seekers and immigrants are subject to the state's probing, which is often based on narrow assumptions about sexuality and the attendant identity boxes. The scrutiny and conservative judging of private lives is built into the process, with the requirement, which started all the way back in 1790, that naturalization applicants have to prove their good "moral character," a stipulation wielded by USCIS as "a powerful exclusionary device."[31]

Marwa faced additional stumbling blocks in obtaining her citizenship but finally prevailed. In the year right after, she traveled to Lebanon. Like many of the asylum seekers I met, she continued to value her connection to family and loved ones in her country of origin, even if she feared government harassment. Her citizenship gave her enough confidence to travel, though she continued to be concerned at some level: "That worry is always there, and it kind of terrorizes you, and you live with that heavy weight, with the uncertainty. And you are always questioning your choices in life because of that. Ten years have lapsed and I need to see people." And, like Fadi, Marwa found her journey "genuinely grounding" and essential to her healing and sense of closure and strength. While she has a new home where she is growing deep roots, despite the pain, exile, and grief, Marwa still wants to hold on to her sense that Beirut is also her home.

PERSISTENT INSECURITY

Though Marwa completed her naturalization process and is now a citizen, there is always a chance, minute as it may be, that her citizenship could be taken away. One prominent example of denaturalization among Arab immigrants is that of activist Rasmea Odeh, who was stripped of her citizenship in 2015 (during the Obama years). The webpage of one of the organizations that Marwa cofounded, the Z collective, features an image of Odeh (in a panel of heroes along with Angela Davis, Comandanta Ramona, and others). Marwa was well aware of the persecution Odeh faced and the eventual revocation of her American citizenship.

Rasmea, like Marwa, was a habitual activist. She first organized in Palestine; then, after she was deported from there, in Lebanon and Jordan; and then in the US, where she built the over eight-hundred-strong Arab Women's Committee of Chicago.[32] There, she worked on projects ranging from challenging "profiling against Arabs and Muslims" to supporting women's empowerment and gathering their oral histories, as well as building alliances with other communities of color to demand "police accountability and immigrant rights to equal access to health and human services and civil liberties."[33] The FBI monitored organizations that Odeh worked with and fished for information on so-called anti-governmental activists.[34] Unable to find anything else on her, the Department of Homeland Security arrested Odeh for "the highly discretionary and rarely prosecuted offense of lying on a naturalization form" ten years prior.[35] The accusation of immigration fraud stated that Odeh "failed to indicate on [that] form ... that an Israeli military court had convicted her in 1970 of an offense she maintains she did not commit and only confessed to under severe torture in prison."[36] According to her supporters, an oversight such as this "would have been forgiven were it a country other than Israel and Rasmea something other than an outspoken Palestinian American activist."[37] The move "reek[ed] of payback," as Angela Davis put it.[38] At the trial, the court allowed the prosecution to present documents from Israel's military (so-called) courts, while forbidding Odeh and her attorneys from referring to the torture and rape she endured while in Israeli custody.[39] Rasmea fought her conviction but in 2017 accepted a plea bargain that led to her deportation.

The threat of denaturalization always lingers somewhere in the background. It can have a chilling effect, causing immigrants to weigh whether their activism might make them targets for silencing. Would Marwa's activism be considered edgy? Edgy enough to make her a target of FBI inquiry? Of course, the history of the FBI's interest in Muslim Americans is notoriously capricious,[40] as is that of the police department of New York, where Marwa now lives.[41]

Though recently ramped up, systematic denaturalization efforts were started under the Obama administration with Operation Janus, in which about one hundred and fifty thousand old immigration and naturalization cases were reviewed for discrepancies in, or missing, fingerprint information. Janus targeted nationals of countries "that are of concern to the national security of the United States,"[42] which is government-speak for "Middle Eastern and Muslim countries." This effort was expanded by the Trump administration, under the name "Operation Second Look," to include a review of over seven hundred thousand cases.[43] Indeed, Trump's Department of Justice announced that it had opened a special standalone section just for denaturalizations in February 2020.[44] According to the *New York Times*, "denaturalization case referrals to the department have increased 600 percent" since 2017.[45]

This effort "underscores the idea that naturalized citizens have fewer rights than those born in the United States."[46] Revocations can be based on misrepresentations, concealment, or omission of information that "had a tendency to affect" the naturalization decision.[47] Though for the last half a century, citizenship, once obtained, has "had an air of finality about it," the Trump administration was seeking to change that and, in the words of Sirine Shebaya, a Muslim Advocates attorney, effectively create "a second class of citizens who no longer feel secure in their belonging to the United States."[48] The Trump administration showcased three denaturalization cases (two Pakistani Americans and one Indian American), but these were not open-and-shut fraud cases. The fact that they continue to be contested in court demonstrates that the administration was willing to go after cases in which the alleged fraud was not obvious or easy to prove, making the campaign scarier to naturalized citizens, especially Muslims.

These attempts have had the overall effect of undermining the "assumption of permanence" previously held by naturalized citizens,[49] and they have also strengthened a tiered vision "of what it means to be American."[50] Marwa's case, of course, was not fraudulent. Earlier, her lawyers had prepared her for questions at her citizenship interview in the form of "Are you in fact gay if you had children with a man?" Now, her travel back to the country from which she initially escaped and sought asylum could present similarly simplistic questions along the lines of "Was your fear credible if you elected to travel back later?"

As Marwa puts it, these doubts terrorize her and cause her to question her decisions every day. She struggles to supplant this fear and questioning with its opposite—a sense of certainty that she is doing the right thing and that she is equipped to face her future in the United States. Adding to Marwa's growing sense of security and confidence in her status is her recently acquired law degree. She completed her law school studies while continuing to struggle financially—she took additional work driving for rideshare companies to pay for some of the fees. She did this while pregnant with her twin boys, in the midst of starting a family, with all its demands on time and energy. The challenges were relentless, but so were her accomplishments. She was quickly hired by a legal aid organization, where she strives to practice the kind of law she is passionate about—centered on abolition and restoration. During the ten years since her exile with no family wealth or educational history, Marwa has journeyed tirelessly. Her accomplishments are part of her healing, and she gives great credit to her community of co-organizers and activists for holding her up along the way.

In November 2020, Marwa participated for the first time in an electoral process as a voter:

> It's a very complicated feeling . . . I couldn't help but remember how, as an immigration fellow eight years ago, some voters told me to my face: 'You shouldn't be here'; 'Muslims destroyed our country. They are terrorists.' I couldn't help but remember the doors slammed in my face while canvassing; I couldn't help but feel all my feelings. Especially that the road to abolition is still very far.

Marwa is deeply inspired by the work of organizer and educator Mariame Kaba, who calls for reacting to violence with transformative justice and community accountability in which survivors are given as much control, autonomy, and self-determination as possible. In her view, prisons and increasing criminalization do not help end violence. Kaba advocates instead for an approach that would take the survivor, the person responsible for the harm, and their communities toward healing while putting power in the hands of those impacted by the harm.[51] Guided by this philosophy and practice, Marwa has worked hard on her relationship with her mother and on her relationship with Lebanon—she seeks not to cut them off or punish them, but rather to prefigure the world in which she wants to live.[52] Faced with nagging fears about the permanence of her citizenship status in the US, Marwa has pushed through toward this place where she determines her choices and desires.

Conclusion
OF STORIES, TRAUMAS, AND HAPPY ENDINGS

IN 2016, I HELPED MY FATHER APPLY FOR A GREEN CARD in the United States. We hired an immigration attorney in New York, who estimated the process would take six to eight months. It actually took over four years. Though interviews are usually waived for adult children sponsoring their parents, such as myself, we were called in for not one, not two, but three separate interviews. With the assistance of a second attorney and multiple FOIA (Freedom of Information Act) requests, we discovered that my dad's application was delayed because of a "background check." As Palestinians, we were not exactly surprised (Dad had been placed on a no-fly list over a decade earlier and had eventually managed to get his name removed) but certainly disappointed. In the meantime, he was not allowed to travel outside of the United States without an advanced parole document. Setting aside the bizarre logic of mandating that someone whose background is somehow suspect must stay in the country, we went through the hassle and expense of applying for an advanced parole document for my dad each year as we awaited a decision on his green card. This document enabled my father to travel to see our family back in Palestine, to go to conferences, and to travel with my nuclear family on yearly holiday trips we had been making together for over twenty years. Until it didn't.

At the end of a family trip to Jamaica in January 2020, we arrived at the airport to fly back to New York. Dad was accustomed to extra scrutiny at airports and promptly showed his advanced parole document, one he had already used to enter back into the US on a previous occasion. However, the airline staff member at the check-in counter was not familiar with the document. He said he had to call his supervisor. It was our bad luck that the supervisor was also unfamiliar with it and decided to call Customs and Border Patrol (CBP) in Miami for guidance. The agent who answered the call that day decided that my father did not have the proper documents—it is not clear why or how, but he was very certain of his view. He threatened the airline supervisor that if she allowed my father to board the plane, her company would be heavily fined and she could lose her job. We explained to the supervisor again that the CBP officer was mistaken, that my dad did have the correct document, and that he had in fact already used it to enter the US before. In the midst of these stressful developments, I was reminded of Tawfiq's experience with his asylum travel document. He was held up at the airport for six hours: "The immigration officers had no idea what these travel documents were and they gave me a hard time.... They looked at the document and were like, 'What is this?' They had no idea; they had never seen one before.... I was like, 'You know, your government issued this document.'" It is no wonder he felt discouraged from traveling.

Though it was a Sunday afternoon, I miraculously managed to get our wonderful attorney on the phone, and he again explained to the supervisor that my father had the proper documentation and that he had used it to enter the US before, as an entry stamp on his passport demonstrated. We also showed her the line on the document that read that the presentation of this document "authorized a transportation line to accept the named bearer on board for travel to the United States"! But she just dismissed us and told us to take it up with the US embassy in Kingston—which was four hours away by car and closed that day. She refused to give us her last name and refused to call CBP back. She even refused to share the telephone number she had for CBP, which seemed to be her personal choice rather than a matter of policy, as another airline agent later gave it to us.

We had to make some quick decisions. We agreed that my husband and daughter would take the flight we were booked on back to New York in time for her to go to school the next day. I would stay back with my dad to help him figure out this mess, and my mom insisted on doing so as well. The airport we were in was small and had only a few uncomfortable chairs in the area where we had to stay for many hours while I made phones calls to figure out how we could leave. I had had the privilege of attending and teaching at top universities in the US and had a wide network of contacts, from law school professors who specialized in immigration law to lead staff members of organizations such as the ACLU (American Civil Liberties Union). One of my close friends had a union job that put her in close communication with the congresswoman in our home district in Brooklyn—the congresswoman answered my friend's call on a Sunday afternoon! Another dear friend, who had worked in the mayor's office in New York, was able to connect me to someone in the Mayor's Office of Immigrant Affairs, and that person also responded immediately. My father was stranded in an airport in Jamaica for no fault of his own, but I was extremely fortunate to be able to mobilize an incredible network of friends in relatively influential positions.

And mobilize they did. The law professors examined images of Dad's documents, looked up his file, and confirmed what our lawyer already knew: we had the correct papers. The ACLU friend advised against going to the embassy the next day as the airline had told us to do, because this issue was usually deemed beyond the embassy's jurisdiction. A top staff person at our congresswoman's office contacted CBP; they were rude to her and unhelpful, even after we signed a form authorizing her to inquire on our behalf. A friend of our friend in the New York City Mayor's Office of Immigrant Affairs kindly reached out to a contact she had at CBP at John F. Kennedy (JFK) airport in New York and had better luck. That CBP officer eventually reviewed Dad's documents and said he would contact CBP Miami to clear his path. That this all happened on a Sunday afternoon is another illustration of the strength of this network and how incredibly lucky we were to get these answers and interventions on my dad's behalf.

We had missed the last flight of the day back to New York. The small airport was emptying out, except for a few cleaning staff members. We had been there all day, and my father, who was then eighty-two, looked tired. He joked that he somehow felt guilty, like he had done something wrong. Of course he had not, but I shared his sense of unease, that somehow him traveling on vacation with his family was a step too far for a green card applicant. We booked a nearby hotel to stay the night.

When we arrived back at the airport early the next morning after a few hours of sleep and a failed attempt to visit the nearby American consulate, I explained to the airline supervisor (a different person than the day before) that CBP had cleared my dad, and I begged him to call them again—both days' supervisors were visibly intimidated by the prospect of speaking to a representative of this agency. At this point, the airline rep claimed they couldn't check my dad into the next flight to New York without hearing from CBP, and CBP said it couldn't evaluate my dad's clearance without having him checked into the flight. It took more than a few additional phone calls to sort this nonsense out. We finally were cleared to depart on an afternoon flight. Our lawyer and our contact at the mayor's office were on high alert in case we needed help upon arrival in

New York. But we made our way through immigration at JFK easily—the mayor's staff contact person at CBP seemed to have indeed smoothed our path. I spent the following day baking several batches of fresh Palestinian bread and hand-delivering them, along with my sincere thanks, to friends, our congresswoman's office, and the Mayor's Office of Immigrant Affairs. Without their help, I am not sure what my dad could have done.

In the end—since I was well connected and had sufficient finances and wherewithal—this incident was inconvenient and expensive but largely inconsequential to me or to my father. We considered lodging a complaint against the CBP officer in Miami who belligerently claimed with great certainty that my dad should not be permitted to board the plane. However, enforcing any kind of accountability at CBP was a long shot; its culture of impunity was notorious.[1] A few weeks later, the incident was not much more than a conversation piece about the dysfunction of our immigration system, though one we avoided around my dad as we sensed his discomfort at having unwittingly been the source of hassle for the family. My younger daughter, then twelve, had cried at the airport and was worried about her grandfather and future travel plans, but I hoped the incident had not left a significant mark in her memory.

My dad actually received his green card seven months after and would no longer have to travel with this document that was apparently unfamiliar to some airline supervisors and even some immigration officials. Of course, we were in a position of privilege, and it was merely a family pleasure vacation that was disrupted by this mishap—that pales in comparison to the consequences of such stumbling blocks for many others. But I recount this experience here to illustrate the unpredictable barriers thrown up in the face of immigrants, even those who succeed in jumping through all the narrow hoops placed in their paths. People familiar with the system will hardly be surprised that a bearer of a government document explicitly created for travel, such as my father, was barred by a representative of that same government from doing the very thing the document authorizes him to do. Representatives of the system routinely ignore or violate its rules by banning immigrants when given the opportunity, with little repercussion to themselves but often severe consequences for immigrants and their families. Recall the relatively minor example of the case worker completely ignoring the interpreter request card, issued by her employer, that Fatima gave her in supposedly immigrant-friendly Brooklyn. This mis-implementation of rules compounds all the barriers already presented by the rules themselves. And although, in our case, we were able to overcome these hurdles, both formal and informal, what happens to others less privileged, who face bigger obstacles?

This book is about a group of asylum seekers who overcame many barriers but could only do so thanks to the help of lawyers and advocacy organizations. Despite this structural advantage of legal representation, Marwa, Fatima, Suad, and Fadi all still faced serious stumbling blocks that are not officially part of asylum. Outside of asylum offices, few people know about the system or about what asylees are legally entitled to—even immigrations agents (recall the border agent asking Tawfiq about his asylee travel document: "What is this?")—and most assume the absolute minimum, that asylees are entitled to nothing. But, in addition to lack of information, some stumbling blocks are products of deliberate anti-immigrant and Islamophobic sentiments. Asylees have faced adversarial questioning at asylum interviews that are supposed to be non-adversarial. Work permits have not been mailed, even after lawyers have submitted all the paperwork and paid the fees. Corporate HR personnel have decided that asylees were ineligible to work, when in fact they were eligible. Staff at a homeless shelter have assumed that asylees were not entitled to housing, even though they were. Asylees have feared neighbors who threatened to call ICE, with the knowledge that agents might not heed a lawyer's letter regarding their legal status.

These unofficial obstacles are piled on top of the heavy burden of the official barriers that asylum seekers must overcome: finding a path to entry to the US; preparing a complex application that requires a trained professional; paying fees; meeting the high threshold of persecution and on very particular grounds; writing a painful personal narrative, and then the retraumatizing practice of retelling it; gathering evidence and proving their well-founded fear; submitting the application within a year; enduring without a work permit for six months longer or more; waiting for an asylum interview that could take years; the stress of the interview; awaiting a decision, and, in case of a negative decision, appealing it and going through a lengthy court process that could stretch for years longer.

The four asylum seekers in the preceding chapters were ultimately able to jump through all of these difficult and narrow hoops, but they faced tremendous stress and uncertainty along the way and after. It should be obvious by now that these barriers, both in the formal rules and in their real-life application, are incredibly burdensome to the majority of asylum seekers who are structurally vulnerable. Marwa, Suad, Fatima, and Fadi were less exposed than others, thanks to their connections to attorneys or organizations. Still, their vulnerability is evident if one considers how seemingly minor incidents and accidents could impact them so powerfully. A fire alarm in a court building set Fatima back months and may have contributed to another mental collapse. A hastily planned holiday party and a government shutdown that ended weeks before each added years to Suad's painful wait. Other asylum cases I saw were thrown off by the sloppy translation of a few words by a court-appointed interpreter (for example, rendering the pejorative term *shadh* in Arabic, meaning pervert, as simply "gay") that thereby jeopardized the applicant's chances of success.

The vulnerability of asylum seekers is also illustrated by their subjection to the odds of "refugee roulette"—where huge disparities in the grant rates of particular judges and cities shape their futures.[2] And of course, the lives of asylum seekers are heavily impacted by larger changes in government, from election results to policy changes, from seemingly distant political upheavals to climate change. In early December 2020, asylum seekers trapped in one of the refugee camps that sprang up just south of the US-Mexico border as a result of Trump's Remain in Mexico policy followed the US presidential election results closely, assuming that their very fates hung in the balance.[3] That Fadi was able to apply for asylum and receive his decision within a few months can be contrasted with Suad's experience of multi-year delays, a disparity that is partly a result of a change in political circumstances: violence in central America, the influx of asylum seekers at the US-Mexico border, and the lack of political will to process them promptly—or, rather, the political desire to slow-walk these decisions. Fadi and Suad's ability to enter the country in the first place has shifted, narrowing in the years following 9/11 and then narrowing further as a result of Trump's Muslim bans and anti-immigrant policies, shifts that had little to do with the merits of their cases and were far beyond their control.

PATTERNS OF SUFFERING

A commonality I observed among all the asylum seekers I met over the past decade was their experiences of isolation and despair, though some were dealt a larger share of this than others. Suad wrote in her asylum application that she had wanted to escape to the United States "because there I would be safe and my human rights would be guaranteed." Yet, it is in this supposed land of the free that she experienced some of the hardest times of her life; it was in New York, not Khartoum, that she was most isolated, afraid, severely depressed, and broke. Even Fadi, with his bubbly gregariousness, went through long periods of "deep funk," loneliness, and isolation, and it took many years to begin to achieve an income approaching the one he made in Jordan. Fatima yearned for her sons and mourned in a homeless shelter the fact that she is "number one and number two and number three." And Marwa, couch surfing and depressed, recounted "just living a hard life" and was encouraged by her lawyer not to contact her family.

The usual networks of fellow immigrants that other Sudanese, Jordanians, Egyptians, or Lebanese in the US typically draw on were not easily accessible to these asylum seekers, as they were often regarded as violators of various social mores—Fatima was shunned by her relatives for having left her husband, Marwa was told she couldn't represent the Arab American community because of her "appearance," Fadi didn't want to risk being discriminated against by Jordanian grocery owners for being gay, and Suad feared fellow Sudanese in New York would judge her for building her case on circumcision, not to mention seeking a restorative surgery. Fadi and Marwa, however, succeeded in connecting to different communities that Richard Mole terms "queer diaspora" communities, revolving to varying degrees around both shared sexual identities and ethno-cultural ones.[4]

The four asylum seekers in this book did benefit from connections to non-governmental organizations that provided support and advocated on their behalf. Various charitable entities attempt to fill the huge gaps left by the absence of government support for asylum seekers. These gaps are, however, intentional and are meant to keep the process of seeking asylum onerous, in order to deter all but the most desperate. But in fact these gaps shut out all but the fortunate few who are educated enough, wealthy enough, or simply lucky enough to enter the country and get connected to the few gap-filling nonprofits. It is hair-raising to consider that "out of the almost 200,000 people whose immigration court cases were completed in Fiscal Year 2019, 77 percent did not have legal representation."[5]

But even with the advantage of attorneys by their sides, asylum seekers must wait. As communications scholar Sara Sharma notes, differentials in power in society produce different temporalities.[6] For asylum seekers, that temporality is slow-moving, and they must suffer long periods in states of limbo and indetermination. And these extended times of waiting or "stuckedness," as anthropologist Ghassan Hage terms it,[7] are normalized; asylum seekers are expected to endure them as a sign that they deserve to be granted asylum. The process requires a persistent, stubborn, almost irrational optimism, which asylum seekers must sustain—despite rejections, failed steps, closed doors, and repeated setbacks—to try to forge futures of possibility.[8]

Built-in periods of prolonged uncertainty are exacerbated by the fact that asylum seekers are not entitled to court-appointed legal assistance that could help them navigate these difficulties. And immigration courts offer few protections to applicants. Seasoned asylum attorney Marty Rosenbluth likens them to "traffic courts with death penalty consequences."[9] Judges have a great deal of discretion and can choose to skip formal proceedings entirely. He notes that "immigration law really is like Alice through the Looking Glass. I half expect a rabbit to run through the court room saying 'I'm late, I'm late, I'm late.'"[10] Simple protections don't apply, and the burden of proof is reversed—making the assistance of an attorney—or, as Rosenbluth suggests, even multiple attorneys—all the more necessary.

Asylum seekers must contend with great uncertainty. As an officer admits, they essentially play "officer roulette": the "chances of getting a grant depend on who you get as much as what your claim is, because everybody has their own threshold, everybody has their own interpretation of the law, everybody has their own willingness to believe or suspend disbelief. It's just the way the system is—it's a human system, and that's the way human people operate."[11] Even with the best of attorneys, asylum seekers face unpredictable odds beyond their control.

PROPER MINDFUCK

The asylum process is built on a series of retraumatizations that asylum seekers must endure, particularly the ones lucky enough to have legal assistance. They must recount painful experiences of persecution and repeat them over and over again with organization gatekeepers, then attorneys, and then, again, for the asylum officer or judge. Assembling the accounts in the first place can be exceedingly difficult, as it was for Marwa, who cried every time she "sat down to write." They can also be incredibly invasive, as when Suad had to invite the system—her lawyers and myself first, and then many others—to discuss her genitalia. Attorneys guide applicants to focus their accounts not on points most emotionally salient to them, but on the most legally impactful aspects. These accounts must then be repeatedly practiced in order to train the asylum seeker to offer a legally forceful and exhaustive account (recall Suad's lawyers reminding her to "go through it systematically" and "remember to list all of the impacts [of FGM], physical and mental"). The repetition is also meant to dull the emotions of the asylum seeker in preparation for the pressures, anxiety, and high stakes of a courtroom (Fadi's lawyer advised him that repeating his account would never be comfortable but would get easier over time). This process of preparation is inevitably taxing and draining.

But after this dulling of emotions, asylum seekers must then offer another recounting in front of the adjudicator, in which their emotions resurface, because these decision-makers are instructed to base their determinations of credibility on "the demeanor, candor, or responsiveness of the applicant."[12] All four of the asylum seekers were told by their lawyers that it would be okay if they got upset at their hearing or interview, as it would be normal to be emotional or cry. Suad's lawyers told her: "Your therapist is probably telling you to forget about the fear, but here we are asking you not to" for the hearing. So, asylum seekers have to balance clarity of mind (for full and impactful recollection) with rawness and fresh "appropriate" emotions—one of many headfucks (and that is a suitable term here) built into asylum.

Another balancing feat required of asylum seekers is the memorization of exact sequences of events and their details and dates—clearly an inorganic way of remembering, especially for traumatic events. One immigration lawyer explains that the law requires "maniacal levels of consistency from those least likely to display it," whereby immigrants must overcome "the natural workings of human psychology and memory to win their cases."[13] Fadi noted that the agent who interviewed him "focused on dates, numbers, names. And she kept repeating them!" Marwa felt attacked at her asylum interview, where she was "made to continuously feel like you are guilty or you are lying," and the officer prodded and dug, over and over, about the date and sequence of beatings Marwa suffered from her mother. Suad had to quantify the number of times she was harassed by the morality police and practice recalling them in order. The consistency of this recollection is used to determine an applicant's credibility, even if the information is tangential.[14] And, as immigration attorneys are well aware, "inconsistency is the guillotine that hangs over every asylum case," even if it is around the color of a sweater.[15] What is more, information sufficiently memorized must then somehow be presented as if it were *not* memorized, because rote memorization is regarded as a sign of inauthenticity. The asylee must delicately balance between being well prepared but not over-rehearsed—another disconcerting feat.

In the end, asylum seekers are required to strategize extensively in order to make their way through the complicated asylum system. However, they must simultaneously present themselves as passive victims, since overly strategic presentations can seem manipulative and undermine their credibility. They need to make many choices, but tactfully appear to have no choice at all, as though their pathways were somehow entirely coerced and did not involve any calculation, especially—god forbid—any economic calculations. This is yet another difficult balancing act shouldered by asylum seekers. All of these paradoxical requirements— to routinize the telling of trauma but then allow emotions to resurface, to memorize information but then present it as if it were spontaneous, to strategize but appear guileless—are absurd and traumatizing in themselves. They require a degree of self-control and the turning on and off of emotional switches, actions that in themselves are cruel.

These mind games, together with unpredictability (the possibility of postponements and re-postponements, as well as frequent system dysfunctions, such as lost files, misdirected submissions, delayed work permits, etc.), all amount to a form of bureaucratic torture that asylum seekers are supposed to be thankful for having the chance to undergo. The system is plodding and sadistic, deliberately crushing many under its clunky, slow, heavy feet and occasionally spitting out some lucky victims who survive.

For asylum cases based on gender or sexuality, the stressful and weighty process also relies on the scrutiny of asylum seekers' bodies. They cannot afford privacy or shame. Suad had to have a doctor document the shape of her genitalia as well as the health consequences of her childhood circumcision, from genital abscesses to menstrual cramps and urinary tract infections. Fadi, like many gay Arab asylees I met, was asked about his sexual behaviors, with questions about whom he had sex with, when, and how. Though, clearly, the anal exam Fadi was forced to undergo in Jordan was far, far worse, this probing about sexual encounters is a light version of a similar interrogation. Marwa had to prepare to defend her asylum status from questioning based on how her children were conceived and with whom. An asylum seeker I translated for was discouraged from applying to bring her husband to the US because she had not "consummated" her marriage. At first glance, that a sex act is required for an immigration benefit seems random and unjust. However, presumed sex acts are at the center of many state mediated benefits, from taxes to insurance to inheritance.[16] Asylum seekers are nonetheless particularly vulnerable to state probing and its narrow assumptions about bodies and sexualities.

This prying into bodies and sex was aggravated by long delays in asylum that sometimes were so extensive that a change in staffing was inevitable. Tahirih, for example, had cases that lasted an entire decade.[17] It is hard enough to build trust and comfort around intimate private details with one lawyer or team of lawyers; it is another thing to have to start from scratch with a new set of people. But, as cases dragged on for multiple years, asylum seekers had to contend with the prospect of having new lawyers assigned to their cases, new judges, or even new rules. This poses another challenge to asylum seekers trying to find balance while the ground shifts beneath their feet.

FORCED STEREOTYPING

By design, the asylum system pushes applicants to present concise and impactful distillations of their life experiences that focus on persecution. Fatima's meandering, multilayered accounts were skillfully distilled by her lawyer into a tight, neat, powerful story, where Fatima was all victim, Egypt was all villain, and the US was savior. This curation work is not a matter of the asylum seeker cheating. Rather, the obligatory distillation cheats Fatima and others out of their complex stories. Sociologist Calogero Giametta argues that this "unwillingness to listen to the contradictions, inconsistencies and tensions within people's narratives reinforces a structural ignorance" and is "in part a product of the sub-humanization of racialized non-Western subjectivities."[18]

Suad's lawyers explained to her that she should not refer to the location of her place of employment in Khartoum, nor to its proximity to where morality policemen were stationed, as this would suggest that Suad could just work in a different neighborhood or city in Sudan. She had to paint the entire country in one brushstroke, as a singular place of danger. This forced homogenization and elimination of nuance is of course compounded by the fact that asylum officers and judges are not experts on all countries. Once again, by design, they must make decisions relying on their limited knowledge, often in the form of crude generalities about entire regions of the world, or neatly compartmentalized, unqueered notions of sexuality. They must go with their gut, or what are essentially deeply ingrained cultural assumptions based in their own lives, to make these decisions. Or, they must rely on the opinions of experts who are hired to declare that the applicant would be in danger of persecution anywhere in her country of origin, and its corollary, that she would be safe and free (by implication anywhere) in the United States.

The high bar of "well-founded fear of persecution" on five bases ensures that no nuance creeps into asylum accounts, though these narratives are then exported out of the narrow adjudication context and taken to represent "women in Sudan who have undergone FGM" or "lesbians in Lebanon." No room is left for the fact that Fadi was both tortured in prison in Jordan on suspicion of having sex with another man *and* was eventually accepted by his brothers along with his American boyfriend. Though Marwa's asylum narrative emphasizes that she has experienced a lot of freedom in the US, it cannot mention the Islamophobia and xenophobia that she has also faced. The framework must remain black and white. Marwa's asylum was premised on her repudiation of her family, culture, and religion and on her forced secularization.

These simplistic narratives leave little room for Fadi to have experienced homophobic persecution in both Jordan and the United States, thus encouraging his legal advisers to frame that menace as something exotic: "honor killing." This animates a narrative of rescuing brown women, or brown gay men, from brown straight bogeymen, melding Islamophobia and the so-called war on terror with queer liberalism and homonationalism.

Such essentialism, strategic as it is for asylum seekers, lends itself to a racist view of the world that supports the very structures of inequality that, in part, produce more asylum seekers. Anti-Arab and anti-Muslim racism undergird a range of policies, from the Muslim travel ban to the Iraq war, the tremendous support for Israel and its occupation of Palestinians, and the propping up of human-rights-stomping regimes in the name of anti-terrorism. As I argued earlier, there is a connection between the stereotypes that ultimately helped Fatima stay in the US and the stereotypes that support the ongoing exclusion of many others, such as her own sons. Lionel Cantú argues that asylum can thus be complexly "double edged."[19]

The use of strategic essentialism in this and other gender and sexuality cases can have costs. Leti Volpp wonders, "Are we using racism to get rid of sexism?"—or are we using sweeping anti-Muslim stereotypes to ameliorate the sexist or homophobic experiences of a small number of Muslim individuals?[20] Janet Halley and others argue that when women's rights are legally institutionalized, they may disappear "into legal technologies that we recognize under other rubrics" like universalism or American hegemony.[21] Aya Gruber also argues that American feminists aiming to protect women from violence have often wound up destructively "expanding the power of police and prosecutors" and fueling mass incarceration that has particularly harmed communities of color.[22] Though, clearly, the burden of undoing racism or American hegemony cannot be placed on the shoulders of asylum seekers, the reliance of many gender or sexuality asylum cases on perpetuating inequality begs for a rethinking of current asylum and immigration systems more generally.

The narrow opening offered to asylum seekers is premised on the exclusion of the majority of others, including those who suffer similar persecution but are unable to get visas to the US because of racist and classist visa policies and practices, not to mention those who suffer other forms of persecution excluded by asylum (such as those caused by poverty and war). One has to have endured the right kind of suffering and be lucky and middle-class enough to make it into the US in order to squeeze through this narrow immigration opening.

FAMILY SEPARATION?

The trauma of going through asylum is compounded by the forced disconnection from family or loved ones in the country of origin. As Marwa insisted, the system was designed to cut her off from both the bad and the good back in Lebanon, and she therefore paid a high price for her asylum—losing precious time with family members, one of whom passed away in the interim. Marwa, along with many others, resisted this asylum prohibition and, a few years later, insisted on reconnecting with family, despite potential risk to her immigration status. Though kids torn from the arms of their parents at the US-Mexico border and placed in cages have received wide attention and often condemnation, family separation takes many more varied—sometimes subtle, but still traumatizing—shapes.

Fatima had long been on a mission to convince her lawyer that, in addition to getting asylum for herself, she should bring her sons back from Egypt, where they had been deported. Minutes after she was granted asylum in an immigration courtroom, Fatima restarted her campaign; the sons had done nothing wrong and surely were deserving of "family reunification." Fadi hated Jordan but still wanted to see the people he loved there. But the asylum system allows only simple good-and-evil stories in which asylees would never want to so much as set foot back in their country. Suad had to prepare to respond to any questions about Saudi Arabia by insisting she had no place to go to except Sudan and that she absolutely could never, ever go there under any circumstances.

Marwa insisted on reconnecting to her parents who had, in fact, harmed her. In her vision of restorative justice, her liberty included the power to work on repairing relationships and the "right to make things right." Indeed, she feels she succeeded in healing with her mother, who became a huge support for her and her new queer family. Asylum had uprooted her, but she struggled to re-root herself on her own terms, even though she recognized that those terms came with a certain degree of uncertainty.

As unlikely as it sounds given their difficult experiences, in the end Fadi, Fatima, Suad, and Marwa are all members of a lucky elite of asylum seekers because of their connections with attorneys and nonprofit organizations. The US government provides no support or guidance during the asylum process, and it would be nearly impossible to divine the specialized information necessary for asylum. Although not all lawyers are equally skilled, experienced, or committed, on average their presence nonetheless does perform relative miracles for navigating the system. Indeed, without legal counsel, asylum seekers would be hard-pressed to figure out the "magic words" they need to use.[23] Nor could they know the right amount of supporting documents they need to present. One asylum officer noted:

> If there is this much documentation, it means that one of the NGOs that knows what they're doing has taken the case and has put a lot of research into it, and they don't take cases which are not good cases, so you know it's a substantive case . . . if it's a pile of paper this big, [pointing to a large file] in my experience, [it] has never been frivolous. Now, if it's a pile of paper that big [pointing to smaller thickness], it could very well be [frivolous]. But after you get over this much, I've never known it to be frivolous."[24]

Asylum seekers would need to know this magical amount of documentation and what to include in it. Most of the asylum seekers I met did not have the wherewithal at that stressful stage of their lives to assemble such a binder. In fact, they couldn't even manage to review or understand the contents of binders assembled by their lawyers on their behalf—even university graduate Suad and college student Marwa.

Without their connection to lawyers and nonprofit organizations, the asylum seekers would not have known about the need for certain types of documentation and expert confirmation, not to mention had the resources and connections to marshal it. Suad was directed to visit doctors and therapists, whose reports then made her situation real to the asylum system. Asylum seekers without legal counsel, with language barriers, or who are too afraid to access the healthcare system would be at a significant disadvantage in their applications. And it is not just a matter of connecting to any doctor or therapist, but connecting to ones who themselves have received specialized training on how to make their reports speak most effectively to asylum—again, using the necessary magic words. Fadi's experienced therapist Ghada, Fatima's Dr. Miller, who wrote about the heat rising from her head, and Marwa's paid expert on Muslim societies—all had experience or training in speaking to the asylum system.

In addition to fluency in the language of asylum, NGOs also offered connection to language interpreters, paid or volunteers such as myself, to help overcome basic language barriers to applying. The skill and comfort level of such interpreters, as well as their familiarity with particular dialects, can significantly smooth the paths of applicants. Alternatively, poor interpreters without knowledge of asylum can introduce an added layer of complexity and muddle the necessary extensive preparation with lawyers and communication with asylum officers. Since the government does not provide interpreters at asylum interviews (though they do provide them for court cases), they are essentially another valuable resource NGOs can provide to asylum seekers not proficient in English.

Without specialized guidance, asylum seekers are unlikely to have the foreknowledge that they should banish all mention of economic suffering and present their gender and sexual victimization in "isolation from other injustices or forms of exploitation."[25] As sociologist Jane Freedman explains, the asylum system is designed based on an artificial premise that there are "'real' refugees fleeing violence and persecution" and "'bogus asylum-seekers' or 'false refugees' coming to benefit from the economic and material benefits available in Western states."[26] In reality, there is a continuum between "forced" and "voluntary" migrations, and the division between the two is usually impossible to make.[27] Fadi left Jordan hoping for more freedom as a gay man but was also attracted by the prospect of more economic opportunities in America—prospects which, in fact, turned out to be worse than he imagined. As Marwa noted, she decided to leave Lebanon at a "time that was really, really not good for me for many reasons"—this included abuse from her mother, persecution by the authorities, and economic pressure from her family. Scholar Eithne Luibhéid argues for an urgent rethinking of this false distinction, as "most migrations in fact straddle choice and coercion."[28] But, of course, until this foundational conception of asylum is changed, lawyers will advise their clients, just as Suad's team at McCormick did, to deflect any suspicion that their motives for coming to the United States are economic. In Suad's case, this meant not dwelling on the fact that she was fired from the laboratory.

Generally, intersectionality has been increasingly recognized as a more accurate understanding of how power operates in societies, with even the Merriam-Webster dictionary offering a definition as "the complex, cumulative way in which the effects of multiple forms of discrimination (such as racism, sexism, and classism) combine, overlap, or intersect especially in the experiences of marginalized individuals or groups."[29] Yet the immigration system remains mired in an old-school, or neoconservative, view of gender or sexuality as somehow operating independently of race, class, and other forms of hierarchies, insisting on the sort of "single-issue analyses" that Kimberlé Crenshaw, who coined the concept of intersectionality, decried back in 1989.[30]

This single-issue perspective holds sway in terms of what is considered qualifying suffering that has taken place back in asylum seekers' countries of origin. Such suffering needs to be presented in isolation from other potentially tainting suffering (especially economic). It also must be presented as separate from any suffering in the so-called rescue country. Sima Shakhsari notes a painful, sometimes deadly irony around what are considered important human rights: for "Sayeh, an Iranian transgender refugee woman who committed suicide in 2008 less than a year after arriving in Toronto . . . [n]either the hardships that she endured while waiting in Turkey, nor the lack of access to housing, work opportunities, and healthcare in Canada entered the register of violation of human rights."[31] This cordoning off of human rights violations is necessary to sustain the "Third World barbarism vs. First World freedom narratives" at the core of asylum.[32]

In the vast sea of government neglect of asylum seekers, various small islands of nonprofit care have sprung up to fill some of the need. These include organizations focusing specifically on asylum as well as others targeting immigrant communities more generally, or even community service organizations that do not exclude noncitizens.

Fadi, for example, connected with a network that helped him find a therapist and then, through her, access to legal assistance. His path to building his life in the US was significantly facilitated by these connections. These NGOs are heavily burdened and can only serve a small portion of potential asylum seekers, who, in the best of cases, are abandoned by the government to struggle through the complicated system on their own—and, in worse cases, are placed in detention or deported. This high demand for limited resources causes organizations to turn away asylum seekers from lower-priority countries or those who have more complicated cases—just as the LGBTQI+-specialized asylum organization did to Marwa.

LONG-TERM INSECURITY

Even for the lucky few at the center of this book, winning asylum is one significant milestone—but only one—along a longer, and not always linear, path to better lives. For Fadi, who had a relatively smooth journey to asylum after meeting Ghada, ongoing financial difficulties made his way onward bumpy and slow. He was fortunate to survive the "brutal math" of the asylum process,[33] and that empowered him to then face the longer-term brutal math of surviving economically in expensive US cities—making for a less happy ending for several years after asylum. As Marwa put it, asylum gave her a handle on "the basics"—it allowed her to be here and start to slowly build a life, working three jobs at a time. For Fatima, asylum was a momentary upturn along her zigzagging path, followed quickly by a mental collapse and a year of homelessness. For years, her economic vulnerability undermined her ability to transcend the "what's asylum?" questions she encountered and apply for the more widely recognized green card.

Even for these lucky asylum seekers, the immigration front continued to contain uncertainty. When Fadi lashed out and punched a guy for an anti-Palestinian slur, he risked losing the job for which he was still training and, had the person pressed charges, his immigration status as well. The Clinton-era immigration bill of 1996 made deportation a "constant and plausible threat to millions of immigrants," while radically expanding "which crimes made an immigrant eligible for deportation."[34] Suad sensed this insecurity deeply and treaded nervously—driving her car slowly into intersections when the lights turned green. Though her life had "started anew," when ICE ramped up its militarized deportation machine after Trump's election, her anxiety heightened and she worried: "Do you think they will stop me if I am walking in New York? Even if I carry my documents?"

While Trump intensified denaturalization efforts, seeping into society at a much wider level was their underlying premise that "America is under attack by malevolent immigrants who cause dangerous harm by finding ways to live here."[35] It remains to be seen in the post-Trump period whether this assault on immigrants will be rolled back significantly and whether the tiered vision of what it means to be American will be weakened. In the meantime, asylum seekers who strive to heal themselves and connect to families continue to experience uncertainty. Although, as permanent residents and then citizens, they are able to travel physically to their countries of origin, they are told that such movement puts their legal status in some jeopardy. For Marwa, these fears terrorize her and cause her to question her decisions every day. But she is adamant not to let such dread govern her decisions and insists on owning her narrative and her relationship to her family and place of birth. Armed with a law degree, she asserts her right to have hope for Lebanon and for other places from which asylees flee.

Asylum seekers are under pressure by the system to tell a simplified and unqualified story, framing themselves as cultural victims who seek emancipation in the discrimination-free United States of America and promising to repudiate their connections to the countries they were born in. But these simple stories make a mess—they set a standard that then endangers the status of asylum seekers and invalidates their frequently complicated relationships to their countries.

OUR STORIES

This book traces the narrow paths of a relatively lucky few, discerning in them—beyond the individual asylum interview or court hearing—the contours of our politics. These are only four stories; they can hardly be expected to represent the full range of Arab gender or sexuality asylum experiences. This "sample," if one were to look at it that way, is too small and too narrow, with, for example, only one gay man and one queer woman represented from the wide spectrum of people gestured to in the acronym "LGBTQI+." But these are examples, such as they are, that suggest that the United States prefers simple stories—about countries of uniform cultural backwardness, where exotic sexual violence threatens passive victims, whom we rescue by allowing them tentative entry into our polity of freedom and opportunity. Suad, Fatima, Fadi, and Marwa each fought hard and long on many fronts to gain admission to this country and, in the end, in their own views, their lives were better for it. But their journeys are premised on narrowness and difficulty and on the almost assured failure of many others to gain similar access, especially generic victims of war and poverty. In the years since they entered the US, policies have shifted, making the narrow openings they squeezed through significantly narrower. That these particular individuals were deemed worthy at a particular point, and their entry (slowly, painfully) legitimized while that of so many others was blocked, points to the arbitrariness and injustice of the rules governing who gets to live where and how.

Considering refugee determination systems in various countries around the world, refugee law specialist David Matas observes that they all "share two common features: complexity and unfairness."[36] A few vulnerable asylum seekers who make their way to the United States are chosen (according to the whims of the politicians of one of the wealthiest countries in the world) to be the objects of pity and to be granted admission—slowly, contingently, with no government assistance, and often at great psychological cost to those individuals. But these asylum seekers made the most out of this deeply flawed and unnecessarily cruel system.

The election of Joe Biden in 2020 offered immigration advocates a modicum of hope for some improvement and, at least, the eventual rollback of some of Trump's most egregious policies. But attorney Marty Rosenbluth points out that even just figuring out what needs to be rolled back "will be a Herculean task."[37] The Immigration Policy Tracking Project (IPTP) documented over one thousand separate immigration-related changes made by the Trump administration.[38] Rosenbluth explains that these include "changes to essential immigration forms, official rule changes, agency directives, dozens of presidential orders, numerous changes in practices by agencies, over a dozen programs that were terminated entirely, and numerous modifications in the way data was gathered and reported on. While the work of undoing these changes has been made easier by the work of the IPTP and other researchers, there are no doubt hidden landmines everywhere." Not to mention that it remains to be seen how committed the new administration will be to enacting fundamental reform.

Given that President Obama was dubbed "deporter in chief" by immigration advocates, even a total rollback to the pre-Trump status will not be sufficient to bring justice to the system. Indeed, the inhumanely lengthy delays experienced by both Suad and Fatima occurred under Democratic administrations, with waits and arbitrary decisions trending upwards during those periods as well. Though the shift to Biden's control is a cause for some optimism, both Democrats and Republicans have been wary of people like Suad and Fatima. Both want the status of saving the victims of other cultures but are unwilling, so far, even in the most optimistic of times, to commit politically to that inclusion, not to mention expanding it further.

This is part of a larger trend beyond the United States. Anthropologist Didier Fassin argues that there has been a shift in Europe, as well, from seeing asylum seeking as a right enshrined in the Geneva Convention to a matter of state discretion, generously granted once claims have been deeply scrutinized.[39] Professor of migration law, Thomas Spijkerboer points out, however, that the very assertions of sexual exceptionalism used to legitimize European or American dominance over, and exclusion of, others are then used by asylum seekers to try to gain minimal inclusion.[40] Though the asylum seekers in this book challenge the global apartheid system by strategizing and maneuvering their ways out of their Bantustans, they can only do so in highly restricted and narrow ways.

Small incremental improvement is better than none, but better intentions among Democratic administrations are not enough to effect necessary change. I remember attending a public lecture last year by a well-known law professor and Palestinian rights advocate whom I admire a great deal. I recognized a young man in the audience at the lecture, whom, for the life of me, I could not place. I wracked my brain to remember where I had met him. As the lecture began, the speaker thanked her wonderful students, gesturing to the mystery audience member and a few others sitting near him. So, where did I know this prominent professor's student from? I wondered. Then it hit me: he was an asylum officer that I had met while interpreting for a case the previous year. It was the case of Nabila, a Libyan woman who had been delayed for several years because of a "security background check"! The applicant had been called in by this asylum officer for a second interview, almost two years after he first interviewed her (I interpreted at both meetings), to follow up on questions regarding her contact with Islamicist groups that had been threatening and persecuting her! That this amazing Palestinian rights professor had a favorite student who was instrumental in enacting this lengthy delay and line of questioning, even if it was required by his supervisor, goes to show that good intentions don't go far in a system broken by design. This was also true of my interpretation work—where I found myself participating at some level in traumatic asylum preparation as well as in cultural essentialism.

I later went back to my jottings from Nabila's interview and was reminded that the asylum officer had impressed me with his knowledge of Arabic and a mug he had on his desk with a line of poetry by Mahmoud Darwish: "We have on this earth what makes life worth living." Palestinians widely quote this poem, reminding ourselves of the small, beautiful things that inspire us to continue our struggle:

> We have on this earth what makes life worth living:
> April's hesitation,
> the aroma of bread at dawn,
> a woman's point of view about men,
> the works of Aeschylus,
> the beginning of love,
> grass on a stone . . .
> the hour of sunlight in prison . . .[41]

My book also pushes on because of small, beautiful things. Marwa's twins toddling around a room, Fadi's eyes lighting up when he talks about paint colors, Fatima's invitation to come for a meal at "mama's house," and Suad's smiling selfies. I hoped that learning of the injustices of asylum through these less bleak "success stories" would make the accounts easier to consume. I could have written a much darker book on, for example, the intake interviews at nonprofits where applicants have been turned away. Or on cases still in limbo after years of capricious delays. Or on a case that was delayed so extensively for a security check that the applicant gave up and left to Canada. Or I could have succeeded in reaching detained asylum seekers languishing in cold private prisons. I hope you see within my "happy ending" accounts all of the pitfalls, coincidences, arbitrary standards, and bizarrely specialized information that comes into play, any of which could have catapulted the successful applicants towards an opposite fate.

Notes

INTRODUCTION

1. I use pseudonyms for all the asylum seekers in this book.
2. "Executive Office for Immigration Review Adjudication Statistics: Total Asylum Applications," United States Department of Justice, April 15, 2020, accessed September 17, 2020, justice.gov/eoir/page/file/1163606/download.
3. Sayantani Dasgupta, "'Your Women Are Oppressed, But Ours Are Awesome': How Nicholas Kristof and *Half the Sky* Use Women Against Each Other," *Racialicious* (blog), 2012, conspireforchange.org/your-women-are-oppressed-but-ours-are-awesome-how-nicolas-kristoff-and-half-the-sky-use-women-against-each-other.
4. Deepa Kumar, *Islamophobia and the Politics of Empire* (Chicago: Haymarket Books, 2012); Moustafa Bayoumi, *This Muslim American Life: Dispatches from the War on Terror* (New York: New York University Press, 2015).
5. Anat Shenker-Osorio, interview by Dahlia Lithwick, *Amicus* (podcast audio), *Slate*, February 13, 2021, accessed November 15, 2021, slate.com/podcasts/amicus/2021/02/incitement-impeachment-inevitable-acquittal. The passage referenced is at 16:55.
6. Gil Loescher, "UNHCR at Fifty: Refugee Protection and World Politics," in *Problems of Protection: The UNHCR, Refugees and Human Rights*, ed. Niklaus Steiner, Mark Gibney, and Gil Loescher (London: Routledge Press, 2003), 7.
7. Meghana Nayak, *Who is Worthy of Protection?: Gender-Based Asylum and U.S. Immigration Politics* (New York: Oxford University Press, 2015).
8. See, for example, Jerry Markon, "Can a 3-Year Old Represent Herself in Immigration Court? This Judge Thinks So," *Washington Post*, March 5, 2016, accessed April 3, 2021, washingtonpost.com/world/national-security/can-a-3-year-old-represent-herself-in-immigration-court-this-judge-thinks-so/2016/03/03/5be59a32-db25-11e5-925f-1d10062cc82d_story.html.
9. In the five-year period leading up to 2012, only 14 percent of detained immigrants and 37 percent of all immigrants secured legal representation in their removal cases. Ingrid Eagly and Steven Shafer, "A National Study of Access to Counsel in Immigration Court," *University of Pennsylvania Law Review* 164, no. 1

(2015): 1–91, accessed April 14, 2021, scholarship.law.upenn.edu/cgi/viewcontent.cgi?article=9502&context=penn_law_review. In 1999 and 2000, one out of three asylum seekers did not have counsel in asylum interviews conducted by asylum officers. Andrew I. Schoenholtz and Jonathan Jacobs, "The State of Asylum Representation: Ideas for Change," *Georgetown Immigration Law Journal* 16, no. 4 (2002): 742, accessed April 23, 2021, scholarship.law.georgetown.edu/facpub/2175.

10. Eunice Hyunhye Cho, Tara Tidwell Cullen, and Clara Long, "Justice-Free Zones: U.S. Immigration Detention Under the Trump Administration," American Civil Liberties Union, 2020, accessed November 15, 2021, aclu.org/report/justice-free-zones-us-immigration-detention-under-trump-administration.

11. In addition to an American passport, as a "'48 Palestinian," I also hold an Israeli one.

12. Mary Harris, "This Immigration Judge Has a Fix for Immigration Courts," *What Next* (podcast audio), *Slate*, April 25, 2019, accessed December 3, 2021, slate.com/news-and-politics/2019/04/immigration-courts-doj-independence-separation.html. The passage referenced is at 12:04.

13. USCIS (United States Citizenship and Immigration Services) implemented a "last in, first out" policy on January 29, 2018. Royce Murray, "USCIS Changes to Asylum Interview Scheduling Allows Long-Pending Cases to Languish," *Immigration Impact*, February 23, 2018, accessed April 13, 2021, immigrationimpact.com/2018/02/23/uscis-changes-asylum-interview-scheduling-allows-long-pending-cases-languish/#.YHch4y2ZPOR; Breanna Cary, "Timing of the Affirmative Asylum Application Process," *Nolo*, accessed October 19, 2020, nolo.com/legal-encyclopedia/timing-the-affirmative-asylum-application-process.html.

14. Jaya Ramji-Nogales, Andrew Schoenholtz, and Philip Schrag, "Refugee Roulette: Disparities in Asylum Adjudication," *Stanford Law Review* 60 (2008): 295–411.

15. *Well-Founded Fear*, directed by Michael Camerini and Shari Robertson (New York: Epidavros Project/Epidoko Pictures, 2000). The quote is at 1:17:00.

16. US DoJ, "Total Asylum Applications."

17. This is not limited to the United States. See Sean Rehaag, "Judicial Review of Refugee Determinations (II): Revisiting the Luck of the Draw" (working paper, 2018), accessed November 1, 2021, s3.amazonaws.com/tld-documents.llnassets.com/0007000/7392/ssrn-id3249723.pdf.

18. Ghassan Hage, "*État de siège*: A Dying Domesticating Colonialism?" *American Ethnologist* 43, no. 1 (2016): 43.

CHAPTER 1: "I'VE ALWAYS BEEN LOOKING FOR MY FREEDOM"

1. Rogaia Mustafa Abusharaf, "Virtuous Cuts: Female Genital Circumcision in an African Ontology," *Differences: A Journal of Feminist Cultural Studies* 12, no. 1 (2001): 112–140.

2. Suad had just provided an account of this meager income to the lawyers for the work permit application.

3. Nancy Kelly, "Gender-Related Persecution: Assessing the Asylum Claims of Women," *Cornell International Law Journal* 26, no. 3 (1993): 630.

4. Jessica Mayo, "Court-Mandated Story Time: The Victim Narrative in U.S. Asylum Law," *Washington University Law Review* 89, no. 6 (2012): 1503.

5. Immigration and Nationality Act. 8 U.S.C. § 1158 (2022). For the pertinent passage, see section (b)(i)(B)(iii).

6. Many scholars have offered nuanced critiques of this western view and the impact of anti-FGM activism. See, for example, Ellen Gruenbaum, "Feminist Activism for the Abolition of FGC in Sudan," *Journal of Middle East Women's Studies* 1, no. 2 (2005): 89–111. See also Sondra Hale, "Colonial Discourse and Ethnographic Residuals: The 'Female Circumcision' Debate and the Politics of Knowledge," *Female Circumcision and the Politics of Knowledge: African Women in Imperialist Discourses*, ed. Obioma Nnaemeka (London: Praeger Press, 2005), 209–218.

7. The caption has recently been changed and, as of last writing, reads: "Kae wanted a future free of violence for both herself and her children. Through her perseverance and with the help of her attorneys, Kae was granted asylum." Tahirih, "Who We Serve," accessed February 1, 2022, tahirih.org/who-we-serve/survivor-voices/page/2. The longer one-page account of Kae's experiences states: "She was taken to an old house where two women, who had no professional training, forcibly performed the surgery." Tahirih, "Survivor Voices," accessed February 1, 2022, tahirih.org/survivor-voices/kae.

8. Michelle A. McKinley, "Cultural Culprits," *Berkeley Journal of Gender, Law and Justice* 24, no. 2 (2013): 159.

9. McKinley, "Cultural Culprits," 159.

10. Ira Glass, "Episode 688: The Out Crowd," *This American Life* (podcast audio), November 17, 2019, accessed December 3, 2021, thisamericanlife.org/688/the-out-crowd. The passage referenced is located at 15:40.

11. In 2010, according to UNFPA. unfpa.org/data/fgm/SD, accessed March 1, 2021.

12. As then attorney general Jeff Sessions put it in a 2018 decision that significantly weakened the ability of women to claim asylum based on domestic violence: "the asylum statute does not provide redress for all misfortune." See Caroline Holliday, "Making Domestic Violence Private Again: Referral Authority and Rights Rollback in Matter of A-B-," *Boston College Law School* 60, no. 7 (2019): 2145–2183.

13. Anaheed al-Hardan, *Palestinians in Syria: Nakba Memories of Shattered Communities* (New York: Columbia University Press, 2016), especially pp. 20–25.

14. Since Suad's first lawyer had used this argument in her initial application, the McCormick team had to also include it in their submission, because deleting it could undermine Suad's credibility.

15. Immigration and Nationality Act.

16. Timothy Randazzo, "Social and Legal Barriers: Sexual Orientation and Asylum in the United States," in *Queer Migrations*, ed. Eithne Luibhéid and Lionel Cantú (Minneapolis: University of Minnesota Press, 2005), 44.

17. The Trump administration tried to take this even further, requiring asylum seekers to not only have political opinions but, much more narrowly, to have been attempting to change the political party in power. See Victoria Neilson, interview by John Khosravi, "Episode 144: Asylum Regulations Update with Victoria Neilson, Esq of CLINIC," *The Immigration Lawyers Podcast* (podcast audio), July 31, 2020, accessed December 3, 2021, audacy.com/podcasts/the-immigration-lawyers-podcast-discussing-visas-green-cards-citizenship-practice-policy-24075/episode-144-asylum-regulations-update-w-victoria-neilson-esq-of-clinic-305795846. The passage referenced is near 04:30.

18. Glass, "Episode 688." The passage referenced is at 26:00.

19. Miriam Ticktin, *Casualties of Care: Immigration and the Politics of Humanitarianism in France* (Berkeley: University of California Press, 2011), 3.

20. Ticktin, *Casualties of Care*, 17.

21. *Asylum Manual*, Immigration Equality (2005), accessed February 1, 2022, immigrationequality.org/asylum/asylum-manual/preparing-the-application-declaration-dos-and-donts.

22. "Public Charge," National Immigration Law Center (2021), accessed February 1, 2022, nilc.org/issues/economic-support/pubcharge.

23. Tahirih, "Policy Briefing: Immigration Actions by the New Administration," virtual event, February 11, 2021.

24. Immigration Equality, "BREAKING: The Trump administration has proposed denying green cards to immigrants who receive government benefits," Facebook, September 22, 2018, facebook.com/ImmigrationEquality/posts/10156807586639595.

25. Sara McKinnon, "Citizenship and the Performance of Credibility: Audiencing Gender-Based Asylum Seekers in U.S. Immigration Courts," *Text and Performance Quarterly* 29, no. 3 (2009): 205–221.

26. Tim Weiner, "U.S. Plans to Delay Work Permits For Immigrants Who Seek Asylum," *New York Times*, February 17, 1994, accessed November 2, 2017, nytimes.com/1994/02/17/us/us-plans-to-delay-work-permits-for-immigrants-who-seek-asylum.html.

27. National Immigrant Justice Center, "Update on Two New Attacks on Asylum Seekers," September 30, 2020, accessed February 23, 2022, immigrantjustice.org/for-attorneys/legal-resources/copy/update-two-new-attacks-asylum-seekers.

28. Brian Jacek and Kristina Hon, "At Least Let Them Work: The Denial of Work Authorization and Assistance for Asylum Seekers in the United States," Human Rights Watch (November 2013), accessed February 12, 2020, hrw.org/sites/default/files/reports/us1113_asylum_forUPload.pdf.

29. Human Rights Watch, "Bad Dreams: Exploitation and Abuse of Migrant Workers in Saudi Arabia," July 13, 2004, accessed February 23, 2022, hrw.org/report/2004/07/13/bad-dreams/exploitation-and-abuse-migrant-workers-saudi-arabia.

30. See Sean Rehaag, "Bisexuals Need Not Apply: A Comparative Appraisal of Refugee Law and Policy in Canada, the United States, and Australia," *International Journal of Human Rights* 13 (2009): 415–436.

31. Kimberly Topel, "'So, What Should I Ask Him to Prove that He's Gay?': How Sincerity, and Not Stereotype, Should Dictate the Outcome of an LGB Asylum Claim in the United States," *Iowa Law Review* 102 (2017): 2376.

32. Detention Watch Network, "Immigration Detention 101," accessed February 23, 2022, detentionwatchnetwork.org/issues/detention-101.

33. As unlikely as it sounds, Suad had both a fingerprinting appointment as well as this hearing scheduled on Muslim holidays.

34. Mahmoud Mamdani, "Sudan: Colonialism, Independence and Secession," in *Neither Settler Nor Native: The Making and Unmaking of Permanent Minorities*, (Cambridge: Harvard University Press, 2020).

35. Juliana Morgan-Trostl, Kexin Zheng, and Carl Lipscombe, "The State of Black Immigrants," Black Alliance for Just Immigration (2020), accessed April 22, 2021, baji.org/wp-content/uploads/2020/03/sobi-fullreport-jan22.pdf. See in particular part II, "Black Immigrants in the Mass Criminalization System."

CHAPTER 2: "MY LIFE IS A BOLLYWOOD FILM"

1. Note that, starting in 1994, the Violence Against Women Act also offered a form of asylum to survivors whose immigration status depended on abusive family members (spouses or partners, children, parents) with citizenship or permanent resident status. Such survivors became potentially eligible—should they be able to find the legal expertise and necessary documentation—for immigration relief and a potential pathway to citizenship independently from their abusers. See Edna Erez and Shannon Harper, "Intersectionality, Immigration, and Domestic Violence," in *The Handbook of Race, Ethnicity, Crime, and Justice*, eds. Ramiro Martínez Jr., Meghan E. Hollis, and Jacob I. Stowell (Hoboken: Wiley, 2018), 457–474.

2. Fatima had far exceeded the deadline (one year from arrival) for submitting an asylum application, but her lawyer was able to argue that her illiteracy and PTSD were extraordinary circumstances allowing her an exception to this rule.

3. Mayo, "Court-Mandated Story Time."

4. Lila Abu Lughod, *Do Muslim Women Need Saving?* (Cambridge: Harvard University Press, 2013); Jasbir Puar, *Terrorist Assemblages: Homonationalism in Queer Times* (Durham: Duke University Press, 2007).

5. Susan Akram and Maritza Karmely, "Immigration and Constitutional Consequences of Post–9/11 Policies Involving Arabs and Muslims in the United States: Is Alienage a Distinction without a Difference?," *UC Davis Law Review* 38 (2005): 609.

6. Several years later, in June 2018, US Attorney General Jeff Sessions issued a precedential decision in an attempt to place a sweeping ban on domestic violence asylum claims. Six months after that, a federal judge "ruled that the administration

could not impose such a ban and that people who make domestic violence claims must have a fair opportunity to apply for asylum." "US: Protect Right to Asylum for Domestic Violence," Human Rights Watch, January 23, 2019, accessed October 31, 2019, hrw.org/news/2019/01/23/us-protect-right-asylum-domestic-violence.

7. This is, sadly, unsurprising. See Make the Road New York and the New York Immigration Coalition, "Still Lost in Translation," July 2010, accessed March 1, 2022, nyf.issuelab.org/resources/15109/15109.pdf.

8. Halal meat is from animals slaughtered according to Islamic law.

9. Smadar Lavie, *Wrapped in the Israeli Flag: Mizrahi Single Mothers and Bureaucratic Torture* (Lincoln: University of Nebraska Press, 2018), 103.

10. Ticktin, *Casualties of Care*, 121.

11. Lavie, *Wrapped in the Israeli Flag*, 98.

CHAPTER 3: "I WISH IT WAS A HAPPIER ENDING"

1. Fadi offered this in English, later explaining that the term Bassem used in Arabic was *manyak*.

2. Throughout my conversations with Fadi, he used the English word "gay" to describe himself, even when speaking in Arabic.

3. "Dignity Debased: Forced Anal Examinations in Homosexuality Prosecutions," Human Rights Watch, July 12, 2016, accessed February 20, 2019 hrw.org/report/2016/07/12/dignity-debased/forced-anal-examinations-homosexuality-prosecutions.

4. Immigration officers have unchecked power at ports of entry, and many instances of abuse and harassment have been documented. Randazzo notes that such abuse was so rampant that a training memorandum had to specify that border agents should refrain from "using derogatory language, racial slurs, verbal abuse, humiliation tactics or accusations of lying when questioning aliens." Randazzo, "Social and Legal Barriers," 50.

5. I was able to view these videos online in 2013, though they have since been deleted.

6. Yasmin Nair, "How to Make Prisons Disappear: Queer Immigrants, the Shackles of Love, and the Invisibility of the Prison Industrial Complex," in *Captive Genders: Trans Embodiment and the Prison Industrial Complex*, ed. Eric Stanley and Nat Smith (Oakland: AK Press, 2011), 130.

7. Mark Trevelyan and Gareth Jones, "Which European Countries Offer the Most Social Benefits to Migrants?," *Euronews*, September 16, 2015, accessed February 11, 2020, euronews.com/2015/09/16/which-european-countries-offer-the-most-social-benefits-to-migrants.

8. Becca Heller, "One Happy Ending," accessed April 4, 2019, heartsonfire.org/becca-heller-irap.

9. Ingrid Eagly and Steven Shafer, *Access to Counsel in Immigration Court*, American Immigration Council, September 2016, accessed April 14, 2021,

americanimmigrationcouncil.org/sites/default/files/research/access_to_counsel_in_immigration_court.pdf.

10. "Evaluation of the New York Immigrant Family Unity Project," Vera Institute of Justice, 2017, accessed November 19, 2019, vera.org/publications/new-york-immigrant-family-unity-project-evaluation.

11. According to the American Immigration Council, 63 percent of all immigrants in 2016 did not have a lawyer in court. Eagly and Shafer, *Access to Counsel*.

12. Immigration Equality, "Asylum Manual," Section 26.4.8.1. accessed February 7, 2022, immigrationequality.org/asylum/asylum-manual.

13. Lambda Legal, "Soto Vega v. Gonzales," accessed Oct 20, 2020, lambdalegal.org/in-court/cases/soto-vega-v-gonzales. The "H" in "LGBTQ/H" stands for "HIV positive."

14. "How Europe Determines Whether Asylum Seekers Are Gay," *The Economist*, September 13, 2018, accessed February 7, 2022, economist.com/europe/2018/09/13/how-europe-determines-whether-asylum-seekers-are-gay.

15. Senthorun Sunil Raj, *Feeling Queer Jurisprudence: Injury, Intimacy, Identity* (London: Routledge, 2020), 95.

16. Raj, *Feeling Queer Jurisprudence*, 97. I use "LGBT" here, rather than "LGBTQ+," as a reflection of some organizations' discomfort with "Q+."

17. US Citizenship and Immigration Services, "Guidance for Adjudicating Lesbian, Gay, Bisexual, Transgender, and Intersex (LGBTI) Refugee and Asylum Claims Training Module," December 28, 2011, 40, accessed February 7, 2022, uscis.gov/sites/default/files/document/guides/RAIO-Training-March-2012.pdf.

18. Topel, "What Should I Ask," 2359.

19. Stefan Vogler, "Legally Queer: The Constructions of Sexuality in LGBQ Asylum Claims," *Law and Society Review* 50, no. 4 (2016): 871. Vogler suggests that that "reliance on stereotypes and Western identity categories has decreased over time" (872) and that there is some ambiguity that skilled lawyers could use to push boundaries, though this raises the dilemma of using people's asylum cases to do so.

20. Carmelo Danisi, Moira Dustin, Nuno Ferreira, and Nina Held, *Queering Asylum in Europe: Legal and Social Experiences of Seeking International Protection on Grounds of Sexual Orientation and Gender Identity*, IMISCOE Research Series (Springer, 2021), 189, accessed Oct 4, 2021, link.springer.com/content/pdf/10.1007%2F978-3-030-69441-8.pdf.

21. Elif Sarı, "Lesbian Refugees in Transit: The Making of Authenticity and Legitimacy in Turkey," *Journal of Lesbian Studies* 24, no. 2 (2020): 146.

22. Rema Hammami, "Follow the Numbers: Global Governmentality and the Violence Against Women Agenda in Occupied Palestine," in *Governance Feminism Notes: From the Field*, ed. Janet Halley, Prabha Kotiswaran, Rachel Rebouché, and Hila Shamir (Minneapolis: University of Minnesota Press, 2019). See also Nadera Shalhoub-Kevorkian and Suhad Daher-Nashif, "The Politics of Killing Women in Colonized Contexts," *Jadaliyya*, December 17, 2012, accessed Oct 7, 2020, h.

23. He used the English word "gay."

24. Amy Shuman and Carol Bohmer, "Gender and Cultural Silences in the Political Asylum Process," *Sexualities* 17, no. 8 (2014): 952.

25. Lila Abu-Lughod, "Seductions of the Honor Crime," *Differences: A Journal of Feminist Cultural Studies* 22, no. 1 (2011): 18.

26. Gayatri Spivak, "Can the Subaltern Speak?," in *Marxism and the Interpretation of Culture*, ed. Cary Nelson and Lawrence Grossberg (Urbana: University of Illinois Press, 1988), 271–313.

27. Anita Sinha, "Domestic Violence and U.S. Asylum Law: Eliminating the 'Cultural Hook' for Claims Involving Gender-Related Persecution," *New York University Law Review* 76, no. 5 (2001): 1562, 1592.

28. Kamala Visweswaran, *Un/common Cultures: Racism and the Rearticulation of Cultural Difference* (Durham: Duke University Press, 2010), 198.

29. Visweswaran, *Un/common Cultures*, 199.

30. Karen Musalo and Stephen Knight, "Gender-Based Asylum: An Analysis of Recent Trends," *Interpreter Releases* 77, no. 42 (2000): 1539–1541.

31. Efrat Arbel, Catherine Dauvergne, and Jenni Millbank, "Introduction: Gender in Refugee Law: From the Margins to the Centre," in *Gender in Refugee Law: From the Margins to the Centre*, ed. Efrat Arbel, Catherine Dauvergne, and Jenni Millbank (London: Routledge, 2014), 12.

32. Connie Oxford, "Protectors and Victims in the Gender Regime of Asylum," *National Women's Studies Association Journal* 17, no. 3 (Fall 2005): 27, 29.

33. Their website states that "OutRight formerly known as IGLHRC closed its longstanding asylum documentation program in mid-2007." Accessed October 19, 2020, outrightinternational.org/content/asylum-resources.

34. Nayak, *Who is Worthy*, 144. Lena Ayoub and Shin-Ming Wong, "Separated and Unequal," *William Mitchell Law Review* 32, no. 2 (2006): 559–597.

35. Nayak, *Who is Worthy*, 144.

36. Ayoub and Wong, "Separated and Unequal," 564–565.

37. Ayoub and Wong, "Separated and Unequal," 565.

38. Ayoub and Wong, "Separated and Unequal," 566.

39. Ayoub and Wong, "Separated and Unequal."

40. Nayak, *Who is Worthy*, 146.

41. Randazzo, "Social and Legal Barriers," 35.

42. Randazzo, "Social and Legal Barriers," 35.

43. Victoria Neilson, "Homosexual or Female—Applying Gender-Based Asylum Jurisprudence to Lesbian Asylum Claims," *Stanford Law and Policy Review* 16, no. 2 (2005) 417: 2.

44. Monica Rhor, "US Grants Asylum to Gay Man: Rules Dominican Faced Threat at Home," *Boston Globe*, September 5, 2003, accessed February 7, 2022, archive.boston.com/news/local/articles/2003/09/05/us_grants_asylum_to_gay_man.

45. Neilson, "Homosexual or Female," 4.

46. Roxana Akbari and Stefan Vogler, "Intersectional Invisibility: Race, Gender, Sexuality, and the Erasure of Sexual Minority Women in US Asylum Law,"

Law and Social Inquiry 46, no. 4 (2021): 1062–1091.

47. Randazzo, "Social and Legal Barriers," 43.

48. Randazzo, "Social and Legal Barriers," 37.

49. Swetha Sridharan, "The Difficulties of U.S. Asylum Claims Based on Sexual Orientation," Migration Policy Institute, October 29, 2008, accessed Oct 19, 2020, migrationpolicy.org/article/difficulties-us-asylum-claims-based-sexual-orientation.

50. Immigration Equality reported that only 5 percent of its almost seven hundred LGBTQ and HIV cases were from the Middle East and North Africa, "Our Work," accessed April 27, 2020, immigrationequality.org/our-work/#.Yf16_i-B1pQ.

51. Randazzo, "Social and Legal Barriers," 52. This uptick is unsurprising, given the overall increase in the number of detained and deported Muslims at that time. For more on post–9/11 detention of Muslims in the US, see Irum Shiekh, *Detained Without Cause: Muslims' Stories of Detention and Deportation in America After 9/11* (New York: Palgrave Macmillan, 2011).

52. Ramji-Nogales, Schoenholtz, and Schrag, "Refugee Roulette."

53. Julia Preston, "Big Disparities in Judging of Asylum Cases," *New York Times*, May 31, 2017, accessed Oct 19, 2020, nytimes.com/2007/05/31/washington/31asylum.html.

54. Preston, "Big Disparities."

55. Deborah Morgan, "Not Gay Enough for the Government: Racial and Sexual Stereotypes in Sexual Orientation Asylum Cases," *Law and Sexuality: A Review of Lesbian, Gay, Bisexual, and Transgender Legal Issues* 15 (2006): 151–152. See also Mengia Tschalaer, "Between Queer Liberalisms and Muslim Masculinities: LGBTQI+ Muslim Asylum Assessment in Germany," *Ethnic and Racial Studies* 43, no. 7 (2019): 1268; Moira Dustin and Nina Held, "In or Out? A Queer Intersectional Approach to 'Particular Social Group' Membership and Credibility in SOGI Asylum Claims in Germany and the UK," *GenIUS-Rivista di studi giuridici sull' orientamento sessuale e l'identità di genere* 2 (2018): 80.

56. Kate Sheill, "Losing Out in the Intersections: Lesbians, Human Rights, Law and Activism," *Contemporary Politics* 15, no. 1 (2009): 56.

57. Mengia Tschalaer notes that similar questions about the details of sex posed to asylum seekers in Germany were not only unlawful but suggest a "Western and heteronormative-dominated imagination of gay sex." Mengia Tschalaer, "Queer Spaces: The Sexual Asylum Story," *Diaphanes*, March 12, 2019, accessed Oct 28, 2021, diaphanes.com/titel/queer-spaces-6169.

58. Dara Lind, "The Disastrous, Forgotten 1996 Law That Created Today's Immigration Problem," *Vox*, April 28, 2016, accessed Oct 14, 2020, vox.com/2016/4/28/11515132/iirira-clinton-immigration.

59. American Immigration Council, *Aggravated Felonies: An Overview*, March 16, 2021, accessed Oct 14, 2020, americanimmigrationcouncil.org/research/aggravated-felonies-overview.

60. US Citizenship and Immigration Services, "Policy Manual," accessed Oct

19, 2020, uscis.gov/policy-manual/volume-7-part-m-chapter-6.

61. Jawziya Zaman, "Why I Left Immigration Law," *Dissent Magazine*, July 12, 2017, accessed February 15, 2021, dissentmagazine.org/online_articles/left-immigration-law.

62. See, for example, Ghaith Hilal, "Eight Questions Palestinian Queers Are Tired of Hearing," November 27, 2013, accessed Oct 14, 2020, alqaws.org/articles/Eight-questions-Palestinian-queers-are-tired-of-hearing; Musa Shadeedi, "Globalizing the Closet: Is 'Coming Out' a Western Concept," *My Kali*, March 30, 2018, accessed Oct 14, 2020, mykalimag.com/en/2018/03/30/globalizing-the-closet-is-coming-out-a-western-concept.

63. Jason Ritchie, "How Do You Say 'Come Out of the Closet' in Arabic?: Queer Activism and the Politics of Visibility in Israel-Palestine," *GLQ: A Journal of Lesbian and Gay Studies* 16, no. 4 (2010): 571.

64. Ritchie, "Politics of Visibility," 571.

65. Ritchie, "Politics of Visibility," 571.

66. Sa'ed Atshan, *Queer Palestine and the Empire of Critique* (Stanford: Stanford University Press, 2020), 55.

67. Atshan, *Queer Palestine*, 55.

68. This point is made by Joseph Massad in an interview with Éwanjé-Épée and Stella Magliani-Belkacem, "The Empire of Sexuality: An Interview with Joseph Massad," *Jadaliyya* March 5, 2013, accessed Oct 14, 2020, jadaliyya.com/Details/28167/The-Empire-of-Sexuality-An-Interview-with-Joseph-Massad.

69. Laurie Berg and Jenni Millbank, "Constructing the Personal Narratives of Lesbian, Gay and Bisexual Asylum Claimants," *Journal of Refugee Studies* 22, no. 1 (2009): 195–223.

70. See, for example, "societal discrimination against LGBT persons" in United States Department of State, *2011 Country Reports on Human Rights Practices—Jordan*, May 24, 2012, accessed October 15, 2020, refworld.org/docid/4fc75a8ec.html.

71. Mayo, "Court-Mandated Story Time."

72. McKinley, "Cultural Culprits," 91–165.

73. Tahirih, "Tahirih Justice Center 10th Anniversary: Voices of Courage, Stories of Justice," Jan 31, 2017, accessed Oct 15, 2020, youtube.com/watch?v=BLz4xjbiI3I; Tahirih, "Tahirih Holds Congressional Briefing for Greater Progress in the Protection of Refugee Women," posted April 29, 2008, accessed Oct 15, 2020, tahirih.org/news/tahirih-holds-congressional-briefing-to-strengthen-protection-for-refugee-women.

74. *Out of Iraq*, directed by Chris McKim and Eva Orner, World of Wonder, 2016.

75. See step 7 in USCIS, "The Affirmative Asylum Process," last updated September 16, 2021, uscis.gov/humanitarian/refugees-and-asylum/asylum/the-affirmative-asylum-process.

76. Eithne Luibhéid, "Queer/Migration: An Unruly Body of Scholarship," *GLQ: A Journal of Lesbian and Gay Studies* 12, nos. 2–3 (2008): 186.

77. According to the published proceedings of an expert roundtable organized by the United Nations High Commissioner for Refugees, held in Geneva, Switzerland, September 30 to October 1, 2010, the UNHCR urges "risk assessment and priority processing for resettlement," including "mechanisms to conduct resettlement on an emergency basis for LGBTI refugees at heightened risk." UNHCR, *Summary Conclusions: Asylum-Seekers and Refugees Seeking Protection on Account of their Sexual Orientation and Gender Identity*, November 2010, 5, accessed February 12, 2020, refworld.org/docid/4cff99a42.html.

78. "Priority Processing for Vulnerable Groups," IRAP, accessed October 15, 2020, refugeerights.org/policy-impact/priority-processing-for-vulnerable-groups. "As part of his memorandum [in 2011] on 'International Initiatives to Advance the Human Rights of Lesbian, Gay, Bisexual, and Transgender Persons,' President Obama directed federal agencies to take steps to protect vulnerable LGBT refugees and asylum seekers." Sharita Gruber, "Obama Administration Makes Refugee Program More LGBT-Inclusive," October 30, 2015, accessed October 15, 2020, americanprogress.org/issues/lgbtq-rights/news/2015/10/30/124632/obama-administration-makes-refugee-program-more-lgbt-inclusive.

79. In 2015, the Canadian government similarly "announced that it was not going to resettle single straight men, but only single gay men." Fadi Saleh, "Resettlement as Securitization: War, Humanitarianism, and the Production of Syrian LGBT Refugees," in *Queer and Trans Migrations: Dynamics of Illegalization, Detention and Deportation*, ed. Eithne Luibhéid and Karma R. Chavez (Urbana: University of Illinois Press, 2020), 80.

80. Saleh, "Resettlement as Securitization," 79.

81. Anne Norton, "Gender, Sexuality and the Iraq of Our Imagination," *Middle East Report*, November/December 1991.

82. "Clumsy Retreat from Afghanistan Would Be 'a Grave Mistake,'" Senate Republican Leader Mitch McConnell, April 13, 2021, accessed April 22, 2021, mcconnell.senate.gov/public/index.cfm/pressreleases?ContentRecord_id=95CA45F7-5D1A-4026-B461-03800894D320.

83. Ratna Kapur, "There's a Problem with the LGBT Rights Movement—It's Limiting Freedom," *The Conversation*, September 17, 2018, accessed April 22, 2021, theconversation.com/theres-a-problem-with-the-lgbt-rights-movement-its-limiting-freedom-101999.

84. Beth Fertig, "A Mother and Daughter Both Have HIV. The U.S. Lets in Only One," *New York Times*, March 6, 2019, accessed April 28, 2021, nytimes.com/2019/03/06/nyregion/family-separation-hiv.html.

85. Alex Johnson, "Corinthian Colleges Shuts Down, Ending Classes for 16,000 Overnight," *NBC News*, April 26, 2015, accessed February 10, 2020, nbcnews.com/news/education/corinthian-colleges-shuts-down-ending-classes-16-000-overnight-n348741.

86. Andrew Kreighbaum, "Growing Price Tag for College Shutdowns," *Inside Higher Ed*, September 4, 2019, accessed February 10, 2020, insidehighered.com/news/2019/09/04/costs-federal-government-mount-profit-college-shutdowns.

CHAPTER 4: "MANY REASONS TO LEAVE"

1. Rachel Lewis, "'Gay? Prove It': The Politics of Queer Anti-Deportation Activism," *Sexualities* 17, no. 8 (2014): 965.

2. Sofian Merabet, *Queer Beirut* (Austin: University of Texas Press, 2014).

3. Proud Lebanon, "The LGBTIQ+ Community in Lebanon," proudlebanon.org/wp-content/uploads/2021/01/UNIVERSAL-PERIODIC-REVIEW-LEBANON-The-LGBTIQ-community-in-Lebanon-by-Proud-Lebanon.pdf.

4. Proud Lebanon, "The LGBTIQ+ Community in Lebanon."

5. On fake immigration lawyers, see the example here: Johnny Diaz, "Florida Man Who Posed as Immigration Lawyer Gets 20-Year Sentence," *New York Times*, April 15, 2021, accessed April 23, 2021, nytimes.com/2021/04/15/us/elvis-harold-reyes-fraud-immigration.html. According to Judge Katzmann, unauthorized practitioners often lead immigrants "astray with incorrect information and terrible advice with lasting, damaging consequences that can fatally prejudice what otherwise would be a proper claim to entry." Robert A. Katzmann, "The Legal Profession and the Unmet Needs of the Immigrant Poor," *The Record* 62, no. 2 (2007): 292, citybarjusticecenter.org/wp-content/uploads/pdf/Katzmann_Lecture.pdf. The American Bar Association's extensive list of resources on notario fraud suggests the scope of the problem. American Bar Association, "Consumer Education," accessed February 9, 2022, americanbar.org/groups/public_interest/immigration/projects_initiatives/fightnotariofraud/consumer_ed. See also Katzmann's comments on licensed lawyers who "render inadequate and incompetent service" in Katzmann, "The Legal Profession," 292.

6. Israel occupied a swath of southern Lebanon from its invasion of the country in 1982 until 2000. See David Hirst, "South Lebanon: The War That Never Ends?" *Journal of Palestine Studies* 28, no. 3 (1999): 5–18; Augustus Richard Norton, *Hezbollah: A Short History* (Princeton: Princeton University Press, 2018), 21, 68.

7. Marty Rosenbluth, "The Uphill Battle to Fix Immigration Courts and Immigrant Rights," March 4, 2021, accessed March 10, 2021, americanbar.org/groups/crsj/publications/human_rights_magazine_home/the-next-four-years/the-uphill-battle-to-fix-immigration-courts-and-immigrant-rights/?fbclid=IwAR1M6ehwTSeXaZBB9jsZAae18fAaXmHxeDyo2tptMI4eZZjRGCBTB0C9NKw.

8. Kirstie Brewer, "How Do I Convince the Home Office I'm a Lesbian?" *BBC*, February 26, 2020, accessed January 28, 2020, bbc.com/news/stories-51636642.

9. Berg and Millbank, "Constructing the Personal Narratives," 10.

10. Hilary Evans Cameron, "Refugee Status Determinations and the Limits of Memory," *International Journal of Refugee Law* 22, no. 4 (2010): 469.

11. US Citizenship and Immigration Services, *Officer Training: Credibility Training Module*, RAIO Directorate, June 20, 2016, 301, accessed December 11, 2020, aila.org/infonet/uscis-guidance-to-raio-officers-on-credibility.

12. César Cuauhtémoc García Hernández, *Migrating to Prison: America's Obsession with Locking Up Immigrants* (New York: The New Press, 2019).

13. Nair, "How to Make Prisons Disappear," 126.

14. Weiner, "U.S. Plans to Delay Work Permits."

15. Camilo Montoya-Galvez, "U.S. Restricts Work Permits for Asylum-Seekers, Raising Fears of Homelessness and Hunger," *CBS News*, August 25, 2020, accessed April 26, 2021, cbsnews.com/news/work-permits-asylum-seekers-trump-administration-rule; National Immigrant Justice Center, "Update On Two New Attacks On Asylum Seekers," September 30, 2020, accessed April 23, 2021, immigrantjustice.org/for-attorneys/legal-resources/copy/update-two-new-attacks-asylum-seekers.

16. K-Sue Park, "Self-Deportation Nation," *Harvard Law Review* 132 (2019): 1878–1941.

17. For more on how the debt economy exacerbates inequalities, see Brett Williams, *Debt for Sale: A Social History of the Credit Trap* (Philadelphia: University of Pennsylvania Press, 2005).

18. Sarah Gualtieri and Pauline Homsi Vinson, "Arab/Americas: Locations and Iterations," *Amerasia Journal* 44, no. 1 (2018): vii–xxi; Kristine J. Ajrouch and Amaney Jamal, "Assimilating to a White Identity: The Case of Arab Americans," *The International Migration Review* 41, no. 4 (2007): 860–879.

19. Dean Spade, *Normal Life: Administrative Violence, Critical Trans Politics, and the Limits of Law* (Brooklyn: South End Press, 2011).

20. Roger Lancaster, "Tolerance and Intolerance in Sexual Cultures in Latin America," in *Passing Lines: Sexuality and Immigration*, ed. Brad Epps, Keja Valens, and Bill Johnson Gonzalez (Cambridge: Harvard University Press, 2005), 255.

21. Lionel Cantú, Eithne Luibhéid, and Alexandra Minna Stern, "Well-Founded Fear: Political Asylum and the Boundaries of Sexual Identity in the U.S.-Mexico Borderlands," in *Queer Migrations: Sexuality, U.S. Citizenship, and Border Crossings*, ed. Eithne Luibhéid and Lionel Cantú (Minneapolis: University of Minnesota Press, 2005), 65–68.

22. Lancaster, "Tolerance and Intolerance," 255.

23. "Importance of the Expert Witnesses with Professional Credentials," Muslim World Expert, accessed December 11, 2020, muslimworldexpert.com/services-offered/expert-witness/credentials-of-an-expert-witnesses.

24. "Difference Between an Expert Witness and a Factual Wtiness," Muslim World Expert, accessed February 8, 2022, muslimworldexpert.com/services-offered/expert-witness/expert-witness-and-a-factual-witness.

25. "Predominant Hardships," Muslim World Expert, accessed April 29, 2020. As of December 11, 2020, his updated website listed his publications as including papers on "Honor Killing in the Muslim World" and "Gays from the Muslim World and Immigration to the United States."

26. Puar, *Terrorist Assemblages*.

27. For example, Gabbay's website lists publications such as "Forensic Sociol-

ogy: Analyzing Social Networks in the Muslim-World for Asylum Immigration Cases" and "Religiously Motivated Violence in North and West Africa (E.g. Nigeria and Egypt): A Forensic Sociology Perspective," Muslim World Expert, accessed December 11, 2020, muslimworldexpert.com/publications.

28. For more on the impact of the eighteen-year Israeli military occupation in southern Lebanon, see Hirst, "South Lebanon"; Norton, *Hezbollah*.

29. Lancaster, "Tolerance and Intolerance," 267–268.

30. Randazzo, "Social and Legal Barriers," 40.

31. Kevin Lapp, "Reforming the Good Moral Character Requirement for U.S. Citizenship," *Indiana Law Journal* 87, no. 4 (2012): 1571.

32. Nehad Khader, "Rasmea Odeh: The Case of an Indomitable Woman," *Journal of Palestine Studies* 46, no. 4 (2020): 62–74.

33. Rasmea Odeh, "Empowering Arab Immigrant Women in Chicago: The Arab Women's Committee," *Journal of Middle East Women's Studies* 15, no. 1 (2019): 117–124.

34. Charles Davis, "How the FBI Goes after Activists," *Vice*, April 1, 2014, accessed December 4, 2020, vice.com/en/article/qvaekb/how-the-fbi-goes-after-activists.

35. Palestine Legal and the Center for Constitutional Rights, "The Palestine Exception to Free Speech: A Movement under Attack in the US," September 2015, accessed December 4, 2020, ccrjustice.org/sites/default/files/attach/2015/09/Palestine%20Exception%20Report%20Final.pdf.

36. Palestine Legal, "Palestine Exception," 41.

37. Davis, "How the FBI Goes after Activists."

38. Khader, "Rasmea Odeh."

39. Palestine Legal, "Palestine Exception," 41.

40. See for example, Chip Gibbons, *Still Spying on Dissent: The Enduring Problem of FBI First Amendment Abuse*, Defending Rights and Dissent, 2019, accessed February 9, 2022, rightsanddissent.org/fbi-spying; Sabrina Alimahomed-Wilson, "When the FBI Knocks: Racialized State Surveillance of Muslims," *Critical Sociology* 45, no. 6 (2018): 871–887.

41. Diala Shamas and Nermeen Arastu, "Mapping Muslims: NYPD Spying and Its Impact on American Muslims," Creating Law Enforcement Accountability & Responsibility (CLEAR) Project, 2013, accessed November 4, 2021, law.cuny.edu/wp-content/uploads/page-assets/academics/clinics/immigration/clear/Mapping-Muslims.pdf.

42. Department of Homeland Security Office of Inspector General, *Potentially Ineligible Individuals Have Been Granted U.S. Citizenship Because of Incomplete Fingerprint Records*, September 8, 2016, accessed December 7, 2020, oig.dhs.gov/assets/Mgmt/2016/OIG-16-130-Sep16.pdf.

43. Seth Freed Wessler, "Is Denaturalization the Next Front in the Trump Administration's War on Immigration?" *New York Times*, December 19, 2018, accessed November 12, 2020, nytimes.com/2018/12/19/magazine/naturalized-citizenship-immigration-trump.html.

44. American Immigration Lawyer's Association, "DOJ Announces Creation of a Section Dedicated to Denaturalization Cases," February 6, 2020, accessed February 9, 2022, aila.org/infonet/doj-announces-creation-of-a-section-dedicated.

45. Katie Benner, "Justice Dept. Establishes Office to Denaturalize Immigrants," *New York Times*, February 26, 2020, accessed December 4, 2020, nytimes.com/2020/02/26/us/politics/denaturalization-immigrants-justice-department.html.

46. Benner, "Justice Dept. Establishes Office."

47. American Immigration Lawyers Association, "Featured Issue: Denaturalization Efforts by USCIS," August 27, 2021, accessed February 9, 2022, aila.org/advo-media/issues/all/featured-issue-denaturalization-efforts-by-uscis.

48. Maryam Saleh, "The Justice Department Singled Out This Man in Expanding Efforts to Strip Citizenship. A Judge Doesn't Think the Case is Open and Shut," *The Intercept*, February 23, 2019, accessed December 7, 2020, theintercept.com/2019/02/23/denaturalization-operation-janus-citizenship-trump.

49. Masha Gessen, "In America, Naturalized Citizens No Longer Have an Assumption of Permanence," *The New Yorker*, June 18, 2018, accessed April 28, 2021, newyorker.com/news/our-columnists/in-america-naturalized-citizens-no-longer-have-an-assumption-of-permanence.

50. Saleh, "Justice Department."

51. Mariame Kaba and Shira Hassan, *Fumbling towards Repair: A Workbook for Community Accountability Facilitators* (Winnipeg, Manitoba: Project NIA/Justice Practice, 2019), 9.

52. Kaba and Hassan, *Fumbling towards Repair*, 40.

CONCLUSION

1. Chris Rickerd, "Whistleblower Says CBP Has Culture of Impunity and Violence," August 15, 2014, accessed April 16, 2021, aclu.org/blog/immigrants-rights/ice-and-border-patrol-abuses/whistleblower-says-cbp-has-culture-impunity-and.

2. Ramji-Nogales, Schoenholtz, and Schrag, "Refugee Roulette."

3. Caitlin Dickerson, interviewed by Michael Barbaro, "Trump Shut the Door on Migrants: Will Biden Open it?" *The Daily* (podcast audio), *New York Times*, December 8, 2020, accessed December 3, 2021 nytimes.com/2020/12/08/podcasts/the-daily/trump-biden-immigration.html. The passage referenced is at 13:56.

4. Richard Mole, "Rethinking Diaspora: Queer Poles, Brazilians and Russians in Berlin," in *Fringe: Queer Migration and Asylum in Europe*, ed. Richard Mole (London: University College London Press, 2021), 75.

5. Rosenbluth, "Uphill Battle."

6. Sarah Sharma, *In the Meantime: Temporality and Cultural Politics* (Durham: Duke University Press, 2014), 196.

7. Ghassan Hage, "Waiting Out the Crisis: On Stuckedness and Governmentality," in *Waiting*, ed. Ghassan Hage (Melbourne: Melbourne University Press, 2009), 97–106.

8. Ilana Feldman, *Life Lived in Relief: Humanitarian Predicaments and Palestinian Refugee Politics* (Berkeley: University of California Press, 2018).

9. Marty Rosenbluth's Facebook page, June 16, 2020, accessed February 9, 2022, facebook.com/marty.rosenbluth/posts/10107908279446418.

10. Marty Rosenbluth's Facebook page, June 17, 2020, accessed February 9, 2022, facebook.com/marty.rosenbluth/posts/10107911973643218.

11. Camerini and Robertson, *Well-Founded Fear*. The passage referenced is at 16:00.

12. 8 U.S.C. § 1158.

13. Zaman, "Why I Left."

14. 8 U.S.C. § 1158.

15. Zaman, "Why I Left."

16. Michael Warner, "Normal and Normaller: Beyond Gay Marriage," *GLQ: A Journal of Lesbian and Gay Studies* 5, no. 2 (1999): 119–171.

17. Tahirih, "Policy Briefing."

18. Calogero Giametta, *The Sexual Politics of Asylum: Sexual Orientation and Gender Identity in the UK Asylum System* (Abingdon: Routledge, 2017), 151.

19. Cantú et al., "Well-Founded Fear," 69.

20. Leti Volpp, "Cultural Defenses in the Criminal Legal System," Asian Pacific Institute on Gender-Based Violence, 2002, accessed November 1, 2021, 4, api-gbv.org/resources/cultural-defenses-criminal-legal-system.

21. Janet Halley, Prabha Kotiswaran, Chantal Thomas, and Hila Shamir, "From the International to the Local in Feminist Legal Responses to Rape, Prostitution/Sex Work and Sex Trafficking: Four Studies in Contemporary Governance Feminism," *Harvard Journal of Law and Gender* 29 (2006): 422.

22. Aya Gruber, *The Feminist War on Crime: The Unexpected Role of Women's Liberation in Mass Incarceration* (Berkeley: University of California Press, 2021).

23. Glass, "Episode 688." The passage referenced is at 26:00.

24. Camerini and Robertson, *Well-Founded Fear*. The passage referenced is at 37:00.

25. Ticktin, *Casualties of Care*, 17.

26. Jane Freedman, *Gender and the International Asylum and Refugee Debate* (New York: Palgrave Macmillan, 200), 1.

27. Freedman, *Asylum and Refugee Debate*, 4.

28. Luibhéid, "Queer/Migration," 178.

29. Accessed November 2, 2021, merriam-webster.com/dictionary/intersectionality.

30. Kimberlé Crenshaw, "Demarginalizing the Intersection of Race and Sex: A Black Feminist Critique of Antidiscrimination Doctrine, Feminist Theory and Antiracist Politics," *University of Chicago Legal Forum*, no. 1 (1989): 139–167.

31. Sima Shakhsari, "The Irony of Rights: Healthcare for Queer and Transgender Refugee Applicants in Turkey," *Jadaliyya*, September 2, 2013, accessed November 11, 2021, jadaliyya.com/Details/29441/The-Irony-of-Rights-Healthcare-for-Queer-and-Transgender-Refugee-Applicants-in-Turkey.

32. Sima Shakhsari, "Killing Me Softly with Your Right: Queer Death and the Politics of Rightful Killing," in *Queer Necropolitics*, ed. Jin Haritaworn, Adi Kunstman, and Silvia Posocco (London: Routledge, 2014), 93–110.

33. Fertig, "Mother and Daughter."

34. Lind, "The Disastrous, Forgotten 1996 Law."

35. Gessen, "Naturalized Citizens."

36. David Matas, "Refugee Determination Complexity," *Refuge: Canada's Journal of Refugees* 19, no. 4 (2001): 48.

37. Rosenbluth, "The Uphill Battle."

38. Immigration Policy Tracking Project, "1,059 Trump-era Immigration Policies (and Their Current Status)," February 13, 2022, accessed March 2, 2022, immpolicytracking.org/home.

39. Didier Fassin, "The Precarious Truth of Asylum," *Public Culture* 25, no. 1, 69 (2013): 39–63.

40. Thomas Spijkerboer, "Gender, Sexuality, Asylum and European Human Rights," *Law Critique* 29 (2018): 222.

41. Mahmoud Darwish, *Unfortunately, It Was Paradise: Selected Poems*, trans. and ed. Munir Akash and Carolyn Forché with Sinan Antoon and Amira El-Zein (Berkeley: University of California Press, 2003), 6.

Index

Abu-Lughod, Lila, 95
ACLU. *See* American Civil Liberties Union
Afghanistan, 95, 115
Afghan women, asylum for, 95
African Americans, 44
Akbari, Roxana, 99
American Civil Liberties Union (ACLU), 146–147
American dream, 82
American Psychiatric Association, 98
anal exams, as torture, 83
anti-Arab and anti-Muslim racism, 156
anti-black discrimination, 33, 44
anti-immigrant policies, of Trump administration, 3, 9, 12, 31–32, 43, 98, 130, 141, 150, 162–163
anti-immigrant sentiment, 43, 149
Arab Americans, 61; activists, 122, 132–133; assimilation to whiteness, 132; discrimination, in community, 151; on queer people, 136
Arab countries, 3–4; "honor killings" in, 94; LGBTQI+ asylum applicants from, 54, 154–155
Arab feminist organizations, 94, 120
Arabs: gay men, 82, 94–97, 112, 154; immigrants, denaturalization of, 140; immigration pathways for, blocked, 88; LGBTQI+ asylum seekers, 97, 123, 129; men, stereotypes of, 3–4; profiling, 140
Arab Women's Committee, Chicago, 140
asylees: access to basic services, 70, 72; anti-immigrant sentiment toward, 43, 149; benefits for, 63–67, 73; bodies of, inspecting, 16; citizenship for, 99–100, 108, 115–116, 139–143; as cultural victims, rather than political dissidents, 95; green cards for, 76, 138; home countries of, 104–105, 107–108, 136–138, 157–158; homeless, 62–63, 67–75, 78, 103, 130, 151; housing for, 74–76; immigration status of, 69–70, 73; judges, in disparities among, 100; legal representation for, 76–77; persistent insecurity of, 140–143; poor, 115–116; successful, as "worthy victims," 7; Tahirih Justice Center descriptions, of successful, 110; traveling home, reentry to US and, 104, 107–108, 138–140; work permits for, 102–103
asylum: for Afghan women, 95; case law, exoticized violence in, 96; case law, FGM in, 13–14, 20–21, 33–34; case law, gender expressions and sexuality in, 91; central bases

185

186 Index

for granting, 30; domestic violence and, 169n12, 171n1; freedom and, 11–12; gender-based, 16, 19, 53, 94–96; Geneva Convention on, 164; "homosexual identity," as basis for, 101; immigration and, 88; labor and, 88; laws, as inaccessible, 121; loss of, 104; poverty excluded as basis for, 30; stereotypes perpetuated in, 119; trauma of, family separation and, 157; US policy, 3–6; since World War II, 6

asylum attorneys, 8, 155, 158; on background checks, 111–112; on documentation, 158–159; expert witnesses and, 133–135; for Fadi, 88–92, 98, 101–102, 160–161; for Fatima, 48–49, 51–63, 65, 67, 76–77; Immigration Equality manual for, 26–27, 30, 90; on judges, in asylee disparities, 100; Lawyer's Committee for Civil Rights and, 89–90; for Marwa, 122–125, 132–135, 138–139; pro bono, 1–2, 8, 11, 14, 18, 22, 33, 41, 51, 54, 62, 82, 89–90, 92, 122, 134; on simplified identities, 119; for Suad, 14–17, 19, 22–44, 46, 109, 134, 152–153, 160

asylum seekers, 1–6; background checks of, 81, 111–114; birth dates of, 55–56; bodies of, examinations and discussions of, 15, 152–155; in broken system, 8–10; bureaucratic torture of, 63–67, 73, 78, 154; credit history of, lacking, 132; cultural complexity, edited out of narratives, 55; detained, 129; documentation for, 18, 60, 158–159; domestic violence against, 49–50, 52–53, 55–58, 61, 64–65, 95–96; excluding, 61–63, 78; expert opinions on, triggering for, 133–135; on family members, uniting with, 61–62, 77, 104–105, 136–138, 157–158, 162; on FGM, 12–16, 18–24, 152–153; financial difficulties of, 129–132, 161; gender and sexuality of, 5–7, 16, 19–20, 23, 25–28, 30, 33, 53–54, 90–95, 99–101, 114–115, 122, 124, 139, 154, 156–157, 159, 164; government lawyers and, 28–30, 35–36, 39, 59; on healing, 136–137, 162; on hijab and dress code, 25–28, 30; homesickness of, 128–129; humanizing, 3–4, 66; illiteracy and, 47–48, 72–74; Islam and, 54, 58, 125; isolation and loneliness of, 128–129, 150–151; language barriers for, 18, 47–48, 69–70, 72, 159; Lawyer's Committee for Civil Rights for, 89–90; from Lebanon, 119–120, 123, 125–126, 137–139; without legal counsel, 18, 158–159; "looking gay," 90–92; memories and memorization, in accounts of, 22–28, 55, 126–128, 153–154; mental illness and, 57, 62–63, 65, 72, 78–79, 161; from Middle East, 3–4, 87, 95–97, 99, 111–115, 134; mindfucks of, 152–155; from Muslim-majority countries, 4, 111–115, 134; NGOs, for assisting, 89, 97, 106, 129, 151, 158–161; number and sequence, in credibility of accounts of, 2, 25–28, 55, 126–128, 153; official documents carried by, 73, 146, 149, 161–162; patterns of suffering, 150–152; persecution of, 2, 5, 16–17, 55, 88, 97, 122, 152, 156; on personal lives and traumas, 15–18, 22, 25–26, 49–53, 56–58, 82, 93, 97, 126–127, 133, 152–153; presented as contributing members of society, 30–33; PTSD of, 57–58, 69, 97; refugees and, 87; rescue narratives of, 94–95; resourcefulness of, 48–49; "Restrictive Social Mores," in claims of, 96; retraumatization of, 7, 17, 29–30, 37, 45–46, 50, 125, 149, 152–153; short and sensational narratives of, favored in asylum system, 110–111; simplified narratives, favored for cases of, 33–34, 50–56, 108–109, 124–126, 162; stories of, editing, 55–58; support for, lacking, 89, 124, 130; therapists for, 81–82, 86–87, 89, 97, 153, 159–161; torture by delay, 34–40; Trump on, 3, 9, 32, 46, 77, 114–115, 130, 170n17; unofficial barriers, to overcome, 149; on US, 45–46, 135–136; at US-Mexico border, 3, 6, 8, 150; visas and, 8; vulnerability of, 150, 161; work permits for, 31–32, 81, 114, 130–131. *See also* LGBTQI+ asylum seekers

asylum system: appeal process, 35, 58, 149; as broken and dysfunctional, 8–10, 37, 46, 73–74; as bureaucratic torture, 63–67, 73, 78, 154; delays and cancellations in, 34–40, 43, 46, 59–60, 151–152, 163–164; as deliberately arduous, 130; documents from government agencies, arriving by mail, 72–73; exclusions by, 62; expert testimony in, 133–134, 156; on families, of asylum seekers, 137; FGM and, 12–13, 18, 20, 25, 33–34; gender disparity in, 99, 122; on home countries, of asylum seekers and asylees, 105, 107–109, 133, 157; immigration agents and, 149; judges in, 35–36, 39–42, 54, 56, 58–61, 90, 100, 155; on mental illness, 57; as mindfuck, 152–153; NGOs assisting asylum seekers in, 89; after 9/11/2001, 98; retraumatization in, 37; short and sensational narratives, favored in, 110–111; simple narratives, favored in, 33–34, 50–56, 108–109, 162; stereotypical narratives, favored in, 54–55, 155; stereotyping in, forced, 155–157; vocabulary of, 11–12
Atshan, Sa'ed, 105–106

background checks, 81, 111–114, 145, 164
Berg, Laurie, 126–127
Biden, Joe, 4, 163–164
Black immigrants, in US, 44
Board of Immigration Appeals, 58
Boston Marathon bombing, 70
British Mandate Criminal Code in Jordan, 93
bureaucratic torture, 63–67, 73, 78, 154

Cameron, Hilary, 127
Canada, 160, 177n79
Cantú, Lionel, 133, 156
Catholic Charities, 4–5, 8; Refugee Resettlement section of, 63–64
CBP. *See* Customs and Border Patrol
child separation policy, of Trump administration, 3, 157
circumcision, 15–16, 18, 42; as FGM, 19–23; as *khitan*, 13; memories and accounts of, 22–23; pharaonic, 20, 23; recircumcision, 24–25, 41; in Sudan, 21–25
citizens: denaturalization of, 140–142; as sponsors for same-sex partners, 88
citizenship, 4–7, 9, 20, 46, 171n1; for asylees, 99–100, 108, 115–116, 139–143; denaturalization and, 140–142
class discrimination, 99
classism, 157
Clinton, Bill, 161
Cold War, 7
coming out, 105–106
Crenshaw, Kimberlé, 160
Cuba, 99

188 *Index*

Customs and Border Patrol (CBP), 145–148

Darwish, Mahmoud, 165
Davis, Angela, 140
denaturalization, 140–142, 162
Department of Homeland Security, US, 140
Department of Justice, US, 98, 101, 141
deportation, 38, 43–44, 53, 57–58, 61, 73, 161–162; Immigration Bill of 1996 and, 103–104, 161; under Obama administration, 163
discrimination: anti-black, 33, 44; in Arab American community, 151; against gay men, 99, 108, 151; gender and class, 99; intersectionality and, 160; against LGBTQI+ people, 123, 133, 136; against Muslims, 119; against Muslims in LGBTQI+ circles, 136; against queer people, in Muslim American organizations, 136; against women, 23, 53
domestic violence, 171n1; against asylum seekers, 49–50, 52–53, 55–58, 61, 64–65, 95–96; Sessions, on asylum and, 169n12, 171n6; US protections, 61
dress code, in Sudan, 27–28, 30
drug addiction, 79
due process, 9, 100, 126

Egypt, 52–56, 58, 60–62, 73, 109, 128–129
Eid, 1, 22, 42
environmentalists, 119–121, 125
essentialism, 54, 96, 156, 164–165
ethnocentrism, 91, 106
expert testimony, in asylum cases, 133–135, 156

family reunification, 61, 157
family separation, 3, 157–161
Fassin, Didier, 164

FBI, 140–141
Feinstein, Diane, 130
"female genital mutilation" (FGM): activism against, 20; American views of, 19; asylum case law on, 13–14, 20–21, 33–34; asylum seekers on, 12–16, 18–24, 152–153; asylum system and, 12–13, 18, 20, 25, 33–34; circumcision as, 19–21; fear of, 19–21; in gender oppression, 23; "Matter of Kasinga" case on, 13, 21; memories and accounts of, 22–24; in Sudan, 21–22, 134, 156. *See also* circumcision
feminism, 27, 30
feminists: activists, 3, 5, 19, 121–122; organizations, Arab, 94, 120; queer environmentalist, 119–121, 125
FGM. *See* "female genital mutilation"
FOIA. *See* Freedom of Information Act of 1967
food stamps, 65, 67
forced migration, 88, 159
forensic sociology, 134
Freedom of Information Act of 1967 (FOIA), 145

Gabbay, Shaul, 134
gay marriage, 117
gay men: Arab, 82, 94–97, 112, 154; Canada, on resettling, 177n79; discrimination against, 99, 108, 151; in Egypt, 109; families of, 79–81, 83–84, 92, 97, 105–107, 109–111; "honor killings" and, 93–95, 97–98, 111, 156; immigration law on, 98–99; in Iraq, 110; in Jordan, 82–83, 93–94, 97–98, 105–108, 112, 154; Muslim, 87, 96, 123; persecution of, 99, 106, 108–109; in Saudi Arabia, 112; sexual practices of, inquiring about, 101; torture of, 83, 87, 102, 109, 156. *See also* men who have sex with men

gay Muslims, 87, 96, 99, 114, 123–124
gay rights activists, 3, 5, 97
gay rights movement, US, 88
gender: discrimination, 99; disparity, in asylum process, 99, 122; oppression, FGM in, 23
gender and sexuality: asylum, 16, 19, 53, 94–96; of asylum seekers, 5–7, 16, 19–20, 23, 25–28, 30, 33, 53–54, 90–95, 99–101, 114–115, 122, 124, 139, 154, 156–157, 159, 164; in immigration system, neoconservative view of, 160; MSGD, 136–137; persecution for, 5, 7, 97, 99, 112. *See also* LGBTQI+; women
Geneva Convention, 164
Giametta, Calogero, 155
government attorneys, 28–30, 35–36, 39, 59
green cards, 58, 77, 104–105, 145, 148; for asylees, 76, 138; for immigrants, Trump against, 31; sponsors for, 79
Gruber, Aya, 157

Hage, Ghassan, 151–152
Halley, Janet, 156–157
Hamas, 96
health care, human rights and, 160
Helem, 123
heteronormativity, 83–84
Hezbollah, 54, 114
hijab and dress code, 25–28, 30
homelessness and homeless shelters, 62–63, 67–75, 78, 103, 130, 151
homesickness, 128–129
homophobia, 2, 79–80, 93–98, 156
homosexuality, laws on: in Jordan, 83, 93–94, 97–98, 100; in Lebanon, 123
"honor killings," 54, 96, 134; in Arab countries, 94; gay men and, 93–95, 97–98, 111, 156; violence against women, Muslims and, 94
housing, 74–76, 81
humanitarianism, 73

human rights, 43, 45, 101, 138–139; health care, 160; IGLHRC on, 97, 99, 174n33; US and, 150; violations, 156, 160
human rights organizations, 14, 53, 97, 99

ICE. *See* Immigration and Customs Enforcement
IGLHRC. *See* International Gay and Lesbian Human Rights Commission
illegal termination, 103
illiteracy, 47–48, 72–74
immigrants: on American dream, 82; Arab, denaturalization of, 140; Black, in US, 44; denaturalization of, 140–142, 162; deportation of, Immigration Bill of 1996 and, 103–104, 161; detained, legal representation for, 167n9; green cards for, 31; lesbian, 130; LGBTQI+, 88, 90; networks of, 151; sexuality of, 139; TPS program for, 38; "wealth test" for, 31
immigration: agents, 84–85, 149; arrests, 49, 51; asylum and, 88; attorneys, 8, 14, 29, 43, 89–90, 122, 145, 147–148, 153, 178; attorneys, fake, 123, 178n5; detention, 4–5, 8, 13; documents, 146–147; law, 98–99, 152; Muslim, 54; officers, abuse and harassment by, 54, 172n4; politics, stereotypes in, 3–4; queer, 130; raids, 12, 43–44, 51, 57–58; status, 81, 103, 113, 157, 161, 171n1; status, of asylees, 69–70, 73
Immigration Act of 1917, 98
Immigration Act of 1990, 98
Immigration and Customs Enforcement (ICE), 12, 43–44, 149, 161–162
Immigration and Nationality Act of 1952, 98
Immigration and Nationality Act of 1965, 17, 98

Immigration Bill of 1996, 103–104, 161
immigration court: asylum cases in, 29, 49; cultural differences in, 91; due process and, 126; government attorneys in, 36; judges, in disparities of, 100; memories and narratives in, 23; people lacking legal representation in, 151; protections for applicants, lacking, 152; simplistic and strategic narratives in, 110; under Trump administration, 9
Immigration Equality, 99, 175n50; manual, for asylum lawyers, 26–27, 30, 90
immigration policies (various administrations): of Biden, 4, 163–164; of Obama, 91, 115, 141, 163; of Trump, 43, 98, 150, 162–163
Immigration Policy Tracking Project (IPTP), 163
immigration system, 2–3, 36–37, 157; agents at border, 84–85; neoconservative view of gender and sexuality in, 160; representatives of, violating rules, 148–149; trauma and, 82
immunizations, 76
IndyAct, 120
International Gay and Lesbian Human Rights Commission (IGLHRC), 97, 99, 174n33
intersectionality, discrimination and, 160
IPTP. *See* Immigration Policy Tracking Project
Iraq, 110, 112–115
Islam, 54, 58, 115, 125
Islamophobia: anti-immigrant sentiments and, 149; after Boston Marathon bombing, 70; of immigration officers, 54; xenophobia and, 119, 132, 138, 156
Israel, 125, 140–141
Israeli Defense Forces, in Lebanon, 135

Jamaica, 97
Jordan, 3, 84, 92, 104; gay men in, 82–83, 93–94, 97–98, 105–108, 112, 154; homosexuality laws and, 83, 93–94, 97–98, 100; Iraq and, 112–113; torture in, 2, 83, 87, 102, 156
judges, in asylum system, 35–36, 39–42, 54, 56, 58–61, 90, 100, 155

Kaba, Mariame, 142–143
Kapur, Ratna, 115
Katzmann, Robert A., 178n5
khitan (circumcision), 13
Knight, Stephen, 95–96

Lancaster, Roger, 133, 135
language barriers, 18, 47–48, 69–70, 72, 159
Lavie, Smadar, 72–73
Lawyer's Committee for Civil Rights, 89–90
Lebanon, 121; asylum seekers from, 119–120, 123, 125–126, 137–139; homosexuality laws in, 123; Israeli Defense Forces in, 135
Lesbian and Gay Immigration Rights Task Force, 99. *See also* Immigration Equality
lesbians, 156; asylum cases of, 126; asylum officers on, 124, 139, 142; immigrants, 130; immigration law on, 98–99; persecution of, 99; as term, "queer" *versus*, 124
Lewis, Rachel, 122
LGBTQI+: activism, 136; asylum organizations, 97, 106, 123, 161; rights organizations, 94, 123; US politics of, 125; vocabulary of, 132–133
LGBTQI+ asylum seekers, 81, 87–88, 93, 96, 99–102, 109; Arab, 97, 123, 129; from Arab countries, 54, 154–155; asylum adjudicators scruti-

nizing, 126–127; language, in applications of, 124–126; from Lebanon, 123; organizations for assisting, 97, 106, 123, 161; in pinkwashing US foreign policy, 135; on stereotypes and "looking gay," 90–92
LGBTQI+ people: activists, 120–121; on coming out, 105–106; discrimination against, 123, 133, 136; immigrants, to US, 88, 90; in Jordan, 93; in Lebanon, 123; "looking gay," 90–92; from Middle East, 54, 96, 99, 105, 111–115, 135; Muslims, 87, 96, 99, 114, 123–124; Palestinians, 105–106; refugees, 177n77, 177n79; stereotypes, 91–92; violence against, 94–96. *See also* gay men; lesbians; queer
"looking gay," 90–92
Luibhéid, Eithne, 133, 160

Magnet, 86
Matas, David, 163
"Matter of Kasinga" case, 13, 21
Mayo, Jessica, 53, 108–109
McConnell, Mitch, 115
McKinley, Michelle, 109
McKinnon, Sara, 31
Mead, Margaret, 136
Medicaid, 76
Meem, 120–121
mental illness, 71, 77; asylum seekers and, 57, 62–63, 65, 72, 78–79, 161; asylum system on, 57; depression and anxiety, 86
men who have sex with men, 93–94, 101, 106–107, 111. *See also* gay men
Mexico, border with US, 3, 6, 8, 84–85, 150, 157
"Middle East": asylum seekers from, 3–4, 87, 95–97, 99, 111–115, 134; LGBTQI+ people from, 54, 96, 99, 105, 111–115, 135; stereotypes and simplistic accounts of, 54–55, 60, 96–97, 135
migration, forced, 88, 159
Millbank, Jenni, 126–127
Miller-Muro, Layli, 19
Mole, Richard, 151
Morgan, Deborah, 101
Morris, Aaron, 91–92
Morsi, Mohamed, 60
MSGD. *See* Muslim Alliance for Sexual and Gender Diversity
Musalo, Karen, 95–96
Muslim Alliance for Sexual and Gender Diversity (MSGD), 136–137
Muslim Americans: attacks against, 43–44; FBI targeting activists, 140–141; organizations, discrimination against queer Muslims in, 136; persecution of, 136
Muslim Brotherhood, 60
Muslim-majority countries, asylum seekers from, 4, 111–115, 134
Muslims: gay, 87, 96, 99, 114, 123–124; immigration, 54; Islamophobia against, 70; profiling, 140; queer, 125, 136; stereotypes of, 111, 114, 156; travel ban, under Trump administration, 43, 98, 114, 150; violence against women, "honor killings" and, 94

Nair, Yasmin, 88
Nasawiyya, 120
National Association of Immigration Judges, 9
National Security Entry-Exit Registration System, 99
naturalization process, 139–142
Neilsen, Victoria, 99
New York Times, 141
9/11/2001, 4, 85–86, 98, 111
non-governmental organizations (NGOs): for asylum seekers, 89,

97, 106, 129, 151, 158–161; "honor killing," in vocabulary of, 94; for LGBTQI+ asylum seekers, 97, 106, 123, 161

Obama, Barack, 91, 114–115, 140–141, 163
Obergefell v. Hodges (2015), 117
Odeh, Rasmea, 140–141
Operation Janus, 141
Operation Second Look, 141
Out of Iraq, 110–111
Oxford, Connie, 96

Palestine, 97, 112, 145
Palestinians, 86, 89–90, 94, 112–113, 164–165; activists, in Israel, torture of, 140–141; background checks on, 145; in Israel, 125; queer, 105–106; refugees, 87
panic attacks, 49–50
Park, K-Sue, 130
patriarchy, 57
persecution: asylum seekers on, 2, 5, 16–17, 55, 88, 97, 122, 152, 156; of gay men, 99, 106, 108–109; for gender and sexuality, 5, 7, 97, 99, 112; homophobic, 156; of lesbians, 99; of Muslim Americans, 136; of women, for sexuality, 122
personal memories, family accounts and, 23
Pessolano, Sergio, 19
pharaonic circumcision, 20, 23
pinkwashing, 115, 135
political asylum, 122
post-traumatic stress disorder (PTSD), 57–58, 69, 97
public and subsidized housing, 74–75

queer: activists, 105, 121–122; diaspora, 151; feminist environmentalist, 119–121, 125; immigration, 130;
Muslims, 125, 136; Palestinians, 105–106; spaces, in Lebanon, 123; as term, "lesbian" *versus*, 124; women, 121–122

racism, 28, 43, 54, 74; anti-Arab and anti-Muslim, 156; classism and, 157; stereotypes and, 111; xenophobia and, 44
Raj, Senthorun Sunil, 91
Ramadan, 107
Randazzo, Timothy, 136, 172n4
recircumcision, 24–25, 41
Refugee and Immigrant Job Center, Brooklyn, 64–67
Refugee Resettlement section, of Catholic Charities, 63–64
"refugee roulette," 9, 29, 150
refugees: assistance for, 63–64, 74; asylum seekers and, 87; determination systems, 163; LGBTQI+, 177n77, 177n79; Palestinian, 87; resettlement, 114–115; status, 101, 127; UNHCR on, 177n77
Remain in Mexico policy, of Trump administration, 150
Reno, Janet, 99
repressive social norms, 95
restorative justice, 138, 158
Ritchie, Jason, 105
Rosenbluth, Marty, 126, 152, 163

Sari, Elif, 92–93
Saudi Arabia, 33, 44, 109, 112
Sessions, Jeff, 169n12, 171n6
sexism, 57, 156, 160
sexual harassment, 89–90
sexuality. *See* gender and sexuality; LGBTQI+
sexual violence, 52, 162–163
Shakhsari, Sima, 160
Sharia dress code in Sudan, 27
Sharma, Sara, 151

Shebaya, Sirine, 141
Sheill, Kate, 101
Sinha, Anita, 95
social service agencies, 74
social workers, 51, 68, 71–72, 86
Spade, Dean, 119, 132
Spijkerboer, Thomas, 164
Spivak, Gayatri, 95
State Department, US, 21, 53, 108
stereotypes: in asylum system, 54–55, 119, 155–157; in immigration politics, 3–4; "looking gay," 90–92; of Middle East, 54–55, 60, 96–97, 135; of Muslims, 111, 114, 156; racism and, 111
Stern, Alexandra Minna, 133
Sudan, 1, 3, 33, 84, 109; circumcision in, 21–25; conceptions of race in, 44; dress code in, 27–28, 30; FGM in, 21–22, 134, 156
Syrian civil war, 6
Syrian refugees, 6, 114–115

Tahirih Justice Center, 19, 110
Tajik woman, in Afghanistan, 95
Taliban, 95
Tan, Shirley, 130
Temporary Protected Status (TPS), 38
therapy and therapists, 81–82, 86–87, 89, 97, 153, 159–161
Ticktin, Miriam, 30, 73
Toboso-Alfonso case, 99
Togo, 21
Topel, Kimberly, 91
torture: anal exams as, 83; bureaucratic, 63–67, 73, 78, 154; by delay, 34–40; documents as implements of, 72; of gay men, 83, 87, 102, 109, 156; in Jordan, 2, 83, 87, 102, 156; of Palestinian activists, in Israel, 140–141; retraumatization and, 7
tourist visas, 2, 50–51, 58, 84–85, 114
TPS. *See* Temporary Protected Status

trauma: asylum seekers, on personal lives and, 15–18, 22, 25–26, 49–53, 56–58, 82, 93, 97, 126–127, 133, 152–153; of family separation, 157; immigration system and, 82; PTSD, 57–58, 69, 97; retraumatization, 7, 17, 29–30, 37, 45–46, 50, 125, 149, 152–153
Trump, Donald: anti-immigrant policies of, 98, 150, 162–163; on asylum and asylum seekers, 3, 9, 32, 46, 77, 114–115, 130, 170n17; on denaturalization, 141, 162; family separation policy, 3, 157; against green cards, for immigrants, 31; ICE and, 12, 161–162; immigration court under, 9; immigration policy under, 43, 98, 150, 162–163; Muslim travel ban, 43, 98, 114, 150; Remain in Mexico policy, 150
Tschalaer, Mengia, 175n57

undocumented status, 130
United Nations High Commissioner for Refugees (UNHCR), 177n77
United States (US): asylum seekers on, 45–46, 135–136; Citizenship and Immigration Services, 1; on cultural victims, of Islam, 115; Department of Homeland Security, 140; Department of Justice, 98, 101, 141; domestic abuse protections in, 61; gay rights movement in, 88; human rights and, 150; immigration law, 98; law, on FGM, 13; LGBTQI+ asylum advocacy in, 97; LGBTQI+ politics in, 125; Middle East stereotypes in, 54–55; State Department, 21, 53, 108; views of FGM in, 19. *See also specific topics*
Uniting American Families Act of 2009, 88
US. *See* United States

USCIS, 104, 139
US-Mexico border, 3, 6, 8, 84–85, 150, 157

Vega, Jorge Soto, 90
violence: exoticizing, 94–96; homophobic, 95; "honor killings," 54, 93–96, 98, 111, 134, 156; against LGBTQI+ people, 94–96; against women, 93–95, 171n1. *See also* domestic violence
Violence Against Women Act of 1994, 171n1
visibility, coming out and, 105–106
Visweswaran, Kamala, 95
Vogler, Stefan, 99, 173n19
Volpp, Leti, 156

whiteness, Arab American assimilation to, 132

women: Afghan, 95; discrimination against, 23, 53; persecution of, 122; queer, 121–122; rights of, 27, 57, 156–157; violence against, 93–95, 171n1. *See also* female genital mutilation; lesbians
work permits, 2, 14; for asylees, 102–103; for asylum seekers, 31–32, 81, 114, 130–131
World War II, 6

xenophobia: Islamophobia and, 119, 132, 138, 156; racism and, 44

Zaman, Jawzia, 105
Z collective, 136, 140

www.ingramcontent.com/pod-product-compliance
Lightning Source LLC
Chambersburg PA
CBHW021109090525
26348CB00002B/2